T0382142

TRAVELS OF A CONSULAR OFFICER
IN NORTH-WEST CHINA

THE " DANCE OF THE BLACK HAT "

TRAVELS OF A CONSULAR OFFICER IN NORTH-WEST CHINA

BY

ERIC TEICHMAN, C.I.E., B.A. (CANTAB.)

OF HIS BRITANNIC MAJESTY'S CONSULAR SERVICE IN CHINA

WITH ORIGINAL MAPS OF SHENSI AND KANSU
AND ILLUSTRATED BY PHOTOGRAPHS TAKEN
BY THE AUTHOR

CAMBRIDGE
AT THE UNIVERSITY PRESS
1921

CAMBRIDGE
UNIVERSITY PRESS

University Printing House, Cambridge CB2 8BS, United Kingdom

Cambridge University Press is part of the University of Cambridge.

It furthers the University's mission by disseminating knowledge in the pursuit of education, learning and research at the highest international levels of excellence.

www.cambridge.org
Information on this title: www.cambridge.org/9781107455597

© Cambridge University Press 1921

First published 1921
First paperback edition 2014

A catalogue record for this publication is available from the British Library

ISBN 978-1-107-45559-7 Paperback

PREFACE

THE following chapters give some account of a series of journeys through the North-Western Provinces of China, undertaken in connection with the Anglo-Chinese Opium Treaty and other matters requiring investigation on the spot in conjunction with Chinese officials.

Shensi and Kansu are not very well known to foreigners generally owing to their isolation and to the absence of any towns open to foreign trade therein; but they contain many regions well worth visiting, and Kansu especially, with its profusion of game, European climate, and interesting mixed population of Chinese, Mahomedans, Tibetans, and Mongols, is in many respects one of the most attractive of the eighteen Provinces.

We were greatly indebted to the Chinese officials, both those who accompanied us and those of the districts through which we passed, for their constant courtesy and assistance, which did much to mitigate the hardships of these long journeys through the mountains and deserts of the North West. In all we covered a distance of 14,200 li (about 4000 miles) by road in Shensi and Kansu, the journeys occupying some ten months of almost continuous travel, divided over two summers.

This book was written three years ago, in 1917, when affairs in China were in great disorder after the troubles consequent on the collapse of Yuan Shih-k'ai's imperial dream in 1916. Unfortunately the hopes that China would soon pull herself together again and put her house in order have not yet been realised, and the country continues to drift on down stream, torn by internal strife and preyed upon by countless hordes of brigands and those Frankenstein monsters, the Armies of the North and South, created by the militarists for their own profit and advancement.

Conditions in Shensi have become worse rather than better during the past two years. The neighbouring Province of Szechuan, usually the chief bone of contention between North and South, after changing hands again and again,

settled down towards the end of 1917 in possession of the
Southerners. Shensi then became the principal scene of
conflict between the Northern and Southern Armies, and
during 1918 and 1919 the Province suffered terribly at the
hands of the rival forces, in most cases indistinguishable
from the brigand hordes. Towns and villages were again
pillaged and burnt, and the countryside laid waste. The
Military Governor, who *more sinico* started his career as a
Southern revolutionary, but subsequently gravitated towards
the reactionary North and became one of the staunchest of
the Northern militarists, has survived many vicissitudes and
is still in the saddle; but the next two most prominent
officials in the Province at the time of our visits, both
progressive and enlightened men, have since met with a
violent end at the hands of one side or the other.

Kansu has remained peaceful. General Ma An-liang
died in the summer of 1918, and is said to have been succeeded, as Head of the Moslems of the North West, by
General Ma Fu-hsiang.

The remarks about the successful suppression of opium
cultivation, which reached its high-water mark in 1916 and
1917, contained in Chapter XI unfortunately no longer hold
good. At the time of writing the poppy is again being
extensively cultivated in the distant provinces of the interior,
notably in Shensi and Szechuan, under the open encourage-
ment of the local officials, who derive their principal revenues
from the taxation of the opium produced. In the spring
of 1919 the writer travelled for days through districts in
Western Szechuan, where the cultivation of opium had
previously been completely eradicated, without ever being
out of sight of the countless fields of red and white poppy
in full bloom; the price of opium was everywhere rapidly
falling, and the populations of the out of the way cities
were again sodden with the drug. This flagrant violation of
the country's treaty engagements is not the fault of the
Central Government, who continue to do their best to
carry out suppression of production and consumption. But
the various semi-independent military chiefs in the distant
interior care nothing for the orders of the Peking administration or for China's treaty obligations, and aim only at their
own enrichment.

The present trouble in China is not so much the issue between North and South as the question of civil *versus* military government throughout the country. If the latter, a heritage of the revolution of 1911, can ever be got rid of, peace and progress will return. Though all signs of good and efficient government in the interior are now lacking, yet no one acquainted with the sterling qualities of the Chinese people (as distinguished from their rulers) and with the boundless resources of their great country, can doubt that they will make good in the end. Even as it is, so vast is the country, that the troubles in the far interior have comparatively little effect on the trade of the country at the Treaty Ports, which continues to expand from year to year.

The chapter on railways is, it is to be hoped, already out of date, the Powers interested in the economic development of China having evolved a new policy, that of the internationalisation of railway construction. This scheme, if it is realised, will mean the abolition of spheres of interest, the surrender of all special railway claims, and the pooling of all existing rights for railways yet unbuilt. Unfortunately it is meeting with opposition from certain interested quarters; but the hopes of all real well-wishers of China are at the moment centred in its ultimate realisation.

E. T.

PEKING, *August* 1920.

CONTENTS

CONTENTS

LIST OF ILLUSTRATIONS

LIST OF MAPS

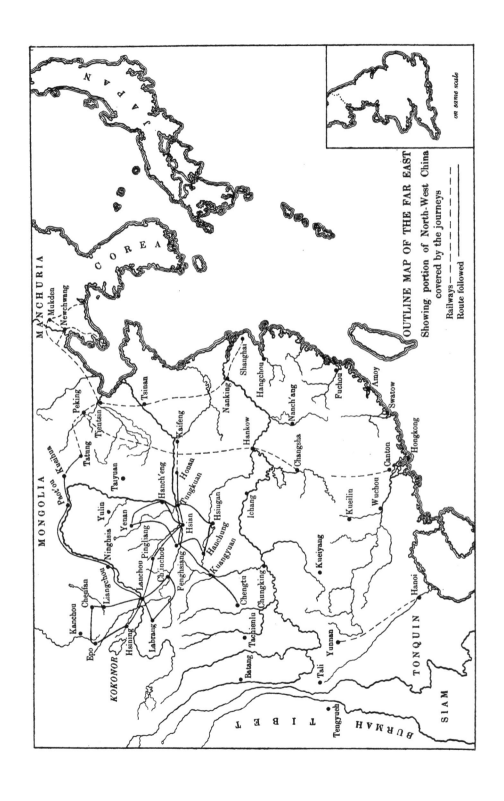

OUTLINE MAP OF THE FAR EAST

Showing portion of North-West China
covered by the journeys

Railways - - - - -
Route followed ————

on same scale

CHAPTER I

FROM RAILHEAD IN HONAN TO HSIAN FU,
THE CAPITAL OF SHENSI

Approaches to the North West—By train to railhead at Kuanyint'ang—Along the Yellow River to T'ungkuan—Road and railway construction in China—Up the Wei valley plain past Huayin, Huachou, Weinan, and Lint'ung to Hsian—Antiquities—Recent events in Shensi.

THERE are a certain limited number of trails leading into Shensi and Kansu from the coast, namely, from Honan *via* the T'ungkuan passage, from Hankow up the Han river, from T'aiyuan in Shansi *via* Suitê to Ninghsia, and from Kueihuach'eng *via* the Yellow River and the Ordos to Northern Kansu. We entered the North West by the first named route and eventually returned by the last named. The T'ungkuan trail, which nowadays carries most of the traffic, follows the valleys of the Yellow and Wei rivers through a natural gap in the mountains leading into the heart of the North West. Along this road has passed much of the traffic with Central and Western Asia since the dawn of history, and along it is one day to be built a trunk railway from the coast to the confines of Turkestan.

Starting from Peking, the Peking-Hankow railway is followed as far as Cheng Chou, the junction with the Kaifeng Fu Honan Fu line, which used to be known as the Pien Lo railway, but is now a section of the great East and West trunk line called the Lung Hai, meaning that it connects (or rather will one day in the distant future connect) Hai Chou on the coast of Kiangsu with Lung, the classical name for Kansu. Cheng Chou is a busy railway settlement attached to a little walled city; on a windy day in the spring it is an indescribably beastly spot, the whole place being shrouded in whirling dust, sand, and loess.

Leaving Cheng Chou the train soon enters a maze of loess hills through which it crawls to emerge near Kung Hsien on the valley plain of the Lo River, which is followed to Honan Fu (Loyang). The rolling stock on this section is in the last stages of decay, and the carriages are usually overrun with soldiers, Honan being one of the military reservoirs of man power for the Northern armies. The plain of the Lo Ho in early April, covered with vividly green winter wheat and dotted with pink and white fruit trees, all against the background of everlasting brown loess, forms a striking picture. The loess scenery between Cheng Chou and Kung Hsien is most remarkable, and the tourist who wishes to see a good example of this weird formation, with its perpendicular precipices and chasms, need not go further afield than this corner of N.E. Honan.

From Honan Fu a construction train, consisting of a string of open trucks packed with Chinese clinging like flies to every available spot, crawls slowly through the loess, which gradually gives way to reddish hills, past the little city of Miench'ih Hsien to the village of Kuanyint'ang, where the famous Lung Hai railway comes to an abrupt end, as though aghast at the appalling distances ahead. Immediately in front is a mountain range which will presumably have to be tunnelled to reach Shen Chou on the Yellow River. No more construction work has been undertaken at the time of writing, though surveys have been made up to Lanchou Fu. It is said that the plans allow for over 40 kilometers of tunnels before that place is reached. The concession is a Belgian one. The sight of the swarms of Chinese packed into the string of open trucks running backwards and forwards on this incomplete section testifies to the popularity of railway travel on this road and to the great number of travellers.

At Kuanyint'ang the traveller must hire carts or pack mules for the journey to Hsian. The latter are preferable, especially if it is likely to rain, as the mud in the loess cuttings on this much travelled road defies description. If the traveller has not brought his own ponies, a mule litter (*chiaowotzu* or *shantzu*) is a necessary accessory to a train of pack mules. This is a rough litter made of sticks and matting in which the passenger reclines carried by two mules, and is not likely to appeal to a foreigner as a pleasant method of travel. A Chinese is satisfied to be carried like a recumbent log in this contrivance for weeks on end, emerging at intervals for his meals; but the more active-minded foreigner is apt to find it intensely wearisome. A pony which can pace a little (the five mile an hour amble, in Chinese, *tsou*) provides on the whole the least tiring method of travel in the North Western provinces; chairs are little used except in the Southern portions, and always entail trouble in getting bearers. We used ponies and pack mules throughout our journeys.

Leaving Kuanyint'ang there is a drop into a ravine and then a stiff climb of a few hundred feet to reach the pass over a range of mountains, the watershed between the Lo and Yellow rivers. This ridge is really the end of one of the principal ranges of the Ch'inling Shan, the one which runs east and west right across Shensi immediately south of the Wei River. From the pass the road descends through undulating country to the township of Changmao Chen, where one is once more in the loess. From here it crosses a loess plateau, with typical valley rifts on either side, finally descending for the last mile to the village of Tzuchung. Changmao and Tzuchung, called 40 and 65 li from Kuan- yint'ang respectively, are both used as stages for halts, but if the journey to Hsian is to be done in good time it is best to try and reach Shen Chou, another 50 li further on, on the first day's march. The road descends through deep loess cuttings to reach the latter, a little city on the banks of the Yellow River.

The traffic on this road is immense and an almost constant stream of carts and pack mules, laden mostly with cotton and hides on their way from Shensi to the coast, is met. In wet weather the mud is appalling; in dry weather the dust is if anything worse. There may be a happy mean, but the traveller who strikes it can consider himself lucky. The first time we travelled this road was in the mud; the second time, during the dry weather in early April, in the dust. In such weather the road is entirely hidden in vast clouds of dust in which the traffic is permanently shrouded. Those who have had experience of loess dust, which is so fine that it can be almost rubbed into the pores of the skin, will know what this means. The horseman can some- times get away from the main road and its ankle-deep layer of dust by following small paths through the fields; but the passengers in carts and mule litters have to put up with it and not infrequently arrive at T'ungkuan in a state of collapse.

From Shen Chou to Lingpao Hsien, a distance of 45 li, the road runs through deep cuttings in the loess near the right bank, but out of sight, of the Yellow River; and from Lingpao to Wenhsiang Hsien, called 60 li, it runs across a series of bluffs high up above the river; for the first 20 li of this latter stage horsemen can follow a footpath along the river itself, which here rolls its pea-soupy waters through a gorge in the loess hills; wild fowl of all kinds abound here in the spring and can be easily shot. Lingpao and Wenhsiang lie right on the river. Round the latter the loess is much mixed with sand. The barrier range on the traveller's left hand here begins to draw in towards the Yellow River to form the famous narrows at T'ungkuan. From Wenhsiang to T'ungkuan, called 60 li, the road continues through the loess not far from the river. Finally T'ungkuan itself is approached through a deep cutting in the loess hills with gates and walls appearing at intervals after the manner of the Nank'ou Pass in the Peking mountains, with which this famous stronghold may be compared.

The narrows of T'ungkuan are formed by the Northern barrier range of the Ch'inling Shan and the Yellow River, which here approach to within a few miles of one another, the intervening space being filled by a thick layer of loess hundreds of feet deep, intersected by impassable rifts. Here the Peking road through Shansi *via* T'aiyuan Fu meets the Honan road and continues as one to Hsian Fu, where it bifurcates again, one branch leading south-west to Chengtu and Tibet, and the other north-west to Lanchow and Turkestan. The fortress of T'ungkuan commands the meeting-point of these four highways, and is now and always has been one of the most important strategical points in the interior of China. It will one day be also a considerable railway centre as trunk lines are projected along all these roads. The number of roads leading east and west, north of the Yangtzu, is extraordinarily small, and railways usually seem to find that the ancient highways of traffic and commerce offer the easiest routes through mountainous country. T'ungkuan has from time immemorial served as the gateway from China to Central and Western Asia, and has played

PLATE I

EAST GATE OF THE FORTRESS OF T'UNGKUAN

WEST GATE OF THE FORTRESS OF T'UNGKUAN

PLATE II

FOUR-WHEELED OX CARTS NEAR T'UNGKUAN

STONE BRIDGE ON THE ROAD TO HSIAN FU

a correspondingly important part in Chinese history. In more recent days too, during the troubles since the fall of the Manchus in 1911, it has once more figured prominently in the manœuvres of Imperial, Revolutionary, and Republican armies, brigands, and train bands, while in times of peace it lends itself admirably, flanked as it is by river and mountain, to the levying of likin and other barrier tolls dear to the Chinese official. It is a compact little place, with ramparts and gates remarkable for their massive size even in China, the land of walls, overlooking the Yellow River, which pouring down from the north in a turgid yellow flood here strikes the Ch'inling Shan and turns sharply to the east.

As we approached T'ungkuan some one noticed three strange pack mules which had attached themselves to our caravan. Enquiries elicited the fact that they belonged to a merchant who was endeavouring to smuggle three loads of Price's candles through the frontier barrier into Shensi by this means. We had unwillingly to cut him adrift. Unless accompanied by transit passes goods in transport through the interior of China are taxed again and again at every point where a barrier can be erected until the prospective profit on their sale is eaten up by these tolls and their further transport becomes futile.

From the railhead at Kuanyint'ang to T'ungkuan is called a distance of 280 li, and can be done in three days. As far as Lingpao the li are "short li"; thence to T'ungkuan they are "long li"; the difference is most marked, the short and the long li averaging about a quarter and a third of a mile respectively. This absurd and typically Chinese arrangement is said to be due to the fact that the authorities of Honan Fu endeavoured in days gone by to lay claim to the fortress of T'ungkuan on the ground that it was nearer to their city than to Hsian Fu.

A peculiar four-wheeled cart of prehistoric appearance is used round T'ungkuan, the only place in China where I have seen a four-wheeled native vehicle. Even the huge carts which one meets on the grasslands of the Mongolian border or in the sands of Western Kansu, regular ships of the desert, and often accommodating whole families, are always of the familiar two-wheeled type.

From T'ungkuan to Hsian is a distance of 290 li, which

can be covered in three long marches. The road, a broad tree-lined cart track, lies up the valley plain of the Wei River, with the great barrier range of the Ch'inling Shan on the left hand and the river on the right. The plain is one vast wheat-field, dotted with peculiar walled farms, each a formidable little fortress in itself; they are relics of the great Mahomedan rebellion and form a characteristic feature of the landscape in most parts of Shensi and Kansu. Nowadays the Mahomedans of Shensi are a negligible quantity, the majority having withdrawn westwards into Kansu, where they form an exceedingly important and powerful element in the population.

Forty li from T'ungkuan the district city of Huayin Hsien is reached, the inns lying in the suburb of Huayin Miao, five li east of the walled town. This latter village is the starting-point for the sacred mountain, the Hua Shan, a portion of the Ch'inling range. Seventy li further on the empty city of Hua Chou is passed, and 50 li beyond that Weinan Hsien, the centre of a particularly rich agricultural district, is reached.

The traffic on the roads of this fertile and populous plain is very great, and it is one of the absurdities of modern China that no railway should yet connect Hsian, the metropolis of the North West, with the coast. Railway construction on the plains of Central Shensi means little more than laying the rails on the necessary embankment and building a number of small bridges across the streams which flow down from the Ch'inling Shan into the Wei River. And while these rich and populous plains in the centre of China are innocent of every vestige of railway construction, a line has been built at great difficulty and expense through the mountains north of Peking past Kalgan to end in the air beyond Tatung in Northern Shensi. The Hsian line is a section of the Belgian Lung Hai railway referred to above, which has for the moment come to a stop at Kuanyint'ang in Honan. Failing railways the construction of a few good trunk roads fit for motor traffic would be of enormous advantage to the province and could be undertaken, as far as the plains of Central Shensi are concerned, at comparatively small cost. There can scarcely be another civilized country in the world which would be content at the present day to put up with the prehistoric means of communication which are still the only ones in existence throughout Shensi and Kansu. This absence of proper means of communication is an absolute hindrance to any real progress, and the speedy construction of more railways in China would seem to be of more importance than all the other contemplated reforms thrown together. Road building seems to be past praying for in these days of railways, but it is not at all certain that a portion of the enormous sums spent in railway construction would not be more profitably expended in the construction of a few trunk roads; the latter could at any rate be built by the Chinese themselves without incurring loans.

From Weinan to Lint'ung is a distance of 80 li, the latter being another important wheat and cotton-growing centre. It is not necessary to make these district cities the stages, as villages with inns are numerous all the way from T'ungkuan, and travellers can regulate the length of their marches according to their choice. The following is a list of the usual stopping places, which lie at intervals of 20 to 30 li one from another; T'ungkuan, Huayin Miao, Fushui Chen, Liutzu, Hua Chou, Ch'ihshui Chen, Weinan, Linkou, Lint'ung.

Lint'ung lies close under an outlying spur of the Ch'inling Shan, whence issues a hot medicinal spring. Over these springs is built an elaborate rest-house to accommodate the guests who come to take the baths, and it is thus a popular resort for the rank and fashion of Hsian. The establishment, or rather previous constructions, date from the time when Hsian was the capital of China, Lint'ung having been a pleasure resort for the Emperors of those days. The Emperor who designed the Great Wall and destroyed the scholars and their books (about B.C. 200), and whose name is therefore supposed to be execrated by literary men, is buried in the neighbourhood. We revelled in the baths, after having been smothered in dust for ten days.

On the following day a long half stage of 50 li brings one to Hsian Fu, now officially known by its old name of Ch'angan Hsien, the capital of the province. It is an immense city, of the Tartar type, comparable only to Peking before the introduction of modern improvements. In size and importance, political, commercial, and military, it entirely overshadows all the other towns in Shensi and Kansu, and is altogether the metropolis of the great agricultural North West, the land of loess and wheat.

Hsian is a backward place as regards the improvements of modern civilization, no macadamized roads, no electric light, no foreign carriages. Amongst other conveniences waterworks are required, as the water from most of the wells in the city is very brackish; good water could easily be brought from one of the many clear streams which emerge from the Ch'inling Shan a few miles to the south. There should be a boom in big contracts in Hsian when the railway gets there, or before.

We were too busy during our short stay to do much sight-seeing, but felt constrained to visit the Pei Lin ("forest of stone tablets") where the Nestorian Tablet now is. A large rubbing industry has sprung up (or perhaps it has existed for centuries or thousands of years) and almost every other stone has its attendant Chinese busy taking an impression. One would imagine that the more important inscriptions would get seriously damaged by this incessant rubbing, and indeed such appears to be the case. Outside is a shop where these myriad rubbings are busily sold, and their export from Shensi is quite a trade. The Chinese are, of course, great amateurs of ancient curios, inscriptions, and other historical records, and Hsian and Central Shensi is for them a happy hunting ground in this respect. It seems curious that this region has not received more attention from European scholars interested in these matters, since it contains the beginnings of everything as far as Chinese history is concerned, and the latter is hard to beat for an early start; sand-buried cities in the heart of the deserts of Central Asia are ransacked at great difficulty and expense by scholars of various nations, but it does not appear that much if any excavating has been done on the Hsian plain, which contained the capital of ancient dynasties which flourished three to four thousand years ago. The Nestorian Tablet, which dates back eleven to twelve hundred years, records the propagation of Christianity in China by Nestorian missionaries from Western Asia in those days. It is curious that this faith should have so completely disappeared, while Mahomedanism, an equally alien religion, has become so firmly rooted in many parts of the country. The Chinese show more interest in the inscriptions relating to their classic works in the Pei Lin than in the famous Nestorian Tablet, and indeed the latter was only moved into that select enclosure recently because of an alleged attempt by a foreigner to remove the original stone under the pretext of having a copy made for a foreign museum.

We stayed in Hsian twice in the course of our journeys, an interval of two years elapsing between the two visits. On the first occasion, which was during Yuan Shih-k'ai's regime as President-Dictator, the city and province were in the hands of one of the Northern Generals supported by a Northern army; two years later the situation had completely changed, the province was enjoying a kind of home rule under native officials of its own choice, and was practically independent of Peking. In the interval Yuan Shih-k'ai had been dragged under in the collapse of his monarchical scheme, and with him had vanished, it would seem, all hope of a stable government in China. Many provincial capitals have had a rough time during the years which have elapsed since the Revolution of 1911, but few or none have suffered more than Hsian Fu. The history of events in Shensi during these years is interesting and not uninstructive for those concerned with the future of the Republic, and is here briefly related.

The Revolution of 1911 took a particularly violent form in Shensi, largely owing to the fact that it was engineered by the local members of the notorious secret society known as the Ko Lao Hui, and was ushered in by an outbreak at Hsian, in which the Manchu inhabitants of the Manchu city were massacred, and some missionaries murdered by the uncontrollable mob. For some months afterwards a state of chaos reigned everywhere, and to make matters worse the province was for a considerable time threatened by an invasion of Mahomedan troops from Kansu, under Sheng Yün, the ex-Viceroy of the North West, and Ma An-liang, the leader of the Kansu moslems, both of whom refused to acknowledge the Republic even after the abdication of the Emperor. These Mahomedan troops did in fact cross the border and sacked a few cities in Shensi, but were stopped just in time by the explanations of Yuan Shih-k'ai; for it is unlikely that the revolutionary levies of Shensi would have been able to withstand them, and had it not been for Yuan Shih-k'ai's hand at the helm, the devastation of the whole North West by the Mahomedans, and possibly the establishment of an independent Mahomedan State in Kansu, might have been added to the general chaos of those days.

During 1913 things began to settle down under a loose home rule sort of government composed of natives of the province and strongly influenced by the Ko Lao Hui, but early in 1914 Shensi was once more thrown into a state of turmoil by the raid of the so-called "White Wolf" brigands. Hsian was saved by its walls, by no means for the first time in its history, and this terrible horde swept by, almost within sight of the city, westwards into Kansu, whence they straggled back again across Shensi into Honan laden with silver and opium before the close of the year. Yuan Shih-k'ai, however, had in the meantime taken advantage of the opportunity created by these disturbances to send a Northern army into the province on the pretext of fighting the White Wolf brigands, and having thus secured control of the situation, he proceeded to remove the local Tutu, or provincial Governor, and his native administration, and to replace them by one of his Northern generals as Governor with a staff of Northern officials. Shensi thus emerged from the White Wolf ordeal to see its home rule episode at an end and to find itself once again under the strong hand of Peking.

This action of Yuan Shih-k'ai's in Shensi was only a part of a far-sighted scheme which he was then carrying out for replacing the post-revolution Governors, mostly men of the extreme republican type, by his own nominees, stout soldiers from the North on whom he could rely, in preparation for the great day, the existence of which was totally unsuspected by the vast majority of Chinese and foreigners in the country, when he would ascend the Imperial Throne "at the will of the people." He carried out this policy with extraordinary success and tact in province after province, though in most cases it was a case of playing with fire, but for some reason or other he omitted to do so in the case of

Yunnan, an omission which was to cost him his throne and his life. When the crash came in 1916 many of these stalwarts put up a splendid fight in the interests of their Imperial master, notably the Governor at Canton (who was not, as it happened, a Northerner at all, but a Yunnanese of aboriginal stock); but one by one they gave way before the overwhelming wave of a really popular rebellion; and it is said that it was the receipt of a telegram from one of the most trusted of them all, the Governor of Szechuan, announcing his abandonment of the Imperial cause, which finally brought home to Yuan Shih-k'ai the hopelessness of the position, and caused him to renounce his throne and sink soon after into the grave.

Returning, however, to the history of events in Shensi; during 1915 Yuan Shih-k'ai's hold over the province continued to tighten, and at this time many of the former revolutionary leaders and Ko Lao Hui chiefs were compelled to go into exile abroad, or to join the bands of brigands, composed largely of ex-soldiers disbanded since the Revolution, who began at that time to infest the Northern districts, and who have practically controlled the North of the province ever since.

At the end of 1915 Yuan proclaimed himself Emperor under the dynastic title of Hung Hsien, and on Christmas Day his great antagonist, the late General Tsai Ao, perhaps after Yuan Shih-k'ai the greatest Chinese of modern times, raised the standard of revolt in Yunnan in the name of the Republic. Scarcely anyone, Chinese or foreigner, in Peking when they heard this news suspected that this movement in a far distant corner of the Empire would grow into a rebellion which would overturn Yuan Shih-k'ai within six months. But General Tsai had laid his plans well, and carried them out with a courage and energy not always found amongst the revolutionary leaders, and as the year wore on and the Northern armies failed to defeat him in the mountains of the south west, province after province threw in their lot with the rebellion. The power of Yuan's military governor in Shensi rested purely and simply on his few Northern troops, and it was not surprising that, when in the early summer of 1916 the anti-monarchical rebellion assumed serious proportions, the situation in so turbulent a province soon became critical. The crisis was eventually precipitated by the action of a young military officer of high rank, a native of the province, who revolted with the troops under his command, and having collected a large force from amongst the brigands and secret society men in hiding in the north of the province, marched on Hsian Fu as a supporter of the Republic. The Governor, who was not as staunch an individual as many of Yuan Shih-k'ai's other Northern Generals, promptly threw up the sponge and surrendered the city to save his own life. Shortly afterwards Yuan Shih-k'ai died, and Shensi thus reverted to the state of independent home rule existing after the Revolution of 1911, under the leadership of the young General who had successfully headed the rebellion.

Shensi is in rather a peculiar position. Though geographically it is one of the Northern provinces like Chihli, Shantung, Honan, and Anhui, from which the Northern Military Party draw their power and their troops, it has yet of recent years always exhibited a strong revolutionary and republican spirit. The proximity of Szechuan, a Southern province, may have something to do with this. But the main reason is probably not so much a feeling of sympathy with the Southern republicans, as the independent and somewhat turbulent nature of the population, strongly infected with Ko Lao Hui influence, which renders them impatient of Central Government control and desirous of managing their own affairs[1]. This desire for provincial independence is natural and laudable, being perhaps a preliminary step towards a spirit of true patriotism in which the Chinese are as a people, with a few exceptions, so extraordinarily lacking. But the actual results of provincial home rule are altogether bad, and consist in increased brigandage, a corrupt and inefficient administration, an uncontrolled soldiery preying on the people, and other evils too numerous to mention. The problem now facing the country is how to unite a truly republican form of government with a strong central administration.

[1] Shensi has since nominally joined the North, remaining, however, to all intents and purposes independent.

PLATE III

NORTH CHINA CART INN

ARRIVAL AT HSIAN FU

PLATE IV

GORGES OF THE CH'IENYU RIVER BELOW CHENAN

FORDING THE CH'IENYU RIVER BELOW CHENAN

CHAPTER II

FROM T'UNGKUAN ON THE YELLOW RIVER ACROSS THE EASTERN CH'INLING SHAN TO HSINGAN ON THE HAN RIVER

Departure from T'ungkuan—Passage of the Ch'inling Shan—Lonan—Shang Chou—The Ko Lao Hui—Shanyang—Chenan—Chaitzu, or hill forts—The White Wolf rebels of 1914—Hsingan—The Eastern Ch'inling Shan.

WE arrived in T'ungkuan one day in early April after a terribly dusty journey from railhead in Honan, and were met there by a large party of officials deputed by the Provincial Government at Hsian to accompany us on our tour round Shensi. When, after the ceremonies of reception were over, I announced to these gentlemen that our destination was to be Hsingan in the Han valley, and that we proposed proceeding there by the shortest possible route, all asserted categorically (though none of them had any knowledge whatever of the country in question) that there was no road from T'ungkuan to Hsingan, and that we must first proceed to Hsian, the provincial capital, whence a suitable road could be found.

As soon as one leaves the recognized highways one always meets with the same protest in China—that there is no road in the direction in which one wishes to proceed. But there is a sovereign remedy for this particular difficulty to travel in China which I have scarcely ever known to fail and which I have made use of on many occasions. One sends for a map of the province and notes the next district city to one's starting-point in the direction in which one wishes to proceed; for practically speaking all district cities in China Proper are connected with one another by trails of some kind. In this case an examination of the map showed the city of Lonan due south of T'ungkuan. "Very well," we remark to our Chinese friends, "there may, as you assert, be no road from here to Hsingan, but we will in the first instance proceed to the neighbouring district city of Lonan."

The local magistrate then has to admit that there is certainly a road to Lonan, but adds that it passes over a terrible mountain. Further enquiries show that it is of course a much used trail of two stages of 90 li each.

We left T'ungkuan at daybreak on April 9th, an immense procession of ponies, mules, chairs, baggage coolies, soldiers, and miscellaneous hangers-on, of which my share amounted to three riding ponies and five pack mules. There are no cart roads in Shensi south of the Ch'inling Shan, and the Chinese always travel where possible in chairs. Having tried all methods of travel in North China I have come to the conclusion that a pacing pony with an American saddle and mules for the baggage are best and quickest, comparative rapidity of movement being an important point in the avoidance of undue fatigue; this method of travel is also far cheaper than chairs and baggage coolies and entails a minimum of friction over transport arrangements. But the tracks of Southern Shensi are very hard on the animals, and it is advisable to carry a good supply of shoes and to have a man in the caravan who can put them on.

The trail runs due south for 40 li ascending gradually over the loess foothills to the hamlet of Haoch'ayu lying at the mouth of a gloomy gorge in the rocky barrier range of mountains which bound the Wei River valley on the south. This range, the backbone of China, starts from the highlands of Northern Tibet and finally loses itself in the plains of Honan, serving all the way as the watershed between the Yangtzu and Yellow River basins, and marking the dividing line between Central and North China; that is to say between rice-eating peoples who cultivate alluvial valleys with water buffaloes and employ coolies for transport, and wheat-eating peoples who cultivate loess plains and uplands and use ponies, mules, and camels for transport. We call these mountains Ch'inling, which is really the Chinese name for the passes across the watershed range.

Entering the narrow stony gorge we followed it for about 20 li till it ended in a steep zigzag climb leading to the pass, which like most passes in China is not a saddle but just the ordinary ridge of the range crossed at the most direct point. Chinese trails always prefer where possible to go straight from point to point across the intervening obstacle rather than to make a detour along an easier line. The summit is about 6000 feet high. A little further along this range to the west is the famous Hua Shan, one of the sacred mountains of China. The Chinese call this pass Ch'inling, though as a matter of fact it is not the watershed.

Travel in China always seems to consist either in trekking across infinite plains or of following up and down river valleys and gorges to and from an endless succession of passes.

This pass is the boundary between the districts of T'ungkuan and Lonan, and a better boundary there could hardly be, for one can almost stand with a foot on either side of the range.

From the top of the pass the path drops steeply for a few hundred feet and then continues for 15 li down a picturesque well-timbered valley to the market village of Hsünchien Ssu, a pleasant little place lying at the junction of two clear mountain streams and surrounded by wooded slopes with pheasants calling in the maize fields. Though one is still in the Yellow River basin, i.e. on the headwaters of the Honan Lo, the bare stony mountains and loess plains of the North have been exchanged for the well-watered pine-clad valleys of Central China.

The next day's march, another long one, brought us to Lonan Hsien. The road continued down the wooded valley for three or four hours' march to the market village of Shihchia P'o where rice cultivation appeared (rice is grown up to about 4000 feet in Shensi), and then turned up a side ravine and crossed a low pass in a range of bare hills giving access to the valley of the Lo Ho, which was followed up to Lonan Hsien. The latter is a small place lying well away from the main roads amongst flat open valleys of red clay backed by mountains, a sort of plateau supported between two series of ranges of the Ch'inling Shan. These shallow valleys contain the headwaters of the River Lo (sometimes referred to by the Chinese as the Honan Lo to distinguish it from the Shensi Lo, the chief river of the latter Province), which flows east past Honan Fu (the old Loyang) to join the Yellow River.

A glance at the map showed our next objective to be the district city of Shang Chou, and as there did not appear to

be any main roads leading anywhere from Lonan no difficulties were raised except over the prevalence of brigandage.
Brigands are of course almost universal in China nowadays,
but they are always supposed to be worst in districts
marching with a provincial border line, such as those we
were now traversing. But our party was too formidable a
one to have anything to fear from local brigands such as
these.

A long day's march brought us to Shang Chou. The
track follows up the flat valley of one of the headwaters of
the Lo Ho for 20 li, and then crossing a low rise, drops
over the edge of the red plateau of Lonan into a narrow
winding gorge hemmed in by bare mountains of red sandstone, which is followed until it debouches on to the valley
of the Tan Chiang a little above Shang Chou.

Shang Chou is nowadays a decayed little place, though
formerly quite an important centre, a *Chou* in charge of
four surrounding *Hsien*. After the Revolution of 1911
the former *Fu*, *Chou*, *T'ing*, etc. (Prefectures, sub-
Prefectures, and so on) were all reduced to the rank of
Hsien, or district, of the 1st, 2nd, and 3rd class, the class
being determined largely, it seems, by the land-tax receipts,
and, as many districts have been entirely renamed, most of
the existing maps of China are in this respect out of date.
Shang Chou, now called Shang Hsien, is a 1st class district.
It lies in the valley of the Tan Chiang, an affluent of the
Han River, on one of the most important trade routes in
and out of Shensi, that from Hsian Fu to Lant'ien, across
the Ch'inling Shan by two low passes, and down the valley
of the Tan Chiang to the mart of Lungchuchai, whence
boats ply *via* Chingtzu Kuan in Honan to the Han River,
Laoho K'ou, and Hankow; though the importance of this
route has somewhat declined since the railway from Honan
Fu has reached to within three and a half days of T'ungkuan.

At Shang Chou we were in the basin of the Yangtzu,
the insignificant rise on the edge of the plateau of Lonan
being the Yangtzu Yellow River watershed.

We were here quartered in the local school, which, as
we usually found to be the case, was easily the best and
cleanest building in the place. The existence of a comparatively well-kept school house, with maps and educational

pictures on the walls, in practically every district city throughout China (of which there are nearly 2000) evidences the excellence of the principles governing the administration of the country. In the middle schools English, the official "foreign" language, is taught. Unfortunately in too many cases the local school does little more than represent the principle of education. The Chinese have a well-known saying *Yu Ming Wu Shih*, which means "theory without practice"; this saying holds good of most things in China, especially those connected with the Government of the country.

The magistrate of Shang Chou at the time of our visit was rather a remarkable character, and a "Ta Ko" (lodge-master) in the notorious secret society called the Ko Lao Hui. It is improbable that any foreigner knows much about the secrets, the history, doings, and aims of the Ko Lao Hui, but during and since the Revolution it has been the great power in Western China, particularly in Shensi and Szechuan. Originally anti-dynastic, it worked very much in the dark in the days of the Manchus, and for a magistrate then to have been a member would have been an unheard-of scandal. With the overthrow of the Manchus the Ko Lao Hui came out more into the open. The revolution in the West was largely their work, and the bands of the T'ung Chih Hui who rose in Szechuan against Chao Erh-feng in August 1911, and whose rising brought about the military revolt at Hankow which ultimately swept away the Manchu Dynasty, were Ko Lao Hui partisans under another name. On the coast the revolution was to a large extent a matter of hoisting republican flags, and whole provinces joined the republican cause with their Generals and Governors at their heads. In the West, thanks to the Ko Lao Hui, the revolution was a real rising of the people, led by some of their least desirable representatives, against their rulers, and was accompanied by much more bloodshed, including the terrible massacre of the Manchus at Hsian Fu.

After the fall of the Manchus the Ko Lao Hui reckoned Yuan Shih-k'ai as their chief enemy, and perhaps this was not the least of the latter's many admirable qualities. After his death their power and influence rose almost unchallenged, and at present they are in many parts an absolute curse to the more respectable inhabitants. At the time of writing nearly all the soldiers and brigands in Shensi, as well as many civil and military officials, and in certain districts a high proportion of the entire adult male population, are members, and the administration of the province is largely in their hands. There may be some good in the Ko Lao Hui, but the writer, who has seen their pernicious influence at work throughout Szechuan, Shensi, and parts of Kansu, has never heard of it. To the ordinary observer the society appears to exist for the purpose of practising blackmail and terrorism, and securing mutual protection in the com- mission of every variety of crime. Amongst its members are special bands expert in gambling, kidnapping, piracy, highway robbery, and similar pursuits. Others join merely in order to secure immunity from the depredations of more active members. Offences against the rules of the society are drastically dealt with by punishments such as death, mutilation, gouging out of eyes, etc., carried into effect by members specially told off for that purpose; while should these avenging angels fall by some mischance into the grips of the law, the society will see to it that they do not come to any harm and are well supplied with wine and opium while in prison. The Ko Lao Hui has many aliases, Chiang Hu Hui, Hu Kuo Chun, etc., and they are brigands one day, patriot rebels the next, regular soldiers the next, and so on. One of the first reforms to be carried into effect by a strong administration in Western China is to extir- pate them root and branch, as the Manchus were always endeavouring to do.

The next stage in our journey southwards to the Han valley was the district city of Shanyang, distant 140 li, two days' march. The trail leaves the valley of the Tan Chiang and strikes into the mountains to the south. For half a day we marched up a winding gorge, and then crossing three sandstone ridges one after the other, the highest about 4000 feet, descended to the market village of Heishan Chieh, 70 li from Shang Chou, where we halted for the night. The mountains in this neighbourhood are most intricate, with streams flowing in all directions, but the general feature seems to be a series of ridges trending from N.W. to S.E. The scenery is very agreeable, red sandy mountains, pine trees, and clear streams flowing through narrow cultivated valleys abounding in pheasants.

The following day we crossed another low pass, the boundary between Shang Chou and Shanyang districts, and then followed down a winding ravine for the rest of the way to Shanyang Hsien. The latter is a tiny place hidden away in a wilderness of red sandstone hills and mountains.

At Shanyang we struck a recognized road of sorts leading south to a place called Manch'uan Kuan on the Hupei border, whence boats can be taken down a stream called the Chia Ho across a corner of N.W. Hupei to Paiho Hsien on the Han River, and thence up stream again to Hsingan. To get into a boat wherever possible is the aim of every Chinese traveller, which, though rarely attainable in North China, is very natural considering the state of the so-called roads and the hardships of long overland journeys, and my Chinese companions were unanimous in discovering that this was the only possible route to Hsingan. But the object of our journey being—to use the expression of one of my French-speaking colleagues from the Wai Chiao Pu—"de parcourir toute la province de Shensi aussi rapidement que possible," I had no intention of taking a boat journey across N.W. Hupei, nor to waste a week in being dragged up the Han from Paiho Hsien to Hsingan; and therefore announced Chenan Hsien to be the next stage in our journey, this place lying to the S.W. and appearing to offer an alternative route. This produced a flood of expostulations and protests in regard to the difficulties of that road, which subsequently proved not unfounded. The district magistrate on being referred to admitted that there was quite a good trail to Chenan, and said that the difficulties of this route were reported to lie between the latter place and Hsingan. However, adhering to our usual practice, we made Chenan, distant about 230 li, three days' march, our immediate objective.

The first stage was an easy one of about 60 li. The trail lay down the valley for three hours' march to a point where the latter ended abruptly in an impassable gorge, and then turned up a ravine to the west, which was followed to a low pass with a steep descent the other side to the hamlet of Niuerhch'uan, lying in a small valley in the usual red sandstone mountains.

All along this road across the eastern end of the Ch'inling ranges a large proportion of the hill tops are crowned with walled strongholds called *Chai* which serve as refuges for the inhabitants of the farms and villages in the valleys in times of trouble. These fortified hill tops are a characteristic feature of S.E. Shensi and N.E. Szechuan. The better ones contain houses all ready for receiving the refugees, while others are merely walled shells inside which the owners erect mat sheds or temporary huts. Nearly all are unapproachable except by most precipitous footpaths. Six years ago, in the comparatively peaceful days of Manchu rule, these *chaitzu* were generally in ruins and fallen into disuse; nowadays they have mostly been repaired at a cost of many thousands of taels and have been in pretty constant use during the troubles which have afflicted these parts ever since the revolution of 1911. It is a regrettable but indisputable fact that public security in the interior of China has steadily deteriorated and that the ravages of brigands have everywhere increased during recent years since the establishment of the Republic.

Leaving Niuerhch'uan on the next day, we followed down the valley, which contracts to a gorge and is rather difficult for loaded mules, for an hour's march. Here the gorge debouches on to the valley of a considerable stream, the Shêch'uan Ho (lower down called apparently the Chia Ho), flowing like most of the rivers of Shensi from N.W. to S.E. Our path turned up the valley of this stream and followed it in a westerly direction for the rest of the way to the large market village of Fenghuangtsui, 80 li from Niuerhch'uan. The valley is hemmed in by rocky jungle-clad mountains and is uncultivated till within 15 li of Fenghuangtsui, where a tributary of equal volume from the north joins the stream. From this point on there are rice fields and a succession of hamlets. Fenghuangtsui is the largest village in the district and contains many more families than Chenan itself. Apart from these occasional townships there is marked absence of villages in these mountains, and one usually travels all day long without passing anything but scattered farmsteads and huts.

The next day's march was a long and tiring one called 90 li. The trail leaves the main valley of the Shêch'uan Ho and enters a gorge which soon ends in a stiff climb up to a pass, about 5000 feet high and two hours' scramble from Fenghuangtsui. There is a similar steep descent for a thousand feet or so down the other side into a ravine where farmsteads and rice fields reappear, and then a weary three hours' march down a stony gorge which debouches on to the narrow valley of the Ch'ienyu Ho, a considerable stream for these mountains, which takes its rise in the watershed ranges north of Hsiaoyi T'ing and flows south past Chenan to join the Han near Hsünyang Hsien. The trail continues down this stream, which has to be crossed and recrossed though barely fordable, for another hour's march through precipitous limestone gorges, and then turns up a small tributary to the west for a few li to reach the city of Chenan, a dilapidated little place lying hidden away in the mountains just round the corner from the canyon of the Ch'ienyu Ho.

We had had nine days' continuous travel over the most appalling mountain tracks since leaving T'ungkuan, and as we were well housed in the Yamen of the Chief of Police, and were informed that the trail on to Hsingan was much worse, we decided to rest in Chenan for a day. The fourteen days between T'ungkuan and Hsingan by this route constituted one of the hardest journeys we made in all our wanderings through Shensi and Kansu owing to the roughness of the mountain trail. Travelling as we were with the assistance of the local officials we did not have to sample the inns, if there were any, *en route*; without such assistance it would of course have been very much harder and more fatiguing.

Chenan has practically no city wall left, which is unusual. The explanation lies in the fact that the inhabitants own a particularly fine *chaitzu* on a neighbouring mountain top in which they prefer to take refuge, with their magistrate and his police, in times of trouble rather than defend their city. A large proportion of the population were there at the time of our visit, for at that early period of our journey our party was so formidable in size that when we descended on these small mountain towns like a swarm of locusts the people used often to fly at our approach as though from a band of brigands. Chinese officials travelling on what used to be, and often still is, called an Imperial Mission, such as

that on which we were engaged, must according to immemorial custom be provided with food and accommodation
free of charge by the towns and villages through which they
pass, and not only they themselves, but the cloud of parasites
who accompany them, servants, soldiers, coolies, and animals
as well. The local magistrates of course try and recoup
themselves from the people, but in a very poor post they
might almost be ruined by the passage of such a party.

There are patches of rice fields round Chenan, but most
of the district is composed of a maze of wild mountains, the
lower slopes of which are often dotted with the valuable
wood oil tree, a pretty sight in blossom in April. The Chinese
assert that the district is rich in minerals, copper, iron,
asbestos, and antimony. It is a third class district and the
post of magistrate is of course a poor one, as the land tax
receipts amount to less than a thousand taels per annum.
But amongst our party was an official who had been
magistrate at Hsiaoyi, a day's journey further north in the
mountains, who affirmed that compared to the latter district,
Chenan was a garden; for Hsiaoyi, it seems, has no land
tax receipts, and practically no population. It should be
explained that the land tax is usually collected in grain and
remitted to the provincial treasury in silver, the process of
exchange from the one into the other not being effected
without a certain percentage remaining in the hands of the
local official; hence the amount of the land tax is usually
considered the standard by which the wealth of a post may
be measured.

A road runs due south from Hsian, the provincial
capital, through the Ch'inling Shan *via* Hsiaoyi and Chenan
to Hsingan on the Han River, being the most direct route
between these two important cities, but it is so rough as to
be little used. It is bad enough in the dry season when it
follows up and down the stream beds in the simple manner
of so many mountain trails in China, but when the water
rises and the path has to take to the cliffs of the gorges it is
very much worse and probably quite impassable for pack
animals and chairs. We found the stream bed still just
practicable in April.

The number of burnt-out ruins of hamlets, farmsteads,
and huts along the trail we had just traversed could not fail

to attract one's notice, and enquiries elicited the fact that these were the result of the passage of the terrible "White Wolf" rebels, who passed in and out of Shensi in scattered bands by these out of the way mountain trails in 1914. During our wanderings through Shensi and Kansu we often found ourselves travelling in the footsteps of this devastating horde, whose trail of desolation could be traced in the ruins of farms, villages and towns from the borders of Honan to the confines of the Kokonor. Their lootings, burnings, and killings recall the depredations of the T'aip'ing and Mahomedan rebels who devastated N.W. China, south and north of the Ch'inling Shan respectively, fifty years ago.

This terrible horde of bandits or rebels was an aftermath of the rebellion of 1913. It consisted of an organized and well-equipped nucleus of a few thousand fighting men, disbanded soldiery from the Yangtzu Valley and Secret Society men from Honan, together with many thousands of local adherents drawn from amongst the brigands, soldiers and bad characters of the provinces through which they passed. The four words "Pai Lang Chao Liang" (White Wolf is recruiting) passed secretly up and down the Han Valley, and recruits from all quarters flocked to join the band. After 30,000 of Yuan Shih-k'ai's best Northern troops had failed to crush these rebels in Honan, they burst through into the Han Valley *via* the rich mart of Laoho K'ou, where a foreign missionary was murdered in the sacking of the city, and early in 1914 worked through the mountains into Central Shensi. Hsian, with its mighty walls, withstood the raiders as it had withstood the Mahomedans fifty years earlier, and the horde drove on almost unopposed through Western Shensi into Southern Kansu, looting, burning and killing. The massacres of Chinese non-combatants were appalling, and the raiders, many of them mere youths, richly dressed in looted silks and jewellery and armed with modern rifles and Mauser pistols, rivalled in their cruelty and lust for indiscriminate slaughter the most terrible of Chinese rebels of days gone by. The object of the raid into the North West seems to have been the stocks of opium in Shensi and Kansu. The resistance they met with and the measures taken to deal with them reflect no credit on the Chinese Government of the time and it is a common rumour that many high officials were privy to the raid and shared in the loot which was brought back to Honan. It was not until they reached the Mahomedan districts of Kansu near the Kokonor border that they suffered any serious loss, and that was mainly at the hands of the Mahomedan population of those parts, who are not accustomed to permit themselves to be looted and killed without showing fight, and from the hardships of the long forced marches through that wild region, rather than owing to the action of any Government troops. Eventually the survivors straggled back with their loot through Shensi to their homes in Honan and Anhui. The Chinese officials assert that White Wolf himself, who appears to have been an ex-military officer from the Yangtzu armies, was captured and executed.

The failure of the Shensi troops, mostly revolutionary levies of Ko Lao Hui men and ex-brigands, of much the same type as the raiders, to deal with the White Wolf rebels was to be expected; but the failure of the Northern Army opposed to them in Honan in the winter of 1913–14 seems at first sight difficult to account for. The rebels were of course much more mobile than the Government troops, as they lived on the country by taking what they wanted and impressed men and animals everywhere to carry their transport. Then again their lives being at stake, they could be depended on to fight when cornered, whereas it is difficult to induce the Chinese soldier to close with his enemy in a fight of this kind in which he has no interest. Where not an ex-brigand, the Chinese soldier is often a good fellow in most respects, but he is apt to be too sensible to be willing to run the risk of getting killed without adequate reason. Hence battles between rebels and Government troops in China usually consist in the discharge of large quantities of ammunition at a safe distance from one another. It is the civilian inhabitant of the raided towns and villages who gets killed if he does not manage to escape in time to his *chaitzu* in the mountains.

We left Chenan on April 19th for Hsingan, distant, we were told, five hard days' march over the worst possible roads. The first stage was 80 li to the village of Ch'ingt'ung Kuan. The trail lay all the way down the steep winding gorges of the Ch'ienyu River and was terribly rough and

tiring. A path fit for carrying coolies is ledged in the cliff
side, but mules and ponies have to pick their way over the
stones and boulders in the stream bed, constantly crossing
and recrossing the river, which is only just fordable, as it
washes the base of the cliffs alternately on either side. The
following day's march, called 60 li, to the village of Hsiaoho
K'ou is precisely the same and most tiring. The district of
Hsünyang is entered rather more than half-way near a
picturesque temple overhanging the water. Hsiaoho K'ou
lies at a point where the river, making the most intricate
turns and twists on itself and almost surrounding a precipitous hill crowned by a fine *chaitzu*, is joined by a tributary
from the east.

Ten li lower down, at a hamlet called Liangho Kuan, the
Ch'ienyu Ho is joined by another stream from the west
called the Hsün Ho, which issues from a similar gloomy
gorge in the mountains. This latter river seems to contain
the greater volume of water and is considered the main
stream.

From Liangho Kuan small boats can descend the Hsün
Ho to its junction with the Han at Hsünyang Hsien, whence
the latter can be reascended to Hsingan. It was of course
suggested by everyone that we should here take to boats,
but as it would have taken about a week to get to Hsingan
by water as against three days by road across the mountains,
we decided to continue overland. Since the trail continued,
however, to descend the river gorges for another 40 li, we
were able to avail ourselves of boats for that distance. The
magistrate of Hsünyang had provided a regular flotilla for
our huge party, and the boatmen were obviously relieved
to find that we were only going to take them for a short
distance instead of descending to the Han; for the supply
of boats was of course a sort of official corvée for which they
got little or no remuneration. The best boat, a brand new
one, had been laboriously dragged up the rapids of the
Hsün Ho and hidden away round a bend to prevent its
being impressed; but the magistrate's underlings soon got
wind of it and it was unearthed together with its morose
and disappointed owner, and placed at our disposal. As
our mules and ponies were all tired and footsore from the
rough trails they had been travelling on, I tried to ship them

for a rest; but having embarked them with difficulty in the largest boat, the boatmen pronounced it too dangerous a proposition in the rapids, and they had to continue their overland scramble. We had a pleasant journey downstream, passing through deep gorges and shooting a succession of small rapids, but as we ran aground periodically it took about three hours to do the 40 li to the village of Chaochia Wan, where the gorges open out into a pleasant little valley with cultivated slopes dotted with wood oil trees.

At Chaochia Wan the Hsingan trail leaves the gorge of the Hsün Ho to cut across the mountains to the S.W. for two days' march. The first stage to the village of Map'ing Ho is only 50 li, but it is a hard day's march. It is only when one starts to climb out of these Han valley gorges that one realises their depth. For three hours after leaving Chaochia Wan we scrambled up a mountain side, most of the way too steep to ride, in a downpour of rain. On reaching the pass (about 4200 feet) the weather cleared somewhat, allowing fleeting views through the clouds over a maze of wild reddish mountains patched with trees and jungle vividly green in their spring foliage. From the pass there was a steep drop of a few li, like the ascent by slippery clay paths and flights of irregular stone steps, then an easy descent along a ridge, and finally a precipitous drop straight down the mountain side to the hamlet of Map'ing Ho lying in a ravine running S.E.

From here there was only one stage left, called 90 li, to Hsingan. The magistrate of the latter city, who met us here, suggested an early start, as the 90 li were, he said, "very big and over several mountains." Fortunately we took his advice, for what with the passes, the badness of the road, and the rain, we were nearly twelve hours *en route*.

Leaving the valley of Map'ing Ho the trail enters a defile to the S.W. which leads up to a pass (3300 feet), the boundary between Hsünyang and Hsingan districts, and then drops down into a stony gorge which is followed to the hamlet of Liuli Kou. From this place there are still 60 li left to Hsingan, and the weary traveller feels entitled to hope for a run down the valley for the rest of the way. But it is still the same story of an endless succession of ridges trending from N.W. to S.E. across a road running S.W. and the trail only follows down this gorge for a few li before it turns up the mountain to the S.W. to cross another ridge; and descending into a similar gorge the other side, it soon strikes again S.W. up another mountain slope. This, the last range to be crossed, is a stiff climb of a thousand feet by a rough zigzag track. From the summit (about 2600 feet) there is a fine view over the Han valley. Some 1800 feet below and 25 li away to the S.W. lies the city of Hsingan, with the Han River emerging from its mountain gorges, flowing past the foreground of the picture through a small plain, and disappearing in the mountains to the left; across the river rise tier on tier of hills and mountains towards the Szechuan frontier; on the right hand across a range of red hills a glimpse is caught of the valley plain of the Yo River stretching away towards Hanyin T'ing; and in the immediate foreground are low flat-topped hills of red clay, covered with wheat, peas, and lucerne, across which the path descends, climbing in and out of two deep narrow nullahs, before finally debouching at the ferry on the banks of the Han opposite Hsingan Fu.

The route followed from T'ungkuan to Hsingan, a distance of 960 li, gives one a good general idea of the nature of the ranges of mountains known to foreigners as the Ch'in-ling Shan at their eastern and lower end. All the way one is crossing ridge after ridge trending south-east composed of red sandstone, shale and limestone, the first named pre-dominating on the lower slopes and in the valleys. These red clays and sandstones bound the loess formations on the south all the way from Honan to the Kokonor. The south-easterly trend of these ridges seems to start from the culminating point of the range, the T'aipai Shan, whence one series of ranges runs east along the southern edge of the Wei valley plains, and another strikes south-east right across the Han basin and causes the succession of gorges through which the Han River flows from below Yang Hsien to the Hupei border; between these two series of ranges lies the red plateau of Lonan and the headwaters of the Honan Lo. West of T'aipai Shan there is a similar split, one series of ranges running west into Kansu as the Yangtzu Yellow River divide, and another running south-west as the watershed between the Han and Chialing rivers. From T'aipai

Shan itself streams flow down in all directions. The Chinese apply the name Ch'inling strictly speaking only to the passes in the Yangtzu Yellow River watershed range. The mass of mountains which fill up the whole of Southern Shensi from south of the Wei River to the Szechuan border, and through which the Han flows in a deep and narrow trough, are universally known locally as the Nan Shan.

PLATE V

CHAITZU (HILL FORT) ON THE CH'IENYU RIVER

CANOE BOAT ON THE CH'IENYU RIVER

PLATE VI

GLEN ON THE ROAD BETWEEN HANYIN AND SHIHCH'UAN

GORGES OF HAN RIVER ABOVE SHIHCH'UAN

CHAPTER III

FROM HSINGAN UP THE HAN VALLEY TO HANCHUNG

Hsingan and the resources of the Han valley—Hanyin—Shihch'uan—
Hsihsiang—Kulupa—Catholics and Protestants—Hanchung—Northern
troops in the Han valley.

HSINGAN FU is now a first class district city known as
Ank'ang Hsien. It lies on the southern bank of the Han
River at the head of a small but very fertile plain, where
the river emerging from gorges flows for a few miles through
more open country before disappearing into the mountains
again. It consists of two cities, called the old and the new.
The old city which is the commercial centre and contains
most of the shops and general population is built right on
the river from which it is protected by an embankment.
A mile to the south lies the new city, a much smaller enclosure, containing residences of gentry and retired officials,
Government schools, etc. The new city lies on higher ground
and is said to have been built as a refuge in time of flood.
The alluvial plain between the two cities is enclosed by
stoutly built dykes running from the river up to the rising
ground to the south. We were well housed in a Government
building in the new city which forms a pleasant residential
quarter as compared with the crowded streets of the old.

Hsingan is an important commercial centre and serves
as a gateway into the whole basin of the upper Han, the
Yangtzu's longest tributary. This upper Han basin may be
likened to a miniature edition of the province of Szechuan,
an extremely rich mountain region intersected by innumerable little fertile valleys and plains, with Hanchung, the
administrative capital, comparable to Chengtu, Hsingan, the
commercial gateway, to Chungking, and the Han with its
gorges and rapids to the Yangtzu. To complete the likeness
many parts of the Han basin are just as red as the famous
"red basin" of Szechuan. A great variety of products are
collected at Hsingan from this rich region and shipped
down river to Laoho K'ou and Hankow, such as cereals,
vegetable oils, fruits, nuts, varnish, wood oil, silk, tea,

vegetable wax, cotton, hemp, hides, bristles, edible wood fungus, tobacco, indigo, paper, cane sugar, straw braid, etc., of which the most important is the wood oil[1], crushed out of the seeds of an apple-like fruit ripe in the autumn. Coal, iron, copper, gold, silver, antimony, and asbestos, and perhaps other minerals, exist in the neighbourhood. As a result the basin of the upper Han is one of the most prosperous regions in the whole of China and the population one of the wealthiest. Rice is usually cheaper even than in Szechuan. But in spite of its prosperity the region is isolated and backward as regards foreign improvements, and will probably undergo a very rapid development when tapped by a railway. It is one of the anomalies of modern China that this rich well-populated region and also the productive wheat and cotton-growing prairies of the Wei River valley should still be without railway communication, though neither are really difficult to get at.

The population of Hsingan is somewhat rough, not over friendly to foreigners, and strongly tainted with secret society influence, and compares unfavourably with that of Hanchung and the towns further up the valley, which have been populated by the more kindly Szechuanese. There is a considerable Mahomedan community of immigrants from Kansu, who as elsewhere keep very much to themselves.

The Han River is of course the main artery of communication. To Hankow downstream takes one to three weeks according to the state of the water, and the return journey upstream one to two months. Steam navigation on the upper Han seems to be out of the question owing to the shallows, shifting channels, and rapids. The worst rapids, some of which are very dangerous, lie between Yang Hsien (at the lower end of the Hanchung plain) and Hsingan.

There is good pheasant, partridge, and wild-fowl shooting to be had round Hsingan, and immediately to the south lies a very wild and sparsely-inhabited mountain region on the borders of Shensi, Hupei, and Szechuan, which is said to harbour all kinds of big game, such as deer, goat, pig, bear, leopard, and even the tiger.

[1] Wood oil is nowadays one of the most important articles of the China export trade; the trees flourish on bare stony mountain sides incapable of other cultivation, and are worth studying from the point of view of afforestation generally.

The pronunciation of Hsingan on the Han River and Hsian, the provincial capital in the Wei River basin, is almost identical, and as the Chinese themselves sometimes misunderstand one another when referring to them in conversation, it is rather a hopeless task for the foreigner. The two names are really Hsing-ngan and Hsi-ngan. If one wishes to make certain of being understood one should refer to Hsingan by its old name of Hsingan Chou or its new one of Ank'ang Hsien (not really new as this was always the name of the district), and to Hsian as Hsian Sheng or Ch'angan Hsien.

The American Railway Group, having secured the concession for the construction of a certain mileage of railways in China wherever they could find room between the staked out claims of other Powers, have, according to the newspapers, elected the upper Han valley as one of the scenes of their activities, and propose, it is said, to build a line from Laoho K'ou up the valley of the Han into Shensi, and thence across the mountains into Szechuan. In view of the richness of the country it will tap, and to the fact that it is not unlikely to be the first line to solve the great problem of the railway penetration of Szechuan, the object of so many schemes, this Han Valley Railway constitutes one of the most interesting and attractive of the many railway propositions at present in contemplation in China.

We remained at Hsingan two days, during which it rained incessantly. The climate of the Han valley is rather a treacherous one and fevers are common. We were now bound up the Han basin to Hanchung, a distance of 650 li. The road we followed is the main highway through this region, though much of the way only a mountain footpath eighteen inches wide. Most of the traffic, however, goes by river. Like most of the roads in the Han basin it is really a track for coolie porters, but mules and ponies can travel by it easily enough except for one stage along the Han River beyond Shihch'uan, which is rather dangerous for pack animals. As the main road connecting two such important places as Hsingan and Hanchung it well illustrates the extraordinarily roadless condition of China. Nor in these days of railway construction is it likely that China will ever be provided with roads as the word is understood in other civilized countries. Yet a series of macadamized trunk roads would be an inestimable boon politically and economically to the country and the people and could be constructed at a comparatively small cost; some of the large sums spent annually for the upkeep of unnecessary military forces in the various provinces might with great advantage be diverted to this end.

Leaving Hsingan the Han River is crossed by a ferry above the city and the trail then runs westwards up the valley plain of the Yo River, which is navigable for small boats from Hanyin down. Its valley forms a rich little alluvial plain growing rice and wheat and supporting many farms and villages, and offering an admirable route for a railway westwards, which can thus avoid the gorges of the Han in this neighbourhood. To the south a range of mountains rises steeply to a height of a few thousand feet, separating this little plain from the Han River, while to the north the valley slopes up to low hills of red clay backed by mountains. Seventy li from Hsingan the township of Hengk'ou is reached, the end of the first stage, situated at the junction of the Yo River with the Heng River from the north. It has the honour of being the native place of the present Military Governor of the Province, General Ch'en Shu-fan, the old rule, which has many advantages, that an official is debarred from serving in his native province, no longer holding good.

From Hengk'ou to Hanyin is called 110 li, but the road is good and the li very short (at least four to the mile), so that with ponies and pack mules the distance can easily be done in a day. The Chinese li is commonly considered to be the equivalent of a third of a mile, which, however, is only the case in out of the way parts of Kansu. Elsewhere north of the Ch'inling Shan ten li to three miles may be taken as a fairly accurate average. In the upper Han valley, as in Szechuan, the li averages about four to a mile, or even more in the mountains; the difference north and south of the Ch'inling Shan being probably due to the use of animal and coolie transport in those regions respectively.

Ten li beyond Hengk'ou the hills close in on the river to form a *kuan*, or barrier, and the path crosses a low spur to descend again into the valley, here less than a mile in width, up which it continues past several large villages, crossing and recrossing the stream by fords, for the rest of the way to Hanyin.

Hanyin T'ing, now called Hanyin Hsien, a third class district, is a prosperous little place lying at the head of the fertile Yo River valley, and, like most of the Han basin towns, is more like a Szechuan than a Shensi city.

From Hanyin to Shihch'uan Hsien is a day's march, called 90 li. The path continues westwards up the narrowing valley leaving the main stream which comes down from the north on the right hand. After about 15 li the valley ends in low hills skilfully terraced into rice fields, up which the trail runs to reach a low divide, some 600 feet above and two hours' march from Hanyin. This is the first obstacle to a Hsingan-Hanchung railway, but from here on till it reaches the eastern end of the Hanchung plain near Yang Hsien there will be many difficulties to surmount. From the pass the track, entering the district of Shihch'uan, descends through a defile and then through terraced rice fields amongst the red clay hills to the valley of the Ch'ih Ho, a stream flowing down from the north, and reaches the township of Ch'ihho P'u, 45 li from Hanyin and at about the same elevation. The same mountain range, which is further on pierced by the Ch'ih Ho in a gorge, continues on the left hand and the same red clay hills on the right. The path continues down the valley for an hour's march, and then leaves it to climb over a spur to the north, and so into the valley of the Han, here no wider than the river bed, and flowing from north to south. For the rest of the way to Shihch'uan the trail runs up the Han along the mountain side on the left bank.

Shihch'uan, a third class Hsien, lies right on the river. It is an important strategic point in these parts as the trail from Hsian across the Ch'inling Shan *via* Ningshan T'ing here debouches on to the Han and the Hsingan-Hanchung road.

The next stage to Ch'a Chen, called 80 li, is a rather dangerous one for pack animals. Crossing the Han by a ferry the trail runs up the gorges of the Han, a smaller edition of those of the upper Yangtzu, being ledged in the cliff side some distance above the water. In places it is narrow and there are some corners which are difficult to negotiate; but we met with no accidents, partly because the assistance so constantly rendered to us by the local officials included repairs to bad and dangerous portions of the trail.

Ch'a Chen is a village on the river, already in the district of Hsihsiang, which is an extended one. Here the track, leaving the river, ascends a glen to the S.W., and after reaching a height of about a thousand feet above the Han runs westwards along a mountain slope, with a steep wooded range trending east and west on the left hand, and a series of spurs with intervening glens falling away to the Han on the right. Thirty-five li from Ch'a Chen the path descends some 500 feet to a village lying in the valley of a stream which issues from a gorge in the mountains to the south and flows north towards the Han, and then continuing westwards over another of the lateral ridges descends into a maze of wooded hills and gullies, leaving the mountains to the south out of sight. After two to three hours' march through these hills the trail ascends again to emerge on the top of bare downs, whence there is a fine view over Hsihsiang and the valley plain of the Muma Ho some 500 feet below. After descending into this plain, the Hsuan Ho, issuing from a gorge in the mountains to the south, is forded, and ten li further on, after rounding a low spur separating this stream from the Muma Ho and fording the latter, the district city of Hsihsiang is reached. This is a long day's march of 100 li.

Hsihsiang, the capital of a second class district, lies in another of the fertile valley plains of the Han basin, that of the Muma River. This valley runs from S.W. to N.E. and is here some miles broad. To the south a rocky range of mountains rises some thousands of feet above the plain towards the Szechuan border, and to the north are bare hills separating the valley from the Han. The district is one of the wealthiest in Southern Shensi, though these compare unfavourably, in spite of their apparently greater prosperity, as regards land tax receipts with many of the Wei valley districts, such as Weinan, Lint'ung, P'uch'eng, etc., owing, it is said, to much of the newly reclaimed land in the mountains not being on the old registers. A good deal of silk is produced. This Han valley silk is inferior to the Szechuan product, but is good enough to send to Kansu in exchange for the skins, furs, musk, deer-horns, and medicines of that province. Hsihsiang is also noted as the home of many famous literati and officials, and we were

PLATE VII

HAN RIVER AT CH'A CHEN

MUMA RIVER ABOVE HSIHSIANG

PLATE VIII

TRAIL THROUGH THE FOOTHILLS NEAR KULUPA

APPROACHING KULUPA

palatially lodged in the house of a former provincial governor.

There are at least three roads from Hsihsiang to Hanchung, *via* Yang Hsien, Ch'engku Hsien, and Kulupa respectively. We followed the latter, a three days' march. The path runs up the Muma Ho for some 15 li, where the hills close in on the river and bring the valley to an end, and then runs through the hills and along the river to the village of Matsung T'an, 50 li from Hsihsiang and, owing to a small rapid, the head of navigation for small boats on the Muma Ho, up to this point a placid stream. A little further on the trail leaves the main stream, which here flows down from the south, and turns up a small sandy tributary to the south-west, then turns west through low wooded hills intersected by rice fields, and then runs north-west up a small valley to reach the village of Shaho K'an, 25 li from Matsung T'an. This village lies, as its name implies, in a pleasant region of low sandy hills covered with small woods and intersected by rice fields much resembling Szechuan. For some reason or other it is largely a Mahomedan community with two mosques. In the woods one will often see heaps of old timber, carefully stacked, for the growth of a vegetable fungus called *mu erh* (wood ears), which is a much esteemed delicacy and forms quite an important article of commerce in the Han valley.

The next stage is from Shaho K'an to Kulupa, a distance of 70 li. The path runs up the narrow valley of the stream, occasionally cutting across the low wooded hills, for 30 li to the village of Sunchia P'ing, where the hills open out and encircle a little rice plain. The district of Ch'engku is here entered. The country is a maze of little wooded hills intersected by gullies growing rice, and its chief feature is the sand. The hills are of soft disintegrating sandstone, the stream is a trickle of water in a sandy bed, and the path a firm sand embankment between stream and rice fields. It is evidently an old sandstone plateau cut up into hills and gullies by the action of water, like so much of Szechuan. North of the Ch'inling Shan such a country would be a desert; here with the more abundant rainfall and its resultant vegetation, it is a garden. From Sunchia P'ing the trail continues westwards for a time up the stream, and then, as the latter gradually comes to an end, winds through the same low hills in a northerly direction until, crossing a low divide, it emerges into more open country to reach Kulupa.

The latter is a walled stronghold of the Catholics on the top of a hill and is the centre of Catholic missionary work in Southern Shensi, though the Bishop resides at Hanchung. The Italian Fathers who have been established in this corner of Shensi for a great many years, have attained considerable power and influence in the neighbourhood. They work on different lines to the Protestant Missions, but from their point of view with greater success. Their plan is to collect orphans or other children who are not wanted by their parents, to educate them and teach them all kinds of useful industries, and to bring them up as Catholics. This is the work that is carried on at Kulupa, where there are usually some hundreds of children being brought up as members of the Catholic Church, mostly girls, as these are easier to secure. These old-established Catholic Missions usually own a good deal of land acquired in a variety of ways, and are practically self-supporting. At Kulupa an entire hill top is covered by substantial buildings and the whole surrounded by a good wall. When trouble comes, the gates are shut, the community fetches out its arms, and the brigands, or whoever they may be, pass on to easier prey.

To many Catholics the Protestant missionaries, who are usually married and live as far as possible a comfortable European family life, seem entirely out of touch with the Chinese amongst whom they are working. To many Protestants the life led by the children in such an establishment as Kulupa seems somewhat dreary, inhuman, and lacking in the comforts and interests of home life. The ideas of Catholics and Protestants in regard to Christianity and the converting of the Chinese are certainly very divergent and consequently puzzling to the latter, but they both do an enormous amount of good in different ways. The priest appears perhaps to sacrifice his life more completely to the Chinese, as he usually comes out from Europe never to return, and often lives for the rest of his days practically as a Chinese amongst the Chinese. But no missionaries of any persuasion have done more good for the Chinese people than some of the veterans of the China Inland Mission, who have passed the best part of their lives in isolated stations in Shensi and Kansu, such as Hsingan, Hanchung, Fenghsiang, Lanchou, Liangchou, Hsining, and Ninghsia, where months and years pass by without their ever seeing another foreigner. Their success in securing converts may not have been striking, but it is permissible to speculate on whether those whom they have secured are not more genuine Christians than the native Catholics. Often in spite of the basest ingratitude on the part of the Chinese, whose wounds and illnesses they tend one day, only to be passed by in the street with a scowl on the next, these noble men have laboured on year after year doing good and leavening, in however small a degree, the leaden mass of Chinese materialism. The results of their work may not always be apparent now, but they have sown a seed which cannot fail in time to produce a harvest of some kind, a harvest of which other Missions not infrequently reap the benefit.

We spent the night at Kulupa, where we were most hospitably received and entertained with a banquet.

The distance to Hanchung is called 75 li. After descending for about an hour's march through gullies in the hills the track debouches on to the famous plain of Hanchung, a highly fertile, heavily cultivated, and densely populated region, stretching for a certain distance along both banks of the Han, and entirely surrounded by mountains. Another two hours' march across this plain, past the boundary between Ch'engku and Hanchung (Nanch'eng) districts, brings one to the Han River here a shallow stream flowing in a broad sandy bed, a hundred yards wide and a few feet deep. The path runs along the banks of the Han for a short distance, and then, crossing by a ferry, continues for ten li over the plain to reach the busy township of Shihpali P'u. This village, which, as its name implies, is 18 li from Hanchung, is developing into a large town, and is evidently the centre of the through trade from Szechuan, Kansu, and Northern Shensi, which, as is usually the case in China, is driven to avoid the capital by the various tolls and dues. From here the road runs west for the rest of the way to Hanchung, passing through a rich suburb to reach the East Gate of the city.

Hanchung, now officially known by the name of the district as Nanch'eng, is a first class Hsien, and is one of the three or four wealthiest and most populous cities in the province. It lies in the centre of the rich cigar-shaped plain of the Han valley, surrounded by mountains, and in its situation and general appearance much resembles a smaller edition of Chengtu in Szechuan. Two crops, wheat followed by rice, are regularly raised on the plain. A considerable quantity of silk is also produced and some cotton. The situation of Hanchung in the centre of the most fertile region in the province and at the point of intersection of four trade routes, south to Szechuan, west to Kansu, north to the Wei valley, and east down the Han to the coast, has made it a considerable trade centre. For the same reason it has always been one of the richest and most important likin stations in the province, where the Chinese officials, as elsewhere, do their best to throttle the transit trade and kill the goose which lays the golden eggs by the excessive imposition of dues and tolls. There are few more lucrative offices in the province than that of Superintendent of the Hanchung Likin.

Hanchung is the administrative capital of the upper Han basin, and is the seat of a Taoyin and a Chenshoushih. The position of the former is that of Civil Superintendent of the magistrates in his jurisdiction. It is nowadays less important than it was in the days of the Manchus. Since the abolition of the hierarchical system of Tao, Fu, Chou, and Hsien, the territorial administration is entirely in the hands of the district magistrates acting directly under the Civil Governor of the province. Thus the magistrates correspond directly with the Governor and send copies of their despatches and reports to the Taoyin, so that the latter is short-circuited and the abolition of the post is sometimes advocated as being superfluous. Under the old system the Hsien reported to the Chou, the Chou to the Fu, the Fu to the Tao, and the Tao to the Governor, each being responsible for the acts of his subordinate. The position of Chenshoushih is that of a General with powers of military administration. At the present time, when things are more or less unsettled and the military rule the roost, a Chenshoushih often has powers which amount practically to those of an independent

Military Governor, and the Taoyin, as a civil official, has little importance. This was the state of affairs at the time of our visit, when the upper Han basin was almost a separate province by itself, isolated from the rest of Shensi by the barrier of the Ch'inling Shan. When Yuan Shih-k'ai was busy with his monarchical scheme and was centralizing his rule by posting his own Generals and detachments of his Northern troops at various strategic points in the provinces, he sent a Northern Mixed Brigade into the upper Han valley to hold that region, and to keep open his overland communications with Szechuan. Owing to the geographical isolation of its position this Brigade and its Northern General were still in Hanchung at the time of our visit, a year after Yuan and his short-lived Empire had been swept away by the rebellion of 1916, and were continuing to control the basin of the upper Han though the rest of the province was enjoying a sort of independent home rule. It must be admitted that under the control of these comparatively well-disciplined Northerners the Han valley was much more peaceful and less preyed on by brigands than the rest of the province under home rule. Provincial independence and the loose federal system into which the Republic of China is now again drifting do not tend towards the maintenance of political stability and public security in the interior. So far the history of the past six years in China has proved the absolute necessity of a strong central administration[1], though, in the opinion of many competent Chinese and foreign observers, Peking, tucked away in a far distant corner of the country, with its apparently incurable atmosphere of reaction, is no longer the proper place for the seat of Government.

[1] It is now becoming questionable whether a strong central administration is any longer attainable in China, and whether it would not perhaps be better for the country to develop along the lines of a federation of more or less autonomous provinces.

CHAPTER IV

FROM HANCHUNG IN THE HAN VALLEY ACROSS THE CENTRAL CH'INLING SHAN TO FENGHSIANG IN THE WEI BASIN

Routes across the Ch'inling Shan—Ch'engku—Yanghsien—Across the parallel ridges of the Ch'inling Shan—Big game—The Hsinglung Ling —Fop'ing—Pheasant shooting—More passes—Chouchih—Across the Wei valley plains to Meihsien and Fenghsiang—Wheat, indigo, and cotton.

FROM Hanchung it was our intention to re-cross the Ch'inling Shan back into the Wei valley. The Ch'inling Shan, or Nan Shan, which consist of a series of precipitous parallel ranges trending across the path of anyone travelling between south and north, have always proved an extraordinarily effective barrier to communication between the Han and Wei basins. It was this barrier which prevented the T'aip'ing Rebellion spreading north from the Han valley into Central Shensi, and the Mahomedan Rebellion spreading south from the Wei valley into Southern Shensi; and in recent years it has kept the upper Han basin comparatively peaceful while rebellion and brigandage raged in the Wei valley and Northern Shensi. The Chinese have always rested content with two main routes across this barrier, one at each end; the Hsian-Lungchuchai road in the east, and the Fenghsiang-Liupa-Hanchung road in the extreme west. There is one other route which is considered by Chinese travellers to be just passable, that south from Hsian *via* Ningshan T'ing. The remaining three routes, that in the east *via* Chenan, that in the centre *via* Fop'ing, and that, further west, south from Mei Hsien, the two latter passing over the shoulders of the T'aipai Shan, one on each side, are considered by the Chinese impracticable for ordinary travellers. This is because they are too steep for chairs, and are so rough that even with mules and ponies it is necessary to do the greater portion of the journey on foot. We returned to the Wei valley by the Fop'ing trail, which debouches on to the plain at Chouchih Hsien, whence we turned westwards to Fenghsiang Fu. From Hanchung to Fenghsiang by this route is a distance of about 840 li.

For the first two days from Hanchung the road runs down the valley plain past the district city of Ch'engku Hsien to Yang Hsien, two easy stages of 75 and 60 li respectively. These are two large and flourishing cities, Ch'engku especially rivalling even Hanchung in the wealth and prosperity of its inhabitants. Below Yang Hsien the converging mountains bring this fertile plain to an end and the Han River enters a series of gloomy gorges interrupted by rapids from which it emerges at Hsingan. The latter city is supposed to be about 800 feet only above sea level, whereas Hanchung is credited on some of the best modern maps of China with a height of 2000 feet, thus allowing of a fall of some 1200 feet in the Han between Yang Hsien and Hsingan. As the fall on this portion of the river can hardly be more than 500 feet, Hanchung is probably not more than some 1300 feet above sea level.

The difficulties of this route begin on leaving Yang Hsien. The trail here turns north and reaches the base of the mountains after about 8 li. After following a small valley for a short distance, it leaves the stream and ascends over cultivated downs to reach the edge of a spur between two ravines. There is a steep scramble up this ridge for two hours or more by a very rough rocky track to the top of the first range bounding the valley. The view from this ridge looking north is over a series of steep sparsely timbered ranges, rising one behind the other and blocking the way to Fop'ing. From the pass (4400 feet) there is a steep drop into a winding gorge which debouches after an hour's march into the ravine of a stream flowing S.E.; a short distance up this ravine lies an inn, called Ta Tientzu, 65 li from Yang Hsien, which makes a suitable halting-place for the first stage.

From Ta Tientzu the trail continues up the ravine to the north, past the hamlet of Hohsiatzu, for 35 li to the foot of another range running east and west. There is a stiff climb of about a thousand feet to the pass (5500 feet), followed by a precipitous drop of as much down the other side into a ravine which leads straight down to the unwalled township of Huayang Chen, lying in a basin of sandstone at the junction of several ravines which provide water and space for rice fields, the last seen until the descent into the Wei valley five days further north. The surrounding mountains are much broken, prettily wooded, and full of pheasants. To the north a high range runs east and west across the direction of Fop'ing, while to the south-east there is a large gap in the mountains following the flow of the stream. This stage is also about 65 li.

The trail now continues north up a boulder-strewn valley which soon contracts to a gorge, and then turns up a side glen which leads after a scramble to the pass (6000 feet), two to three hours' march from Huayang. This ridge is the boundary between the districts of Yang Hsien and Fop'ing Hsien and the magistrate of the latter had left his isolated post in the wilds of the Ch'inling Shan to meet us here. There is a fine view to the north over two high rocky ranges running east and west, the further one rising to a height of over 10,000 feet. From the pass the track drops steeply into the gorge of a stream flowing west, where there are some huts called Hot'ao Pa. Crossing the stream the path strikes almost immediately into another glen, which leads up through dense thickets of the dwarf-bamboo to the top of the nearest of the two ranges seen from the last pass. From the summit there are fine views all around over the mountains densely wooded with pine, birch, and other trees; to the north the same high range still blocks the road to Fop'ing. From this pass (7000 feet) there is a precipitous drop of a few hundred feet into the gorge of another stream flowing S.W., up which the trail turns northwards for a few li to reach some huts and a mule inn called Ta P'ing, with a little cultivation, mostly potatoes. We halted here for the night, 60 li from Huayang. This is a tiring march, practically one long scramble up and down the mountains all the way, by very bad tracks much too rough to ride over. The second pass can be avoided by taking an alternative route down one stream and up the other, which is said, however, to be impassable for mules.

Ta P'ing is nearly 7000 feet high, Huayang Chen about 4000, Ta Tientzu about 3000, and Yang Hsien about 1300. The trail thus ascends by a series of steps from valley to valley across the intervening ranges from the Han River to the heart of the Ch'inling Shan.

On the following day's march the trail continues up the stream to the N.E. through forests of pine and birch for about 15 li to reach the pass in the big range. The ascent is comparatively easy except for the last few hundred feet, the valley being flat and open and apparently of glacier origin in contrast to the deep narrow gorges usual in the Ch'inling Shan. A little snow and ice were still lying in the stream bed in the middle of May. From the summit of the pass (9000 feet) there is a fine view to the north towards T'aipai Shan (12,000 feet), which appears as a rocky ridge sprinkled with snow, with a lower range in the immediate foreground over which the path leads to Fop'ing. All around are forest-clad ranges, uninhabited, and abounding in big game, deer, bear, pig, leopard, goral, and takin; but owing to the nature of the country their pursuit would involve great difficulties and hardships. This is near the heart of the Ch'inling Shan, a wild unexplored region, whence the ranges and streams ramify east and south-east on one side, and west and south-west on the other. The pass is called the Hsinglung Ling, and is crowned with an old ruined temple and gateway. There are additional signs that this trail, now unused except by a few isolated coolies carrying salt into the Han valley, smugglers, and others with good reasons for avoiding the main road, was once a much more important route. It is of course the most direct road from Hsian to Hanchung.

From the pass there is an easy descent through another flat open valley, where we saw some silver pheasants (or perhaps they should be referred to as blood pheasants, a species of *Ithagenes*), into the valley of a stream flowing west, where there is some cultivation, as usual mostly potatoes, and some huts, called Huangts'ao P'ing; these valleys are less thickly wooded than those on the southern side of the pass. Here the trail leaves the stream at once and strikes up the opposite slope to the north to reach another pass after an hour's easy climb. This range is the last to be crossed before reaching Fop'ing and is a few hundred feet lower than the Hsinglung Ling. From the pass there is a steep descent by a very rough track through a narrow gorge until one debouches after about 25 li into the broad cultivated valley of the Fop'ing River, up which the road runs eastwards through corn fields swarming with pheasants for ten li to Fop'ing T'ing.

Fop'ing, formerly a T'ing and now a third class Hsien, is a tiny place, a mere walled hamlet, containing only twenty or thirty families, and is probably about the smallest and most miserable of all the Hsien cities in China Proper. It lies in a cultivated valley, on the headwaters of a stream which apparently flows west and then south to join the Han near Ch'engku. This valley, over 6000 feet above sea level, is a quarter to half a mile wide, and surrounded on all sides by lofty mountains; it produces wheat, barley, maize, beans, peas, and potatoes, the latter being a most important crop in these mountains and in many parts the staple food of the people. The wheat was just showing above ground in the middle of May when it is ripe for harvest in the Hanchung plain. This valley appears to be the best and most populous part of the district which is entirely covered by high ranges, including T'aipai Shan in the N.W. corner. The post of magistrate is naturally not sought after. The Chinese consider Fop'ing a "dreadfully bitter" place (*k'u ti hen*), since there is no rice nor pork, nor other desirable food supplies; but to the foreigner the abundance of game, bracing healthy climate, and magnificent mountain scenery combine to make it a delightful spot. When the railway reaches Hanchung a month in Fop'ing in the autumn with dog and gun will form a pleasant way of spending a holiday.

We stayed a couple of days at Fop'ing, during which it rained in the valley and snowed on T'aipai and the higher ranges. The cultivated fields round the city and the brush-covered hills to the south abound in pheasants, and I shot a good many cocks, which in spite of the season were excellent eating and a welcome addition to our food supplies. I have shot a great many cock pheasants in the highlands of Shensi and Kansu in the summer for food, as the parts where supplies are scarce and pheasants abundant always seem to coincide. The game-exporting companies have not yet extended their activities to these parts, which provide probably the best wild pheasant shooting in the world. The pheasants usually met with are the usual Mongolian ring-necked species, with the white ring growing less and less as one goes west till it dies out altogether in the mountains of the Kokonor border. These birds literally swarm in the corn fields in many of the cultivated valleys in the mountains

PLATE IX

GORGE IN THE CH'INLING SHAN ON THE TRAIL TO FOP'ING

ACCIDENT TO A PONY ON THE FOP'ING TRAIL

PLATE X

VIEW FROM THE HSINGLUNG LING ON THE FOP'ING TRAIL

VIEW FROM THE HSINGLUNG LING ON THE FOP'ING TRAIL

of the North West and must consume a great deal of grain. Strangely enough the Chinese peasants, often poor to the verge of starvation, seldom touch them, partly because of the cost of powder and shot, and partly perhaps because of the curious prejudice the Chinese cultivator has to eating anything wild, for fear lest it should make him "wild in the heart." The ordinary Chinese appear much to prefer a skinny old chicken to a nice plump pheasant because the former is not wild. While we were routing out pheasants on these hills we put up four deer, apparently a large kind of roe, which showed very little alarm and kept on reappearing at intervals for the rest of the afternoon.

The T'ing, usually translated "sub-prefecture" and now abolished, appears formerly to have been always the centre of a sort of military district located in mountainous country for the purpose of holding aboriginal tribesmen of some kind in check. Thus one will find many T'ing on the western confines of Yunnan, Szechuan, and Kansu facing the Tibetans; in the Miaotzu country of Kueichou and adjacent provinces; on the borders of Lololand in Szechuan; on the Burma-Yunnan frontier; and in Northern Shensi on the Mongolian border; but not in provinces like Anhui, Kiangsu, Shantung, etc., which have never contained a non-Chinese population. There are quite a number of T'ing in the Nan Shan of Shensi. But every vestige of an aboriginal non-Chinese population seems to have disappeared, if it ever existed. I have a vague recollection that some European scholar has evolved a theory that the non-Chinese tribes now living in Southern China originated in the mountains of Southern Shensi. Incidentally it may be noted that the former T'ing are usually marked in foreign maps of China as more important places than the Hsien. But with the exception of a few larger places such as Tachienlu and T'engyueh, nine out of ten of the T'ing are miserable little walled villages in the mountains, nowadays ranking as the poorest of third class Hsien.

Leaving Fop'ing the track climbs up the range immediately to the north by zigzags to reach the pass about a thousand feet above the valley, whence there is a fine view over a wilderness of mountains all around. To the N. and N.W. lies T'aipai Shan, a bare rocky ridge still carrying a good deal of snow in May. This pass (about 7000 feet) is the watershed between the Yangtzu and Yellow River basins, the streams to the north all flowing down into a river called the Hei Ho, which rises in Fop'ing district and flows through the mountains to join the Wei near Chouchih Hsien. The trail to the latter place, however, does not follow down the gorges of this stream, but passes directly N.E. over a series of spurs running down from T'aipai Shan, and is little if at all less arduous than the portion between Yang Hsien and Fop'ing.

From the pass the path drops steeply through a pine wood into a densely wooded gorge running east. After an hour's march down this ravine the stream is joined by one of greater volume flowing down from the snows of T'aipai Shan. The scenery in this neighbourhood is exceedingly beautiful, the torrent descending in a succession of cascades through a gorge hemmed in by densely wooded heights. Continuing down this winding ravine for another hour's march, the village of Houchentzu is reached, where the valley opens out and there is some cultivation. Here the path leaves the stream, which flows off towards the east to join the Hei Ho, and strikes up a gully which leads after a steep ascent to a pass over a ridge some 1500 feet above Houchentzu, whence it drops precipitously into the cultivated valley of another stream flowing down from T'aipai, and reaches the village of Taima Ho, at about the same elevation as Houchentzu (4500 feet) and 60 li from Fop'ing. This was another hard march, scrambling up and down mountains all day; but the scenery was so fine and the air so bracing that no one seemed too tired, though to be compelled to walk the best part of 60 li in the mountains is not unnaturally considered a terrible hardship by the Chinese upper classes; although these latter appear so utterly unused and averse to all forms of bodily exercise there is yet a curious reserve of strength and of capacity for suffering hardship about them which was frequently noticeable on our long journeys. Our party was now much reduced in size, but it severely taxed the accommodation of these mountain inns and hamlets. Local supplies would of course have been quite inadequate, but large quantities of rice or flour and a few rough tents were always arranged for at our halts by the local officials.

At Taima Ho the track again leaves the stream, which flows east into a deep gorge towards the Hei Ho, and turns northwards up the mountain side to gain a pass over a ridge some 1500 feet above the valley. The ascent is easy, this spur being covered with a sort of clayey loess cultivated in terraces; the appearance of loess so far in the Ch'inling ranges is unusual. From the pass the track drops into the gorge of another stream flowing down from T'aipai Shan; it follows up this gorge for a few li past the hamlet of Ch'enk'ou Wan and then turns up a side ravine to reach the base of a ridge called the Laochün Ling. From here there is a stiff climb for two to three hours, ascending 2500 feet, up a wooded mountain side to reach the pass (7500 feet), T'aipai Shan again becoming visible at intervals. From the summit there is a fine view to the S.W. across the lower ridges traversed by the trail back to the watershed range north of Fop'ing. After a steep drop of 2000 feet through a gorge Watientzu is reached, a few huts and inns, surrounded by precipitous mountains, in the ravine of a stream flowing down from T'aipai. This is another tiring march of 60 li. One is here in the district of Chouchih, the Laochün Ling ridge being the Fop'ing boundary.

From Watientzu the path runs down the narrow wooded gorge for about two hours' march, and then turns north up a gully which leads after a steep climb of 2000 feet to the summit of another ridge trending S.E. This is the last of the eleven passes which have to be crossed on this trail between the Han and Wei valleys. From the northern face of the range there is a very fine view over the Wei valley plain nearly five thousand feet below. From the pass the track descends by steep zigzags and then through a narrow gorge for three hours' march to reach the village of Hsin-k'outzu, lying a little above the plain at the base of the mountains, 80 li from Watientzu. The whole party heaved sighs of relief to find themselves once more on level ground; for the mountains with their fine scenery and bracing air are lost on the Chinese, who only notice the discomforts and hardships they entail for the traveller. The majority of our large party had by this time had enough of the journey, and produced various excuses for returning to the provincial capital, two and a half days' march across the plain. The excuses were unnecessary, as we had throughout raised objections to the size of the party. Carts, which we had not seen since leaving T'ungkuan, were sent to meet us here in case anyone should want them, and the prospect of a return to Hsian reclining in a cart, after scrambling up and down the mountains on foot for so many days, was as attractive to them as a passage in a train *de luxe* would be to a travel-worn European. To me a journey in a Chinese cart is a hideously uncomfortable method of travel, unless it be across absolutely smooth Mongolian grass lands. A Chinese cart travels along a Chinese paved road with a series of bumps sounding like gunshots, which rapidly reduce a European to pulp, but apparently have no effect on a Chinese.

From Hsink'outzu to Chouchih Hsien, a distance of 30 li, the track descends across an undulating plain, which in spring is one vast wheat-field dotted with hamlets and the walled farms peculiar to the Shensi plains. Chouchih, a first class Hsien city and the centre of one of the rich agricultural districts of the Wei valley, lies a few li to the south of the Wei River. It is a regular northern city compared to the crowded little towns of the Han valley, and consists of little more than one long dusty street, open and empty looking. Wheat and cotton are the staples; a little coarse silk is produced, the cocoon season being in full swing at the time of our visit during the latter half of May. The two characters for Chouchih are rather unusual ones, and mean "the winding of mountain streams," which appears to refer to the Hei Ho and its tributaries which flow down from Fop'ing and T'aipai Shan through deep winding gorges to the plains. The district, like all those of Central Shensi, is a very ancient one, dating back to the beginnings of Chinese history. We were as usual quartered in the magistrate's yamen, which happened to be in an unusually good state of repair and provided most comfortable accommodation. A study of the archives of these district yamens of Central Shensi would doubtless prove of great interest to the historian, since, where they have not been destroyed during the revolution or the White Wolf rebellion, they date back to very ancient days.

From Chouchih we turned westwards and travelled across the plain to Mei Hsien, a distance of 100 li. The road, here a good cart track, runs across an undulating wheat prairie, dotted with hamlets and walled farms, with the Wei River out of sight on the right hand, and the great barrier of the Ch'inling mountains on the left. Three townships are passed, Yapei, Hengch'u, and Huaiya, the second being of some interest as the home of a famous Sung Dynasty philosopher. The amount of wheat grown on these plains of Central Shensi is very great, especially nowadays since the suppression of opium cultivation. There is no better wheat flour in China than that of Shensi, and it forms the staple food of the population, eaten in the form of bread (*mo*) and macaroni (*kua mien*). With this excellent wheat flour, good mutton, and plenty of game in the mountains, the foreign traveller is well off as regards food. A sound rule for travel in the interior of China is to avoid all tinned foods and rely on native supplies cooked in foreign style; the former only increase one's baggage loads and are quite unnecessary; native food made up in the native style is unappetising to most foreigners as well as being dangerously dirty.

Mei Hsien, a second class district city, is a small place, but like Chouchih is the centre of a rich agricultural region comprising the plain between the Ch'inling Shan and the River Wei. The latter flows a few li to the north of the town. The city has suffered greatly from rebellions and brigandage during recent years.

From Mei Hsien to Fenghsiang Fu is called 110 li, but the road being good and mostly level, the distance can be covered in one long march. The Wei River, in the dry season a thick yellow stream a hundred yards wide and few feet deep, is crossed by a ferry and the road then runs westwards with the river on the left hand and a loess bluff on the right for 35 li to the village of Ts'aichia P'o. At the time of our visit this low-lying land was almost entirely devoted to indigo and dotted with the peculiar-looking brick pits in which the plants are mashed in preparing the dye. This is an old industry revived on account of the scarcity of aniline dyes. The indigo forms a useful rotation crop for the relief of the land exhausted by the everlasting wheat. We saw little else but wheat, cotton, and indigo during our tour of the loess of Central Shensi, growing on

T. T.   4 the uplands, river plains, and irrigated lands respectively. Leaving Ts'aichia P'o the road climbs the loess bluff to the north, emerging on an undulating plain 500 feet above the river, this being about the usual thickness of the loess deposits in Western Shensi, and then runs N.E. across wheat-growing prairies, past numerous hamlets and walled farms, ascending gradually to reach Fenghsiang Fu.

Fenghsiang Fu, now a first class Hsien, lies at the western end of the open Wei valley, where the mountains of the Kansu border meet the Ch'inling Shan and bring these fertile loess plains to an end. It is a large city and used to be quite an important place, but its commercial prosperity, destroyed during the rebellions and other troubles of the past six years, has not yet revived. The inhabitants have a bad reputation, and, like the town of Paochi on the Wei River a day's journey to the south, it has in the past been a hotbed of the Ko Lao Hui. Its position near the junction of the Ch'in Chou road into Kansu and the high road to Szechuan gives it some importance, and cart tracks radiate from it across the plain in all directions, ceasing abruptly at the foot of the mountains.

CHAPTER V

FROM FENGHSIANG THROUGH THE LOESS OF
WESTERN SHENSI TO YENAN

The loess plateau of Western Shensi—Linyu—Yungshou—Ch'unhua—
Wheat harvest—Rifts in the loess—Yaochou—Origin of loess—Brigands
of North Shensi—T'ungkuan—Yichün—Game in the mountains—Chungpu
—Loch'uan—Fuchou—Ravages of brigands—Kanch'uan—Caves—Yenan.

AFTER a couple of days' rest at Fenghsiang we started on a long tour of the loess country of Northern Shensi, the furthest point of which was to be Yenan Fu. There being nothing in the nature of a main road in that direction from where we found ourselves, and being met with the usual protestations to that effect, we had to apply, as usual with success, the plan of proceeding from one district city to another in the required direction, until we struck the highway from Hsian to Yenan at Yao Chou. Between Fenghsiang and Yao Chou our route took us across a vast plateau of loess, which includes parts or the whole of the districts of Pin Chou, Ch'angwu, Sanshui, Yungshou, and Ch'unhua, and reaches in the N.W. a height of over 4000 feet. It has a marked slope to the S.E. and is intersected by the deep cañon of the Ching River and the ravines of many other streams all flowing in the same direction, and by innumerable rifts and crevasses in the loess from ten to five hundred feet in depth. Travel up and down this plateau along its slope between N.W. and S.E. is easy, but transversely from S.W. to N.E., the line of our march, most trying and arduous, owing to the necessity of constantly crossing the perpendicular rifts in the loess, varying from the tremendous cañon of the Ching River, nearly a thousand feet in depth, to a dry crevasse a hundred feet deep. All these rifts trend in the same direction as the slope of the plateau, i.e. S.E., and all have perpendicular walls. In order to avoid these rifts which increase in size and frequency as the plateau descends, our route kept as much as possible to the high ground and consequently made a long detour to the north.

4—2

From Fenghsiang to Yao Chou by this route is a distance of about 510 li, and thence to Yenan another 530 li.

Leaving Fenghsiang Fu by the East Gate the trail soon turns off the main road to the N.E. and runs across the plain for 20 li to the foot of the hills. Crossing a spur a few hundred feet high the path then descends into the ravine of a stream which is followed up for two hours' march to the hamlet of K'angchia Ho. The surrounding mountains are all of loess terraced for the cultivation of wheat and maize, with the scattered inhabitants living mostly in caves. In this neighbourhood we came across some chikor of exceptionally large size (the handsome red-legged partridge of North China), the only occasion on which I have seen them in the loess. These birds are called *Shih Chi* (stone fowl) in the mountains of Northern Chihli, where they are common, frequenting bare stony slopes. They are found in large coveys, which seldom fail to make their presence known by their characteristic call; but they are most difficult to shoot, as they are inveterate runners, always up hill, and, being very strong, carry a great deal of shot; the only way to get them is to descend on them from above. They are excellent eating, but not so good as the little brown partridge with a black patch on the breast, also fairly common in the mountains of the North. Throughout our journeys in Shensi and Kansu, however, we saw very few partridges compared to pheasants.

From K'angchia Ho the trail runs up a branch of the stream to the N.E. for a few li and then strikes up the hill side, and following a ridge between two ravines ascends gradually to reach a pass (4300 feet), the boundary between Fenghsiang and Linyu districts. There is much uncultivated land on these mountains, the grass-grown terraces gradually becoming obliterated; this is a common sight throughout Northern Shensi and Kansu, and together with the many ruined villages points to a decrease in population, supposed to be due to the ravages of the great Mahomedan rebellion of fifty years ago, but perhaps also due to a gradual desiccation of this region. All around are loess ridges and ravines in bewildering confusion; but there appears to be a sort of watershed trending S.E., a range which is known further east as the Ch'i Shan. From the pass there is no immediate descent, the path following along a winding ridge, and then dropping into the valley of a streamlet, which leads after an hour's march to the hamlet of Liangshê, 80 li from Fenghsiang, where we stopped the night. On the following day an easy march of 40 li down the valley, through corn-fields full of pheasants, brought us to Linyu Hsien. The latter is a tiny city, the centre of a miserably poor third class district, lost in the brigand-infested loess mountains not far from the Kansu border. It is an isolated little place, lying on an unfrequented mule trail into Kansu *via* Lingt'ai. The magistrate, an intelligent young man of the student class, led a lonely and somewhat miserable existence, apart from the danger from brigands, and admitted that he only looked upon this, his first appointment, as a stepping-stone to something better. Most of the many magistrates we met took but little interest in their work, regarding their posts either as a necessary evil to be endured for a short time as a stepping-stone to something better, or as a means of getting rich quick. And yet their work of administration is really most interesting and affords many opportunities of improving the lot of the people. But they can hardly be blamed for taking so little interest in their districts in view of the present system under which they may at any moment have to make way for another place-hunter. Thus it often happened that we came across magistrates who, never leaving their dilapidated little yamens, had only the vaguest knowledge of the geography and inhabitants of their districts.

Life in Linyu city, as in countless other little Hsiens buried in the interior of China, is that of the middle ages, and the appearance of its streets and walls, with ancient cannon and gingals and heaps of stones all ready to hurl on the heads of an attacking force of brigands, has probably changed but little for hundreds of years. Revolutions, rebellions, and battles in the plains below, in which the contending forces pump lead at one another with modern rifles and machine guns, have little effect in these isolated hills, except that the brigands become more and more formidable from year to year.

Linyu lies on a loess bluff overlooking the junction of two streams from the west and north, flowing in beds of shale and sandstone at the bottom of deep narrow valleys in the loess hills. The path, crossing the northern branch, strikes up the hill side between two ravines and emerges on to a wheat covered plateau intersected by rifts and valleys in the loess. It runs across this plateau in a northerly direction, ascending gradually, for a couple of hours, and then, as the cañons on either side close in and the plateau narrows to a spur, it follows along the top of the latter, still ascending, for another hour to reach the village of Tsuimu, 4800 feet, perched up on a ridge with the ground falling away in deep cañons all around, and 40 li from Linyu. Supplies were very scanty in these hills, as the people are miserably poor; but a little wheat flour could usually be obtained, which was good where not mixed with too much loess in the process of threshing and grinding. Cock pheasants could generally be secured out of the corn fields when required.

It is an agreeable peculiarity of loess mountain country that the trails follow where possible along spurs and ridges rather than the valleys (this is so, in spite of a famous and much quoted description of the loess in which the life and traffic of the region is described as moving along the bottoms of the cañons), and Tsuimu lies on a sort of knot, where several ridges and therefore mule trails meet; consequently, though only a dot of a place, it boasts a likin station, and commands two trails into Kansu. The path to Yungshou Hsien, 50 li, follows along the top of one of these winding ridges, this one being actually the summit of a range which runs eastwards from the Kansu border and constitutes the first barrier crossed by the Great West Road between Hsian and Lanchou, and provides a most interesting march owing to the continuous and extensive views on either side over this peculiar loess country. To the south a series of loess spurs and intervening ravines fall away steeply towards the Linyu valley, beyond which the Ch'i Shan range is seen to end, as Yungshou is approached, in the rolling plains of the Wei River and its tributaries; while to the north, across an intervening dip, rises like a wall the edge of the loess plateau country of Eastern Kansu. These loess clad ridges of Western Shensi seem to be pieces broken off from the Kansu plateau, like the mountains on the edge of the Mongolian plateau, south of Dolonor in Northern Chihli.

PLATE XI

CITY OF LINYU FROM THE NORTH

CHAITZU (HILL FORTRESS) OF TSUIMU, WESTERN SHENSI

PLATE XII

CANYON OF THE CHING RIVER, WESTERN SHENSI

FERRY ACROSS THE CHING RIVER

Where the loess has been washed away shales and sandstones
are revealed, and often right on the tops of the spurs there
are outcroppings of a sort of conglomerate of waterworn
pebbles cemented together. The loess mountains in this
neighbourhood are little cultivated, being covered with
poor-looking pasture, which supports scanty herds of cattle
and flocks of sheep. Finally there is a descent of a few
hundred feet to reach the city of Yungshou Hsien, which
lies a little below the crest of the ridge, on the shoulder of
a spur up which ascends the Great West Road from the
Hsian plains.

Yungshou consists of one street running up the ridge
and is merely a walled-in section of the big road; it is a
replica of Linyu, with a little more life in it owing to its
position on the Kansu highway. We had passed through
it two years previously almost to a day on our way to
the latter province, the season of the year being the end of
May.

Our next objective was the district city of Ch'unhua
(locally Shunhua) distant two marches of 90 li each. Leaving
Yungshou we followed up the main road for a few li to
regain the crest of the range, where I shot some cock
pheasants in almost the identical spot as two years before,
and then turned eastwards once more along the top of the
ridge for 25 li to a cave village. Here the ridge ends in
rolling uplands of loess, the beginning, from this side, of
the great loess plateau of Western Shensi. The Belgian
railway (Lung Hai) from Hsian to Lanchou will, it is said,
follow up the Wei River, the line of the cart road being
apparently too difficult; an easier route might perhaps be
found following up the slope of this plateau through
Sanshui district to Ch'ingyang, and thence through Northern
Kansu. The upper portions of these rolling plains where
we met them are uncultivated and covered with poor sheep
pasture, apparently owing to the lack of water, the one
great drawback to the loess; and one might imagine oneself
on the grasslands of Eastern Mongolia, until, on attempting
to cross the plateau in any direction away from the trail,
one almost immediately fetches up against a chasm in the
loess with perpendicular walls perhaps hundreds of feet
deep. Lower down these uplands are one vast cornfield

through which the path descends to reach the township of Ch'angning Chen, winding to and fro to avoid the rifts, the heads of ravines and valleys breaking away south and southeast.

The harvest time on these immense wheat prairies which was now approaching is a period of intense activity. The crops are of course gathered entirely by hand, and large numbers of labourers from Kansu, groups of whom we were constantly meeting, come down to assist; after the harvest is over in the Wei valley plains they work back across the plateau of Western Shensi to their native highlands, harvesting as they go. In good years there must be a large surplus of wheat in Shensi and Kansu available for export; but in the absence of waterways and railways the means of communication are so bad that it would be impossible to move the harvests to any distance.

From Ch'angning the path runs in a northerly direction across the plateau, winding about to avoid the impassable rifts, for about 20 li, where it reaches the Ching River, flowing in a deep narrow cañon some 800 feet deep. There is a steep descent into this gorge, and the Ching River, an unfordable torrent of liquid mud, is crossed by a ferry. This cañon exposes clearly the depth of the loess covering, some five or six hundred feet, the stream having carved itself a bed still deeper down in the underlying rock. The track climbs out of the gorge to the top of the plateau a similar height on the further side, and then runs across the undulating uplands for 15 li to the village of Kao Ts'un in the district of Pin Chou, 90 li from Yungshou. This is a tiring march, including the passage of the Ching Ho, for on the small roads of Northern Shensi the li are apt to be very long.

From Kao Ts'un the track continues N.E. for another 30 li to the village of T'u Ch'iao (4400 feet), in the district of Sanshui, now called Hsünyi Hsien, the highest and most northerly point on the plateau reached between Yungshou and Ch'unhua, whence it runs S.E., descending gradually with the slope of the land, for 45 li, to the large village of T'ungshen Kou. So far the trail by keeping to the north had avoided the crevasses in the loess, but as soon as one turned S.E. they began to be met. Thus between T'u Ch'iao and T'ungshen Kou three streamlets flowing in deep rifts in the loess have to be crossed, the last named place lying on the further edge of the third. The passage of each rift means a precipitous climb down into the gorge of 500 feet or more and a similar ascent the other side (this being the thickness of the loess covering); at the bottom there is usually a streamlet flowing in a rocky bed underneath the loess. The constant crossing of these rifts (called *kou* by the Chinese) was most trying in the dry heat of early June, and at midday the temperature at the bottom of the *kou* was sometimes terrific. Water is very scarce in loess country, and apt to be brackish, and the streamlets at the bottom of the rifts are their only redeeming feature from the traveller's point of view. The passage of these rifts was a constant and arduous feature of our daily marches from now on until we had completed our tour of Northern Shensi. Sometimes marching towards a village after a long day the weary traveller sees his destination apparently only a few hundred yards away, only to find that it is separated from him by a *kou* 500 feet deep which takes at least an hour to cross. From T'ungshen Kou the track continues S.E. across the sloping plateau for 20 li, descending steeply for the last mile or so, to reach Ch'unhua Hsien, a poor little third class district city, lying in a sort of basin formed by the junction of several valleys and rifts in the loess some distance below the level of the plateau. To the south the loess rises steeply to a low rocky range separating the Ch'unhua valley from the Ching Ho.

From Ch'unhua to Yao Chou is a distance of 115 li, two short marches. The trail climbs out of the valley to the level of the plateau a few hundred feet above and continues eastwards, keeping to the high ground and winding round the heads of several rifts in the loess. After two to three hours' march the cañon of a streamlet flowing south is crossed by the usual zigzag descent and ascent, and another hour brings one to the village of Fangli Chen, 40 li from Ch'unhua. Thirty li further on the village of Hsiaoch'u is reached, after crossing two more huge rifts, with streams flowing as usual S. and S.E. The passage of these cañons is the exact inverse of crossing a pass of equal height; instead of the summit of a ridge with the view and breeze to refresh one there is the airless sweltering heat of the bottom of the

kou. Again referring to the well-known description of
the loess which depicts the life and traffic of the region as
moving unseen along the bottoms of the rifts, the converse
holds good on these table lands of Western Shensi, the
villages, farms, and roads lying on the top of the plateau,
and the bottoms of the cañons being often lifeless. From
Hsiaoch'u the track runs eastwards over the plateau, crossing
two more rifts *en route*, for four hours' march to reach Yao
Chou, lying in a valley at the junction of two streams flowing
south.

The region traversed on this route between Yungshou
and Yao Chou must be one of the best examples in the
world of a pure loess plateau. It is dotted with low mountain
outcroppings, and travelling across it one is strongly
impressed with its resemblance to a series of old lake
basins which have been drained off to the south-east. The
loess soil, a sort of very fine sandy loam, which covers
almost the whole of North Western China north of the
Ch'inling Shan to a depth of many hundreds of feet, is
supposed to have been deposited as the result of the dust
storms of countless ages from the Gobi deserts of Mongolia
combined with the decomposition of vegetable matter. The
longer we travelled in the loess country the more difficult
it seemed to credit this theory. The Chinese take it for
granted that these wonderful deposits of *Huang T'u*
(yellow earth, as they call it) were caused by water, that is
to say by the great floods which according to their historical
records once submerged N.W. China at about the same
period as those recorded in the Bible. For anyone well
acquainted with the country it requires but little effort to
imagine these turgid floods of yellow waters washing the
base of the Ch'inling Shan as they poured down from the
N.W., and depositing the loess, even as its redeposit may
nowadays be watched on the banks of the Yellow River
between Ninghsia and Paot'ou. The configuration of the
Wei basin in Shensi is exactly that of the bed of a huge
river washing the base of a rocky cliff on its southern bank
and sloping up in shallows towards the north. Further, in
every rift or ravine, which is cut down through the loess to
the underlying shale or sandstone, a layer of mixed loess
and water-worn pebbles is almost invariably exposed

immediately above the rock on which the loess rests. The regularity of level and depth of the loess over wide areas, the invariable slope of the loess uplands in the same direction as the rivers and streams, i.e. all draining S.E. and the meeting-line of the light sandy loess and the heavier reddish loess, which can often be traced for miles at the same level, may also be noted in support of a water origin; while lastly there is the fact that the loess has nowhere, except in the extreme west, crossed the Ch'inling Shan, a continuous range, whereas it is piled high on either side of other ranges which are not continuous. These lines are written without access to books of reference of any kind, and it should be understood that they represent merely the impressions of a traveller with no scientific training, who has not the least intention of starting a controversy on the subject of a problem which has probably long been settled by competent scientists. But in spite of the fact that we have often seen loess at a height of 6000 feet or more, it is difficult to believe that it was not deposited there by water.

Yao Chou, now a second class Hsien, is quite a large city for Northern Shensi, and about the most prosperous, or rather least miserable, place we came across in that region. It lies, surrounded by indigo fields, in a narrow valley below the level of the loess uplands. We were here joined by a *Lien* (company) of infantry, since the north of Shensi is, at the time of writing, so overrun with brigands, well armed and organized in bands many hundreds strong, that it would have been impossible for a party of Chinese officials to tour those districts with a smaller escort. Curiously enough, owing to the extraordinary change which has occurred in the position of the foreigner in the interior of China since the Revolution of 1911, while no Chinese but brigands, soldiers, or the poorest of coolies can travel on the roads of Northern Shensi without great danger to property and life, a missionary or other foreigner can circulate where he pleases with comparatively little danger of being attacked. We had so far been accompanied by a small mounted escort of a dozen men or so; for though the mountainous districts of Southern and Central Shensi through which we had passed harbour plenty of brigands, these are mostly local robbers who plunder isolated travellers and levy blackmail on the villages. The north of Shensi on the other hand was at the time of our visit in the hands of organized troops of brigands of a semi-political character, robbers one day, rebels the next, and perhaps successful revolutionaries the next.

At Yao Chou we struck the main trail from Hsian Fu to Yenan, Suitê, Yülin, and the north of the province generally; with the exception of the little known and seldom used track by which we returned it is the only trail connecting Central and Northern Shensi. As far as Yenan and Yench'ang it is passable for carts, having been constructed at considerable cost for the transport of the Japanese oil-drilling machinery to Yench'ang in 1906, and again repaired by the Americans during their oil-drilling venture eight years later. This road might at comparatively small cost be made passable for motor traffic, and had the American enterprise succeeded would doubtless long since have been made so. As it is, it nowadays leads into a depopulated, brigand-infested region where there is no trade and traffic, and is gradually reverting to the condition of an ordinary Chinese trail. But it is an example of the ease with which a comparatively good cart track can be constructed through mountainous country, where, without the stimulus of a foreign interest, the Chinese would for ever remain content with the usual villainous mule trail.

The first stage from Yao Chou is a short one, called 60 li, to T'ungkuan Hsien, and lies up the valley to the N.E., which, except at one point about half-way where it contracts into a gorge, is cultivated and bounded by low hills of loess. T'ungkuan is a little third class district city lying at the foot of the first of the mountain ranges which cross Northern Shensi from N.W. to S.E.

The next day's march is from T'ungkuan Hsien to Yichün Hsien, a distance of 80 li. The track runs up the valley to the north, the loess hills gradually becoming more rocky and less cultivated, for 25 li to the barrier hamlet of Chinso Kuan, where an old wall and fort guard the entrance to a gorge. Here the loess is left behind and scrub-covered mountains are entered through a winding gorge, which leads by an easy ascent after three hours' march to the hamlet of Liehch'uan, lying on the top of the range at a height of

PLATE XIII

AT THE BOTTOM OF A LOESS RIFT, WESTERN SHENSI

LOOKING DOWN A LOESS RIFT, WESTERN SHENSI

PLATE XIV

CITY OF CH'UNHUA FROM THE N.E.

CITY OF CHUNGPU FROM THE E.

about 4700 feet. From the pass there is no immediate descent, the track following along a winding ridge in the grass and brush-covered hills for 25 li, and then descending a few hundred feet to reach Yichün, a dilapidated little city, built on the side of the ridge, the centre of a very poor third class district.

The range of mountains crossed on this day's march forms the watershed between the Lo and Wei rivers, the two principal streams draining Northern Shensi, and rises well above the loess covering. Perhaps the soil of no region in the world has been worked by man to the same extent as the loess of Central Shensi, where the Chinese have been scratching, sowing, and reaping uninterruptedly for some 4000 years or more, and the landscape of those plains appears tired and worn out. It is therefore a relief to get out of the loess, with its alternate dust and mud, glaring heat, insufficient and often brackish water, and treeless and monotonous scenery, into these mountains with their clear streams, grassy downs, and brush-covered slopes, haunted by innumerable deer and pheasants. In all our travels we found few spots more teeming with game than the hill sides in the neighbourhood of Yichün, and being now in a country where supplies were practically nil, we bagged quantities of cock pheasants, in pursuit of which it was seldom necessary to go more than a hundred yards from the road. We saw plenty of deer, apparently roe, too, but as we could get as many pheasants as we wanted, we did not trouble to go after them.

This range also marks the dividing line at present between the comparatively peaceful regions of Central Shensi and the brigand infested north. Yichün had been raided but recently, and was generally speaking in a most dilapidated condition from this and previous raids. When leaving the next morning we passed a crowd of the usual emaciated dogs outside the North Gate feasting on the remains of some decapitated brigands, an unpleasant sight at six o'clock in the morning, but one which gave great pleasure to most of the party. For a dead brigand cannot but be a pleasant sight to a peaceful Chinese, and my companions kept on repeating to themselves with real satisfaction *kou ch'ih t'u fei* (dogs eating brigands), as being an entirely suitable and satisfactory state of affairs. Unfortunately my enquiries showed that these decapitated bodies were not those of the real brigands of these regions at all, but of some strangers who arrived at the city gates and could not give a satisfactory account of themselves, and who had accordingly been executed so as to be on the safe side.

Most of the magistrates in Shensi are now natives of the province, young students and military officers of the new school, but in one of the districts on this road we met an official of the old type of magistrate *de carrière*, a Hunanese who had just come down from Chinese Turkestan where he had been serving for years. Though the virtues of the new type of local official in China may be great, it was a pleasure to meet a gentleman of the old school with his many and varied experiences, and we had a long talk about mutual acquaintances serving in the deserts of the far North West.

From Yichün the path follows down the ridge descending gradually for 35 li to the village of P'iench'iao, where the mountains give way once more to loess hills and the ridge flattens out into a plateau. The track continues across this tableland, winding to and fro to avoid the usual rifts in the loess falling away into the valleys on either side, and then descends steeply for the last five li to reach the district city of Chungpu lying in the narrow valley of a stream flowing east.

We were now once more in the loess with its glaring dry heat and choking dust. The season of the year was early June, when all over North China there is a spell of very hot dry weather, corresponding, presumably, to the heat of Northern India before the monsoon. In July and August the rains break, and though the steamy heat is then trying enough, and the loess is turned into slimy mud, the change is a great relief.

At Chungpu we were met by the Taoyin of Northern Shensi, whose seat is at Yülin Fu on the edge of the Ordos. His post is at present a most difficult one owing to the northern districts being so overrun with brigands. He told us that the extreme north of the province was much less desolate and more prosperous than the districts we were now traversing. We had heard much of the terrible "bitter-

ness" of this road, and certainly what with the ravages of
brigands and the natural infertility of the soil, the few
inhabitants were poor to the verge of starvation. Yenan
seems to be the centre of the most desolate area, by far the
poorest region I have traversed in China outside the actual
deserts.

Chungpu, a poor little third class district city half in
ruins, lies on the side of a hill, with a sacred grove of very
ancient trees behind it, which present a remarkable sight
in this treeless country. Near by is a small temple containing
the tomb of the Emperor Huang Ti, who reigned some 4000
years ago, which illustrates the great antiquity of these little
Shensi towns.

The next day's stage to Loch'uan Hsien is a trying
march through the loess. The track follows down the valley
to the east for 20 li, and then turning north climbs up through
a gully on to the plateau a few hundred feet above, across
which it runs for an hour's march to the hamlet of Antzu
T'ou, whence it drops into the valley of the Lo River. This
stream resembles the Ching Ho, a muddy torrent twenty
yards wide, and flows in a narrow valley some hundreds
of feet below the level of the loess plateau. It is crossed by
a ferry at the hamlet of Chiaoho K'ou, and the path then
climbs steeply out of the valley again and runs across the
plateau in a N.E. direction for three hours' march to reach
the district city of Loch'uan. The latter is the usual little
third class Hsien city of Northern Shensi, but appeared to
be rather more prosperous than its neighbours and to show
less signs of the ravages of brigands. It lies on the loess
plateau, intersected as usual by colossal rifts, the heads of
some of which are so close to the city that they threaten
to engulf it in a few years time. These towns and villages
on the loess plateau are quite unapproachable except by
the existing roads owing to the rifts which open up all
around, and could be held by a few men against an army;
perhaps that is why Loch'uan appeared comparatively
immune from brigand raids.

From Loch'uan to Fu Chou is another exhausting march
in the loess of 75 li. The track runs N.E. across the plateau
for an hour's march until it is held up by a huge cañon
with the usual perpendicular walls. Climbing in and out of

this gorge it continues across the plateau, only to meet a few li further on with another and still larger rift, at the bottom of which there is a welcome stream and a hamlet called Chiehtzu Ho, the boundary of Loch'uan district. The crossing of a district boundary was always noticeable throughout our journeys, because it entailed a welcome rest and an exchange of civilities with a new magistrate. After the usual five hundred foot climb out of this cañon the path runs across the plateau northwards for an hour or so, and then drops again into the valley of the Lo River, here containing a considerably less volume of water than where crossed on the preceding stage, the difference being due to a large tributary from the west which joins it in between. Most of the terraced mountain sides in this neighbourhood have gone out of cultivation, and from here north to Yenan Fu the country becomes more and more desolate and depopulated. Another 20 li up the winding valley brings one to Fu Chou.

Fu Chou, now Fu Hsien, a second class district city, is a fortress of great antiquity guarding this highway into the heart of ancient China against the invasions of the hordes of barbarians from the North. It fills up most of the valley with its walls climbing up the hillside. Since the Mongol ceased to threaten Fu Chou has entirely lost its former importance, and is now in a most miserable and decayed condition. A walk on the wall shows the usual dilapidated little city, but a stroll through the streets reveals the fact that it is practically empty, *k'ung ch'eng*, as a Chinese remarked to me. The explanation of this lay in the fact that it had been sacked four times by brigands during the preceding year, and the inhabitants, having given up residence there as hopeless, had emigrated to other parts or provinces. We afterwards passed through many other cities and villages in Northern Shensi in the same condition. The post of magistrate in these districts is an exceedingly unenviable one, and it appears to be difficult to get men to take them up. If the brigands come, the *ching pei tui* (police) are helpless, and the magistrate is lucky if he can save his life by escaping into the mountains. The official of one of these cities informed me that it was inadvisable to arm the local police with modern rifles, as, the

PLATE XV

VIEW ACROSS RIFTS IN THE LOESS PLATEAU NEAR FUCHOU

VIEW ACROSS RIFTS IN THE LOESS PLATEAU NEAR FUCHOU

PLATE XVI

LO RIVER IN A VALLEY IN THE LOESS PLATEAU NEAR FUCHOU

CAVE VILLAGE IN SEMI-DESERT COUNTRY NEAR YENAN

place having long been swept bare of all its valuables, there would be nothing to attract another raid provided there were no modern arms and ammunition in the place. Silver, opium, rifles, and ammunition are what the brigands go for. The only thing that was not utterly decayed in Fu Chou was a brand new *chai* (hill fort) on the top of the mountain behind the town, built by the magistrate and the few remaining inhabitants as a refuge against the next raid. In the centre of the town is an old tower containing an ancient bronze bell of fine workmanship dating from the T'ang Dynasty, the only object of value which survives the periodical raids. From Fu Chou a track leads westwards to Ch'ingyang Fu in Kansu, one of the very few east to west trails in these parts.

From Fu Chou to Kanch'uan Hsien, a distance of 85 to 90 li, the trail runs up the valley of the Lo River through poor-looking crops of maize, millet, hemp, and wheat. The loess hills on either side are mostly uncultivated and the whole region gives the impression of turning into desert. Several miserable hamlets are passed, consisting mostly of caves or cave houses, the latter queer-looking square huts built of earth and stones with tunnel-like interiors. Scarcity of wood for roofing purposes is said to be the reason for constructing these remarkable artificial caves, but probably the people are so used to living in caves that they do not feel at home in anything else. A good cave in the loess is not to be despised as a dwelling, being rain proof, warm in winter and cool in summer. Owing to the vertical cleavage which is always going on in the loess these caves are constantly collapsing, but the owners seem to know by instinct when it is necessary to remove to a new abode. Kanch'uan is a smaller replica of Fu Chou, a ruined empty shell of a city.

Here the trail to Yenan, distant 85 li, leaves the Lo River and follows up a side valley to the N.E. which leads after three to four hours' march by an easy ascent to the pass (4100 feet) in the divide between the Lo Ho and the Yen Shui. This divide is entirely covered by loess, but curiously enough there is a complete change of scenery, and the ascent and descent is through jungle clad ravines and over grassy downs. These mountains are uncultivated and uninhabited, but here and there the remains of old terraces, evidently abandoned for many years, are noticeable. Descending from the pass this curious zone of comparatively rich vegetation is soon left behind and one approaches Yenan by a desolate looking valley between hills of sandy, barren loess. The crops are miserable in the extreme, and consist mostly of millet, little or no wheat being grown. Three to four hours' march down this valley brought us to the gates of Yenan Fu.

CHAPTER VI

FROM YENAN AND YENCH'ANG THROUGH THE
MOUNTAINS OF EASTERN SHENSI BACK TO HSIAN FU

Yenan—American attempt to exploit the oil deposits of Northern Shensi—
Yench'ang—Yich'uan—Brigands and soldiers in Northern Shensi—Han-
ch'eng—How to travel in comfort—Hoyang—Ch'engch'eng—P'uch'eng—
Fup'ing—Sanyuan—Baptist Mission—Cotton cultivation—Back in Hsian.

YENAN FU, now known as Fushih Hsien, a second class
district city, is a large place in area as cities in Northern
Shensi go, but is nowadays extremely poor and dilapidated
as the result of the constant depredations of brigands in
the neighbourhood, most of the shops in the main street
being deserted. It is built in the narrow valley of the Yen
Shui, which it completely fills at this point, and like Fu
Chou it has guarded this passage into China against the
inroads of the Tartar hordes from the North for thousands
of years. On the hill side opposite are some remarkable
cave temples of great antiquity, one of them containing
innumerable (said to be ten thousand) little figures of
Buddha carved out of the sandstone rock. The neighbourhood appears desperately poor and the crops very backward,
the little wheat we saw being still green and barely in ear
during the first half of June, though the elevation is only
about 3000 feet. Northern Shensi and N.E. Kansu appear
to be drying up and turning into desert, perhaps owing to
the existence of a little-known range of mountains in Shansi,
just east of the Yellow River, which, rising in places to a
height of over 10,000 feet, must act as a barrier against the
moisture-laden winds from the coast. Coal and iron are
said to be abundant in the neighbourhood, but lack of means
of communication renders them useless except for local
consumption. Petroleum is also found in Northern Shensi,
and the attempts to exploit these oil deposits have been,
apart from rebellions, revolutions, and brigandage, the most
important events of recent years in this region.

In the past mineral oil used to leak out of the ground

just outside the South Gate of the little city of Yench'ang Hsien, two marches east of Yenan, and about 1906 two wells were sunk on the spot with the assistance of Japanese engineers and Japanese machinery.

Some seven years later the Standard Oil Company of New York conceived the idea of exploiting the supposed oil deposits of North China and negotiated a co-operative agreement with the Chinese Government, which was signed in February 1914, to the following effect.

The Standard Oil Company was to send experts to examine the supposed oil fields in Northern Shensi and Northern Chihli, the expenses of the survey being borne jointly by the Company and the Chinese Government. If the reports of these experts proved favourable, a Sino-American Company was to be formed, which should begin operations within six months of the completion of the survey. Capitalisation of the Company to be 55 per cent. Standard Oil, and 37½ per cent. Chinese Government (the latter being presented with their shares by the Company in exchange for the concession); and 7½ per cent. optional for the Chinese Government to purchase at par. Any increase in capital to be on the same terms, and the management to be Sino-American in the same proportion. The Chinese Government undertook that the exploitation of the oil fields named should be given exclusively to the Standard Oil Company, and that no concession whatsoever for oil-bearing properties in China should be given to any other foreigner until the results of the Company's operations should be apparent to the Chinese Government and the Standard Oil Company, which period should not exceed one year from the date of signing the contract. The agreement to last for sixty years, during which time the Chinese Government would not allow any other foreigners to produce oil in the districts named. In the event of the districts in question (apparently Yenan and Yench'ang in Shensi and Jehol in Chihli) proving worthless, any other districts in Shensi and Chihli to be substituted therefore. Concessions to be granted for the necessary railways and pipe-lines. The Chinese Government to arrange matters with the landowners. The acceptance of the terms of the agreement by the Standard Oil Company to be entirely dependent on the result of the examination by experts.

The above is taken from the newspapers published at the time and may or may not be correct. The remaining facts regarding the history of the enterprise are given from conversations with local Chinese on the subject, and also may or may not accurately represent what occurred.

Anyone acquainted with the vastness of the trade in petroleum, imported from the East Indies by a British Company and from the United States by an American Company, which has come into existence of recent years in China, and the remarkable manner in which this oil penetrates to all but the most distant portions of the country in spite of transport difficulties and likin exactions, will realise what a magnificent proposition this agreement would have been for the Standard Oil Company had the enterprise succeeded; but it is also obvious that it would have been equally of enormous advantage and profit to the Chinese Government, since without foreign assistance the Chinese are at present as incapable of developing such a proposition as they are of building a railway to the moon.

An inspection of the Jehol oilfields in Northern Chihli proved them worthless, but the report of the two geologists sent to Shensi appears to have been favourable, and a careful survey was then made of the whole of the supposed oilfield. A large staff of geologists, engineers, and drillers was subsequently imported, together with quantities of bulky drilling machinery. The transport of the latter from railhead in Honan through the wilds of Northern Shensi to Yenan and Yench'ang entailed difficulties which seemed insuperable, but was nevertheless successfully accomplished by means of American energy, ability, and driving power. When we passed through Central Shensi on our way to Kansu two years previously, the transport of this machinery, which was just then being undertaken, and the adventures which befell it *en route*, seemed the sole topic of conversation and the only subject of interest in the province. We now saw portions of the same huge pieces of machinery lying apparently useless and abandoned in these wild and inaccessible regions.

During 1915 wells were sunk near Yenan and Yench'ang, and also apparently in Ansai, Yichün and Chungpu districts in accordance with the hopes held out by the survey; but no oil was found anywhere except at Yench'ang alongside of the original Japanese well.

Finally in the summer of 1916 work was stopped, the Americans withdrew, and the enterprise was apparently abandoned, the bulky machinery being left behind. Apart from the absence of oil, there must have been many difficulties to contend with in connection with the brigandage and increasing chaos in that region.

The wells have now been filled in, and scarcely a trace of the Americans remains, except for the derelict machinery and the good reputation the surveyors and geologists left behind them amongst the natives, who speak of their departure with great regret and look forward to their ultimate return.

The failure of the enterprise was a bitter disappointment to the local Chinese, for whom the two years were a golden age and who had conjured up visions of railways, roads and pipe-lines, and an era of booming prosperity. Instead of which Northern Shensi now continues as of old to produce little but sand and brigands.

The two original Japanese wells continue to produce oil, and the concern, under official management, flourishes in a small way. Their output is limited by their facilities for refining and transporting the oil, and only one well is therefore usually at work. The oil is sold in the neighbourhood and also across the Yellow River in Shansi, where the people are more prosperous. Transport is by pack mule over the roughest of mountain trails, and the expense of carriage prevents its penetrating any great distance. It was of course owing to the inaccessibility of the region that it was necessary to find oil in really large quantities to make the installation of a pipe-line, say to the Yangtzu, worth the enormous expense entailed.

From Yenan we proposed proceeding east to Yench'ang and to work our way thence somehow or other back to Hsian through Eastern Shensi. Of course everyone said there was no road in that direction, and we knew that the country just west of the Yellow River was likely to prove very rough and poor. But we felt confident that we should as usual always find trails of some kind from one district city to another. As events turned out we found a trail,

PLATE XVII

DIVIDE BETWEEN THE LO HO AND YEN SHUI NEAR YENAN

CAVE TEMPLES IN SANDSTONE CLIFF OPPOSITE YENAN

PLATE XVIII

OIL WELL AT YENCH'ANG

IN THE MOUNTAINS OF E. SHENSI

which, though very arduous and passing through desperately poor mountainous country just inland from the Yellow River, had apparently once been quite an important route. From Yenan to Hsian by this route *via* Yich'uan and Han-ch'eng was a distance of about 1030 li, and took us more than two weeks' hard travelling.

From Yenan to Yench'ang is two days' march, 80 and 60 li respectively. The first stage lies down the valley of the Yen Shui between low hills of loess to the village of Kanku Yi. Ten li out one of the oil wells drilled by the Americans in 1916 is passed in the mouth of a small gorge; it has now been filled in. There are several cave villages on the road, the largest being Yaotientzu 50 li out, where there are inns. Kanku Yi, as its name implies, is the ruin of an old fortified posting stage (*Yi*) such as are common on the main roads of Kansu; here the main trail to the north of the province turns N.E. to Yench'uan and Suitê, while the Yench'ang track continues down the valley to the east.

Twenty-five li from Kanku Yi, at the hamlet of Heichia P'o, the river turns south, and the trail strikes up a ravine to the east to gain the top of the loess plateau some 500 feet above the valley, runs across the level upland for a few li, and then drops steeply into another ravine, which is followed for 20 li till it debouches again into the valley of the Yen Shui at Yench'ang Hsien.

Yench'ang lies in the narrow valley of the Yen Shui, right on the river bank, in the mouth of a tributary ravine. The presence of the petroleum is very apparent from the smell which pervades the whole place, and as we were quartered and entertained on the premises of the oil concern and within a few yards of the principal well, the penetrating smell of mineral oil never seemed to leave us for a moment from the time of our arrival till that of our departure. The two wells lie just outside the city wall to the west; the principal one was pouring forth a steady stream of oil at the time of our visit and apparently never ceases doing so. The city itself is the usual little third class district town of Northern Shensi, but it is less dilapidated than most of its neighbours and the walls are in better repair. This is owing to its not having been sacked by brigands during recent years, for which immunity from the prevailing evil credit is also, it seems, due to the beneficent oil. As the traveller approaches Yench'ang he will note that the city walls appear to be weeping or oozing oil, and the explanation of this curious fact becomes strikingly apparent at night time. For in the embrasures all round the walls every yard or so are placed pans of crude oil, which are lit up when darkness falls and illuminate the whole city and neighbourhood in the most remarkable manner. The effect on anyone not expecting it is extremely startling. Night after night through-out the year this desolate little city lost in the wilds of Northern Shensi indulges in this orgy of illumination. But it costs practically nothing and seems to be very effective in scaring off the brigands, who usually make their raids on moonless nights; doubtless the prospect of having a pan of burning oil upset over their heads deters them also.

The next stage on our journey by this route was the city of Yich'uan Hsien, two long marches due south of Yench'ang. The trail runs down the gorges of the Yen Shui, being ledged in the cliff on the left bank, for about 15 li, and then crossing the river by a ford strikes up the hill side to the south to reach the top of the loess plateau some 600 to 700 feet above the valley; continuing across the plateau for an hour or so it then drops steeply to the hamlet of Ankou Chen in the gorge of a tributary of the Yen Shui, called 35 li from Yench'ang. From Ankou the path strikes im-mediately up the opposite hill to reach the top of the plateau again, the latter here taking the form of a series of flat-topped loess ridges running down towards the Yen Shui from a range trending east and west. A two hours' march to the south up the flat top of one of these ridges brought us to the top of the range (4500 feet), the watershed between the Yen Shui and a stream called the Yunai Ho; the range is composed of grassy downs of loess with occasional out-croppings of rock. From the pass the trail follows a spur to the south, which soon flattens out into the usual square-topped loess ridge, and descends gradually for four to five hours' march, with finally a steep drop into the valley of the Yunai Ho to reach the ruined township of Yunai Chen. The country traversed on this day's march, as also on the following one, consists of loess mountains with a little cultivation on their lower slopes. Villages are very scarce, and the trackless downs and mountains are the haunts of the brigands of these regions, who live in unknown cave villages in the heights, whence they make their forays into the valleys. All the streams, such as the Yunai Ho and others, take their rise in these loess mountains and run eastwards to join the Yellow River, flowing in beds of shale and sandstone at the bottom of narrow valleys in the loess. The Yellow River is said to be reached 100 li down the valley from Yunai Chen. From Yench'ang to Yunai Chen is called 80, 90, or 100 li, according to the fancy of the individual questioned. Distances are not fixed on these small by-roads as they are on the main trails. We found it a very long march; my mule train, composed of particularly good animals which usually averaged well over three miles per hour, took more than ten hours to cover the distance, exclusive of halts. The li on the small roads of Northern Shensi and Kansu are very long. 100 li on a main road in the Han valley is certainly not more than 25 miles at the outside; but the 100 li from Yench'ang to Yunai must be nearer 35 miles.

The next day's march to Yich'uan Hsien is called 80 li. The path runs up a side ravine to the south-west for an hour and then ascends steeply to gain the top of the plateau, which here serves as the divide between the Yunai Ho and the Yich'uan stream. This divide is not a mountain range but a level tableland of loess, the highest point being about 4000 feet. There is the usual view over innumerable flat-topped loess ridges sinking down in the east towards the Yellow River, the trough of which can be vaguely descried; to the north the range crossed on the preceding march bounds the view; and to the south a similar but higher range rises steeply behind the Yich'uan valley. After an hour's march in a southerly direction, descending gradually along the usual flat-topped ridge of loess, the track drops steeply into a ravine which leads down after 20 li to the ruins of a walled village called P'inglo P'u, resembling hundreds of similar dilapidated old forts scattered throughout Northern Shensi and Kansu, most of which have been taken and retaken, sacked and re-sacked, by Mahomedans and Chinese during the days of the great rebellion. Here the path leaves the stream, which flows S.E., and striking again up the slope to the south, runs for two hours' march across the flat-topped hills, descending finally by precipitous zigzags to reach the city of Yich'uan lying in the narrow valley of a stream flowing east to join the Yellow River. The country crossed on this march is again pure loess, very sparsely populated, and with innumerable grass-grown terraces which have gone out of cultivation and render evident the depopulation of the region.

Yich'uan Hsien, lying at the junction of two narrow valleys in the loess, is the capital of a second class district, and was evidently a comparatively large and prosperous city in the past. At the time of our visit it was practically empty, and lying in the heart of that wild and little frequented region which contains the chief haunts of the brigand bands of Northern Shensi, it is at the present time uninhabitable by any but the poorest classes. Northern Shensi, depopulated by the Mahomedan rebellion fifty years ago, and now probably undergoing a process of desiccation, is losing its few remaining inhabitants of the better class through the devastations of the brigands, many having moved across the Yellow River into Shansi, where conditions are much better. Recently a large band of brigands, perhaps finding that Northern Shensi was getting rather bare, also moved across the river; but prompt military measures were taken by the Shansi authorities and they were soon driven back to their original haunts with great loss. The question naturally arises, why should these brigands be left apparently unmolested by the authorities of their own province?

The answer is provided by the history of events in Shensi during the years since the revolution of 1911, which is outlined in another chapter. The brigands of Northern Shensi are mostly ex-soldiers and Ko Lao Hui men, and are composed of the same material as the provincial troops, with whom they exchange rôles from time to time. It is therefore not possible to use the latter against them. Further, they constitute in a way the reserves of the provincial army, which are thus maintained without cost to the provincial Government. The Shensi soldier usually owns his own Mauser and as much ammunition as he can carry wound round and round his body in a cloth bandolier, acquired in the course of some previous rebellion or brigand raid, and thus equipped serves either as a soldier or a brigand according to his own tastes and the military requirements of the local Government. In either character he is about equally obnoxious to the people. Both rôles too have their respective advantages; the life of a Chinese brigand may be rather lean at times, but there is always the possibility of a good haul; the life of a soldier in Shensi may be dull, but he is fed and paid without being asked to do any work. This kind of soldier of fortune is known locally in the province as a *Tao K'o* (guest of the sword); most of the better-class brigands and soldiers are Tao K'o, which is considered a title to be proud of. The Shensi soldier differs widely from and compares unfavourably with his colleagues in the well-organized and disciplined armies of the North (Chihli, Shantung, Anhui, and Honan provide most of the sturdy men for those fine Northern armies on which the power of Peking rests); but it is not his fault, for he is the victim of circumstances and of the Ko Lao Hui. I have been in close contact for months with Shensi soldiers, who were, to use the Chinese euphemism, *Kuei hui pei shan* ("returned from the Northern hills"—a polite way of referring to an ex-brigand locally), and always found them excellent fellows as far as I was concerned, though behaving tyrannically towards the people.

The difficulties of suppressing brigandage in the wild and pathless mountains of Shensi are in any case very great. Measures for the satisfactory pacification of the region would include the complete reorganization of the provincial army, or the garrisoning of the province with three or four brigades of good Northern troops. But the latter is not at present practicable, as the people of the province not unnaturally are great believers in home rule and like to manage their own affairs. Another very necessary but difficult reform is the disarming of the people and the recovery of the large stocks of rifles at present in private hands. In modern China the brigand without a rifle is a negligible quantity. It is chiefly through the various rebellions that these arms have become scattered over the country with such disastrous results, and brigandage grows steadily worse with every such outbreak of civil war. A rebellion is engineered (in Shensi at any rate) by collecting funds and enlisting brigands and secret society men as soldiers; after the rebellion is over, whether it succeeds or not, the soldiers are disbanded and scatter with their arms over the country, with the inevitable result of increased brigandage. The growth of brigandage in Shensi may easily be traced since 1911, the revolution of that year, the rebellion of 1913, the White Wolf rebellion in 1914, the anti-monarchical rebellion of 1916, the troubles of 1917, and so on.

From Yich'uan Hsien to Hanch'eng Hsien is a distance of about 240 li, three hard days' march by a difficult track through the mountains which here hem in the Yellow River. All the way from Yench'ang south to the plains of Central Shensi, which are reached at Hanch'eng, the traveller is crossing a series of parallel ridges trending east and west across his path; but while between Yench'ang and Yich'uan the intervals between these ridges are filled by loess which provides comparatively easy slopes, the region between the latter place and Hanch'eng is covered by mountains which are practically free from loess and entail the crossing of a series of precipitous little passes. The trail slants across these mountains towards the Yümen K'ou, the point where the Yellow River emerges from its gorges on to the plains; the river itself is not touched, though glimpses are caught from the tops of the passes of its huge trough in the mountains.

From Yich'uan the trail runs up the valley to the S.W. for a few li and then turns up a gorge to the south, which leads after a couple of hours' march to the foot of the barrier range which bounds the Yich'uan valley on the south. A steep climb leads to the pass, the Lut'ou Ling (5100 feet). This range and the valleys and spurs leading up to it, though covered with loess on the northern side, are un-cultivated and uninhabited. On the southern side there is practically no loess, and the latter is not met with in any quantity again till the path debouches on to the plains of the Yellow River above Hanch'eng three days later. The absence of loess in the low-lying valley bottoms of these mountains is rather curious, and one may speculate whether perhaps the Lut'ou Ling range, which before the existence of the Yellow River was probably joined to the mountains of Shansi, did not form a barrier keeping the floods which deposited the loess from reaching this region, which con_ stitutes an isolated area sloping S.E. and hemmed in by surrounding mountains; in the case of the similar Yich'uan and Yunai basins further north, the surrounding mountains were perhaps not sufficiently high to keep out the floods, the ranges being themselves nowadays buried in loess.

From the pass there is an easy descent through a gorge for 20 li to Hsiehchia P'ing, the ruins of a hamlet destroyed by brigands, where several ravines join to form a stream flowing east towards the Yellow River. The surrounding mountain slopes are rocky and uncultivated, and except for the scarcity of water resemble the Ch'inling ranges rather than the mountains of Northern Shensi. From Hsiehchia P'ing the path follows up a side ravine which leads after an hour's scramble to another pass (4800 feet); it then drops straight down the mountain side into a gorge which is followed for four hours' march until it expands into a valley at Ch'iyi Chen, a small township called 100 li from Yich'uan, where we passed the night. This is an exceedingly long and tiring day's march over a rough and rocky trail, and my mules were nearly twelve hours on the road; but there is no accommodation short of Ch'iyi Chen, the mountains being almost uninhabited and the few huts passed having mostly been destroyed by the brigands, and we had no tents with us on this journey. Everyone was fairly exhausted when we got in, a tremendous thunderstorm during the last hour completing our discomfiture; but owing, as usual, to the thoughtful assistance of the district magistrate we were comfortably housed in the principal shop of the village. Throughout our long wanderings the preparation of accommodation of some kind at the end of a march by the local official made all the difference to our comfort; schools, yamens, forts, rest-houses, temples, shops, private residences, inns, farms, caves, huts, and tents, have all served us for accommodation at different times, and the order in which they are quoted represents roughly their comparative merits. Starting at daybreak after a cup of tea or cocoa we used usually to march for about three hours and then halt for an hour or two for a good square meal; in the meantime if the march was not too long the pack mules would travel right through, so that the baggage had arrived and was already unpacked by the time we got in in the early afternoon. This is the height of luxury in travel in North Western China. Riding good ambling ponies we used to average four miles or more per hour on a good trail, and a day's journey of 80 li seemed nothing under these conditions. But a few really tiring marches (and this is one of them) stand out in my memory, when we had to cover a hundred li or more over rocky mountain paths where it might be necessary to walk half of the way; the hardest day of all was a march on the Kokonor border, when we started at 6 a.m. and got in at 9 p.m., crossing a pass over 13,000 feet high on the way.

Leaving Ch'iyi Chen the track runs down the valley towards the Yellow River for a few li and then strikes straight up the mountain side to the south to reach the pass (3600 feet). This ridge is the boundary between the districts of Yich'uan and Hanch'eng, which are both very extended ones. From the pass there is a steep drop into a gorge and then a climb over a loess spur to reach the hamlet of Tuch'uan lying in a narrow ravine. From here the trail strikes again up the mountain side to the south, crosses a pass (4100 feet), and descends along a loess ridge with finally a steep drop to reach the walled village of Wangfeng Ch'iao lying in the narrow valley of a stream flowing east. From Ch'iyi Chen to Wangfeng Ch'iao is the middle stage in the three days' march between Yich'uan and Hanch'eng, and though only called 60 li in length is a tiring day's work, consisting of one long scramble up and down the mountains. As this route slants across the ridges to the S.E. and approaches the Yellow River, the passes decrease in altitude and some loess begins to reappear. The mountains in this neighbourhood appear to be full of iron ore.

From Wangfeng Ch'iao the track ascends the mountain side to the south to reach a pass (3400 feet) in the last range which bars the way to the plains. From the previous passes there were extensive views across the cañon of the Yellow River to the mountains of Shansi, but the river itself remained invisible; from this ridge it is seen for the first time, emerging from the mountains at the mouth of the gorge known as Yümen K'ou. This is a very celebrated spot amongst the Chinese, since their annals record that the Emperor Yu (2000 B.C.) here cut a channel through the mountains to drain off the great floods which at that time submerged the whole of North West China, thus bringing into existence the modern Yellow River and the fertile deposits of *Huang T'u* (the "yellow earth," which we call loess); perhaps an earthquake gave rise to this tradition.

From this last pass the track drops steeply into a gorge which is followed for an hour's march to the S.E., and then, crossing the spur which encloses the gorge on the south, drops down into the loess plains on the right bank of the Yellow River. From this point to Hanch'eng Hsien, a distance of 40 li, the trail runs across an undulating plain, which is not really a plain but the usual loess plateau, here of moderate thickness, sloping down from the mountains to the Yellow River, the latter flowing five to ten li away on one's left. This plain between the foot hills and the river is one of the most fertile and densely populated regions in the province, and is thickly dotted with farms, villages, temples, tombs, and pagodas. It is always so in North China, densely peopled fertile plains and barren empty mountains side by side. The largest of the many villages passed is Hsichuang, where there is a likin station to catch the trade coming down from the North by the route we had traversed; but its receipts must be small nowadays, for not only not on this road, but at no time during our tour of Northern Shensi, did we meet a single load of merchandize or a single traveller of the better class, so utterly has all trade and traffic in that region been destroyed by the brigands. Finally there is a short steep descent to reach the city of Hanch'eng, which lies surrounded by fields of indigo in a basin in the loess plateau formed by the valley of a stream flowing S.E.

Hanch'eng, a second class district city, is a large and wealthy town, at least it appeared to us to be so, coming from the poverty-stricken North. The district is one of the most fertile in the province, and is noted for its wheat, cotton, hemp, and indigo. The irrigated fields round the city produce three crops in one summer, maize being sown after a crop of wheat has been harvested, and indigo being then transplanted in early June into the same field, the indigo and the maize growing up together.

The most direct road from Hanch'eng to Hsian lies

through the cities of T'ungchou Fu and Weinan Hsien across the plains along the Yellow River, but we followed a slightly longer route further north across the loess uplands *via* Hoyang, Ch'engch'eng, P'uch'eng, Fup'ing, and San-yuan, a week's journey by a good and mostly level trail. The season of the year was now late June and the rains had not yet broken, so we expected a scorching hot journey across these plains; but fortunately we struck the season of high winds which blow for a few days before the rains break, and had quite a pleasant journey until the last day or two, when we were overtaken by the opening downpours of the rainy season and had a hard struggle to get across the water-logged plain of the Wei River.

From Hanch'eng Hsien to Hoyang Hsien is a long march called 95 li. The road, now a good cart track, leaves Hanch'eng by the South Gate, and crossing a fine stone bridge runs down the valley through indigo fields for 20 li, where it debouches on to the Yellow River at the township of Chihch'uan Chen, a prosperous little city with an important likin station tapping the trade with Shansi. This place, like many other non-official townships we passed on the road to Hsian, is larger and wealthier than any district city we saw in Northern Shensi. At Chihch'uan the road leaves the Yellow River and climbs up on to the loess plateau some hundreds of feet above, across which it runs south-west and west, past the townships of Pailiang Chen (in Hoyang district) and T'ungchia Chuang, a centre of the vegetable oil industry, and many smaller villages, for the rest of the way to Hoyang. This plateau is just like all the other loess uplands, an undulating wheat prairie intersected by rifts and valleys; and the passage of two of these cañons hundreds of feet deep makes the march a long and arduous one.

Hoyang is a fairly large city, the centre of a first class district; but it is a poor-looking place inside, like most of these purely agricultural prairie towns, and is not to be compared with Hanch'eng, which probably does a good deal of trade with prosperous Shansi. It lies in a slight depression of the rolling loess uplands, now covered with short wheat stubble. Supplies of all kinds are abundant on this road, but game is scarce; though an occasional pheasant was to be seen in the bare fields.

From Hoyang to Ch'engch'eng, a short march of 45 li, the trail runs west across the same undulating plains, traversing two deep cañons *en route*. Ch'engch'eng, a second class district city, is a replica of Hoyang.

The next stage to P'uch'eng is a very long march, called 105 li, probably over 30 miles, for the li are long on these prairies. The trail runs south across the plain past numerous hamlets, descending gradually, for three to four hours' march, and then drops by easy gradients in the loess terraces to the walled township of Yungfeng Chen, 50 li from Ch'engch'eng, in the valley of the Lo River. These little walled towns often have the characters for their names inscribed over the gateway, like stations on a railway, a custom which is most useful to the traveller, and which I have not noticed elsewhere.

Five li west of Yungfeng the Lo River, at low water a few feet deep and fifteen yards wide, and of the consistency of liquid mud, is crossed by a ferry. The Lo here flows from north to south; on the right bank rises a loess bluff a few hundred feet high, and on the left the open valley some miles wide stretches up by easy slopes and low terraces to the level of the plateau. From the ferry the trail ascends the bluff constituting the edge of the tableland, and then runs west across the usual undulating wheat prairies, dotted with walled farms and villages, for the rest of the way to P'uch'eng.

P'uch'eng lies in the open plain backed by low mountains about ten miles to the north. It is a large and important place, a first class district city and the centre of a great wheat-growing region. Many prominent men in Shensi have their homes in the district, which therefore, in these days of home rule, exercises considerable influence in the province. These large first class districts in the loess of Central Shensi, such as P'uch'eng, Lint'ung, Weinan, and Fup'ing, the very heart of ancient China, have always been proverbial for their agricultural wealth, and to this day the provincial Government subsists largely off their land tax revenues.

From P'uch'eng to Fup'ing, another long march of 95 li, the trail continues west across the same undulating prairies past many villages including the township of

Hsingshih Chen, a busy place where much of the commerce of P'uch'eng district is carried on. Fup'ing, another important first class district city, lies in a depression in the loess plain caused by the shallow valley of a stream which provides irrigated lands of the richest kind. We chanced to be travelling this trail at a time when political affairs were in a more than usually chaotic state and the authority of the officials more than usually relaxed, and we had been strongly advised not to follow this route owing to the alleged large and turbulent populations of P'uch'eng and Fup'ing, who are said to be noted for their independence and love of managing their own affairs (*P'u Fu jen to*, *pei hsing pu an*, as one member of our party kept repeating); but, as almost everywhere else on our travels, we found the people perfectly friendly.

From Fup'ing to Sanyuan should be an easy march of 60 li; but the rains had now suddenly broken and it was an arduous day ploughing through the loess mud, which has a peculiar slimy character of its own, rendering progress whether on foot or on horseback dreadfully slow. The trail runs S.W. for a few li across low-lying land, apparently the valley of the Yao Chou River, which was largely under cotton, and then continues for 20 li across a wheat-growing plateau to the boundary of the two districts. Here there is a steep drop through a loess cutting into a level plain across which the track runs for the rest of the way to Sanyuan.

Sanyuan, the centre of a second class district, is one of the largest and most important cities in the province, though this is not saying much. Commercially it is an annex to Hsian Fu, much of the commerce which really belongs to the latter being transacted here to avoid the official exactions of the provincial capital. For the same reason most of the trade to and from Kansu passes through Sanyuan. During recent years it has played an important part in the various rebellions and other political events which have so disturbed the province, and its trade has therefore been for the moment destroyed. The city lies on a level loess plain, and is bisected by a stream flowing in a deep rift, which is spanned by a fine stone bridge; the southern portion contains the shops and life of the place, the northern being mostly empty. Cart roads radiate in all directions across the plain.

The English Baptist Mission, apart from the China Inland Mission, the only Protestant Mission working in Shensi, has been established for many years at Sanyuan, in the neighbourhood of which there are quite a number of Christian villages. The history of how they came to the province is of some interest to the student of missionary enterprise in China. The Mission also works in Shantung, and when, after the depopulation caused by rebellion and famine during the latter half of the last century, Shensi was being repopulated from other provinces, some of the Shantung Christians were amongst the immigrants. These appear to have founded Christian communities in the plains of Central Shensi, and to have invited their former foreign teachers to follow them. The story is of interest because it appears to point to the existence at that time of a native Christian church standing on its own legs, which in my experience is a very rare thing in China today. The great obstacle to the spread of Protestant Christianity in China is that the Christian church remains almost everywhere a purely foreign institution. How much Christianity would be found in China in ten years time, if all the foreign support, missionaries and funds, were withdrawn today? There appears to be not the remotest prospect of China ever embracing Christianity on a large scale, until, if ever, a really native Christian church takes root in the same way as the Mahomedan religion has done. All of which, however, in no way detracts from the good work now being done by missionaries of all persuasions throughout the Republic, the benefits of which to the Chinese are incalculable. Since the revolution there has been a great influx of Chinese into the Missions; but it is to be feared that only a very small proportion of these enquirers and converts were actuated by other than material motives, such as a desire to share in the wonderful immunity enjoyed by the foreigner from the evils bred by the lawlessness of the times. There is a story about a veteran missionary in Kansu, who, having baptised several converts and having subsequently had the painful experience of watching them backslide one after the other, swore he would never again baptise a Chinese, and limited himself in future to exhorting them to be good and explaining the sacred books; which seems to the layman to be a thoroughly sound and sensible policy. The conversion of the Chinese is a tough proposition; but there is a far tougher one confronting the missionary in the North West, and that is the conversion of the Mahomedans and Tibetans in Kansu. The Chinese is apathetic towards Christianity, while keeping an open mind towards any aspect of it which may be turned to his material advantage. The Tibetan or Mahomedan on the other hand is usually not at all apathetic, but very actively hostile towards any attempt to convert him.

From Sanyuan to Hsian Fu is a day's march, called 90 li by the Chinese owing to the passage of the two rivers which occupies an hour or so, and is therefore considered the equivalent of 10 li. For us it was a long slow march, floundering through the mud in pouring rain. The road runs due south across the plain, the pagoda of the village of Ch'ingyang T'a being a prominent landmark for the first 30 li. A few li beyond this village the Ching Ho is reached and crossed by a cart ferry, and another 15 li across a low table-land of loess dotted with the curious tumuli, some from fifty to one hundred feet high and said to be the tombs of ancient kings, brings one to the Wei River, varying from a few hundred yards to a mile in width according to the season, and crossed by a cart ferry. These plains along the Wei and Ching rivers are the great cotton-growing areas of Central Shensi. Cotton has always been a staple crop of the province, and is one of the principal exports. It is now being grown more extensively than ever and is being bought up for export by the Japanese. The soil and climate appear well suited to its cultivation, and there seems to be no reason why its quality should not be improved by scientific methods, nor why there should not be a big cotton spinning industry in Hsian and the neighbourhood. As it is the Japanese buy the cotton, take it to Japan to spin, and then return it to the Chinese in the form of yarn.

We found the Wei River in flood and had a hard time crossing it. The ferry took us over the main stream, but two branches in flood had to be forded with the water up to the ponies' bellies and running like a mill race. One of the carts accompanying us, containing the baggage of the soldiers, apparently drove into a hole and disappeared except for its hood; we were too much occupied at the time with our own

PLATE XIX

STONE CAUSEWAY ACROSS LOESS RIFT, E. SHENSI

INDIGO FIELDS IN IRRIGATED LOESS VALLEY NEAR HANCH'ENG

PLATE XX

SUMMIT OF CH'INLING PASS ON MAIN ROAD TO SZECHUAN

TUNG RIVER VALLEY NEAR FENGHSIEN IN S.W. SHENSI

ponies and mules and I never heard what happened to it or whether there was anyone inside. The Chinese pack saddle is made in two parts, the framework containing the baggage resting unattached on the saddle proper, an excellent system permitting of quick and easy loading and unloading; but it has the disadvantage that if the mule falls in fording a difficult river, his load is likely to disappear for good. A few li after crossing the Wei River the village of Tsaot'an is reached, whence the road continues south across the plain for 25 li to reach the north wall of Hsian Fu.

CHAPTER VII

FROM HSIAN FU IN SHENSI TO CHENGTU FU IN SZECHUAN BY THE MAIN ROAD

The Szechuan road—The T'ung Ch'eng Railway—Hsienyang—Hsingp'ing—Wukung—Fufeng—Ch'ishan—Paochi—Shensi mules—Passage of Ch'inling Shan—Fenghsien—Loess—Feng Ling—Ch'aikuan Ling—Liupa—Paoch'eng—Manchu Restoration—Mienhsien—Gold in the Han mountains—Sources of Han River—Ningchiang—Entry into Szechuan—The Chialing Chiang and Kuangyuan—Chaohua—The narrows of Chienmen Kuan—Chienchou—Tzutung—Mienchou—Lochiang and the cities of the Chengtu plain—Chengtu—Szechuanese and Yunnanese.

FROM Hsian, the capital of Shensi, to Chengtu, the capital of Szechuan, by the main road is a distance of 2225 li, say a little over 500 miles (the li in this direction averaging about four to one mile). Travelling the regular stages, it is possible to cover this distance in less than a month, but as our caravan was rather exhausted by its long wanderings, and the heat was at times very oppressive, we journeyed slowly and with occasional rests, and took five to six weeks to reach Chengtu.

This road is about the most important overland route in China, though the traffic on it has somewhat diminished since the introduction of steamers on the upper Yangtzu between Ichang and Chungking, well-to-do travellers nowadays preferring to make a détour by way of Hankow and thus to avoid the hardships of so long an overland journey. As well as being the main and practically the only artery of communication between Shensi and Szechuan, it is a section of the great highway from Peking to Lassa. For the tourist who wishes to see the interior of China, a journey from Peking *via* Hsian to Chengtu by this road, and thence back by river to Shanghai, would provide a tour of great interest through some of the finest scenery in China Proper, besides entailing a minimum of the hardships inseparable from travel in the interior, supplies and accommodation being abundant all the way. After leaving the Wei valley it is a mule trail, paved most of the way and comparatively good in Szechuan, but very rough and rocky through the mountains of Shensi. Lying most of the way through Southern Shensi and Szechuan, where paved paths and flights of irregular stone steps are the rule, it is unsuitable for ponies, and it is advisable to take a chair, at any rate from the Han valley onwards. We started with ponies, having used them on all our journeys through the North West, but were compelled to take to chairs when we got into Szechuan, as the steps and paving stones knocked our ponies' feet to pieces. Walking and chairing is a pleasant enough method of travel, but very slow, the rate of progress in the mountains being only about eight li per hour, which makes the stages long.

The Belgians have secured a concession for the construction of a trunk railway from Tatung in Northern Shansi to Chengtu in Szechuan. It is a peculiar line to have chosen and one which will involve considerable engineering difficulties in Shensi and Szechuan. In nine cases out of ten the railway surveyor is unable to find a better trace for a line than that followed by an ancient highway of commerce, but if this railway is to follow the main trail between Hsian and Chengtu, its constructors are going to have a difficult job. The traveller by this road can therefore beguile the monotony of the journey by speculating as to the feasibility or otherwise of constructing a railway along it; it will certainly not be easy to find a less difficult route.

We left Hsian Fu on the 29th of June in a downpour of rain and floundered through the mud across the plain to reach Hsienyang Hsien, fortunately only 50 li away. This city, a poor-looking place in appearance though the centre of a first class district, is built along the northern bank of the Wei River, which is crossed by a cart ferry. It has some importance as being more or less the head of navigation on the Wei River, and as lying at the point where the great highway from Hsian, T'ungkuan, Peking, and the coast bifurcates, one branch continuing N.W. to Kansu and Turkestan, and the other turning W. and S.W. to Szechuan and Tibet. One cannot but speculate on the innumerable travellers who have passed through its miserable little main street, knee-deep in dust or mud, bound on their weary way to the outposts of Chinese rule in the deserts of

Turkestan or Tibet, at any time during the past few hundred years. Hsienyang is also famous as one of the old capitals of China, having been the seat of no less a person than the Emperor who designed the Great Wall, and who, being annoyed by the supercilious conservatism of the Chinese scholars of those days, buried several hundreds of them alive, and burnt all their books; for which act his name is execrated by the scholars of today.

Starting out from Hsienyang we left the high road to Kansu, which we had followed two years previously, on the right hand, and continued across the level plain to Hsingp'ing Hsien, another short march of 50 li. This is a second class district city lying on a wheat and cotton-growing plain sloping from the north down towards the Wei River.

The next stage to Wukung Hsien is a distance of 90 li, still across the plain. Thirty li out, just beyond the village of Mawei, the local magistrate who was accompanying us suddenly dragged us off the road to visit a dilapidated little temple in the fields, which turned out to be the tomb of a notorious Imperial concubine known to every educated Chinese as Yang Kuei-fei. She was strangled here by her consort, the Emperor, to satisfy his troops in about 170 A.D.; I forget the details of the story, which every Chinese knows. There was nothing to be seen inside the temple except the usual ancient individual busy taking rubbings of inscriptions. Central Shensi is full of these objects of historical interest, dating back sometimes two or three thousand years. Wukung district is entered beyond the walled village of Tungfufeng, which lies half-way, and the plain now begins to rise imperceptibly and becomes the usual undulating loess plateau; so that there is a sudden drop to reach the city of Wukung Hsien lying in a valley a hundred feet or so below the level of the loess. Three streams, from near Fenghsiang, Linyu, and Yungshou, unite here to form a pea-soupy river flowing south to join the Wei. Wukung, a second-class district city, is quite a prosperous little place with busy streets and well-stocked shops.

From Wukung the road climbs out of the valley and runs across the loess uplands to the west. All along this road the traveller is accompanied on his left hand by the

Ch'inling Shan, rising like a wall out of the plain to the south of the Wei River, and affording fine views of its culminating point the T'aipai Shan, snow-clad till mid-summer (12,500 feet). The walled village of Hsinglin Chen is passed half-way out, and 15 li further on the valley of a stream from the north is crossed. Finally there is a drop to reach Fufeng Hsien, 60 li from Wukung, and a replica of the latter, lying in precisely the same sort of hollow below the level of the loess at the junction of two valleys from the north and west.

From Fufeng Hsien to Ch'ishan Hsien is another easy march of 60 li across the uplands, crossing two shallow ravines *en route*, the loess here not being of sufficient thickness to be fissured by the deep rifts and cañons found further north. Ch'ishan lies close under the mountains of the same name, with the loess plain sloping down to the Wei River to the south. The main road here continues west to Fenghsiang, but travellers bound for Szechuan like our-selves, and having no particular concern with the latter place, usually proceed direct to Paochi on the Wei River, a distance of 110 li, which can be covered in a long day's march. Ch'ishan, a second class district city, much resembles Wukung and Fufeng, and seems fairly prosperous for a city of Central Shensi.

The road now runs west and south-west across the loess uplands for about 50 li, and then descends by easy gradients for another 25 li to reach Titien, a village of inns on the Wei River, just beyond the confluence of the latter with the Ch'ien Shui from Ch'ienyang and Lungchou, the passage of which in a flooded state caused us some trouble. On this stretch of road we crossed our previous route from Mei Hsien to Fenghsiang Fu, thus affording an opportunity of checking the route survey, the results of which were not particularly encouraging; but as my instruments consisted of nothing more serious than a prismatic compass, with which I kept up a route survey throughout our journeys, this was perhaps not surprising. From Titien to Paochi the road runs west between the Wei River on the left hand and a high loess bluff on the right. The actual valley plain of the Wei is here quite narrow, as the land on the further bank rises almost immediately to the grim-looking barrier of the

Ch'inling Shan; above the loess bluff on the right hand, however, the undulating uplands stretch northwards to beyond Fenghsiang Fu till they meet the Ch'ishan range; west of Paochi these latter mountains converge on to the Ch'inling Shan, and bring the loess plains of the Wei basin altogether to an end, in much the same way as the cigar-shaped Hanchung plain ends beyond Mien Hsien.

Paochi, a first class district city, lies on rising ground behind the Wei River with its northern wall climbing the loess bluff. It is quite a big place and evidently handles a considerable trade with Szechuan and Kansu. The inhabitants have the reputation of being turbulent and the Ko Lao Hui is very strong in the neighbourhood.

The western districts of Central Shensi through which we had been passing are the breeding grounds for the mules for which Shensi is famous, and which are exported in considerable quantities to the eastern provinces. At the time of our passage the wheat harvest was just over and the fields were being ploughed for the next crop. The endless plains of loess were everywhere dotted with ploughing teams consisting of mules and pony mares, the latter in almost every instance being followed by a mule foal. These Shensi and Kansu mules are the best in China, probably in the world. Fine upstanding animals, they carry loads of over 200 Chinese pounds (say 300 English pounds), travelling stages of 20 miles or more per day for weeks and months on end; the Szechuan and Yunnan mules, though good animals too, carry less than half as much. The secret of mule management in Shensi and Kansu is the feeding, and they are given an enormous amount of grain, which they spend most of the night in eating; a midday feed is not considered necessary, or even advisable, except on a very long march. The jack donkeys by which these fine mules are bred are large upstanding animals, the size of a pony, and very different from the ordinary pack-carrying donkey of North China.

From Paochi to Feng Hsien is a distance of 210 li and includes the passage of the Ch'inling Shan. There are numerous inns *en route*, so that it can be divided into two, three, or more stages as the traveller prefers. Leaving Paochi the Wei River, at high water several hundred yards wide and full of sand-banks, is crossed by a ferry, and the trail then plunges into the Ch'inling Shan by a valley which soon becomes a gorge hemmed in by precipitous mountains. The change from the bare loess plains and hills to these rocky, jungle-clad mountains is strikingly sudden. The road is a well-graded mule path, but very rough going, being irregularly paved with cobbles and boulders. Fifty li from Paochi we reached the hamlet of Kuanyint'ang, nestling underneath a wooded cliff, where we passed the night. Here we were met by some of our old acquaintances from the excellent Northern brigade garrisoning Hanchung and the Han valley, in whose care we were to be till reaching the Szechuan border, and said farewell for good to the picturesque ex-brigands who had formed our escort and who had looked after us so well during our tour of the Northern districts; though their past did not always bear looking into they were the best of fellows.

Crossing the loess of Central Shensi the heat had been terrific, but from now on for the next few days, till we debouched from the mountains on to the Hanchung plain at Paoch'eng, it was delightfully cool though rather rainy. Fifteen li above Kuanyint'ang the gorge ends in the pass over the main Ch'inling range (about 5100 feet); the ascent is easy, the valley leading practically up to the summit. The railway will probably have to cross this pass, but as there is a rise of some 3000 feet from Paochi, there will have to be a pretty stiff gradient or a long tunnel. The gorge resembles the approach to the Nank'ou Pass on the Kalgan railway north of Peking, but is probably more difficult to negotiate.

From the pass there is a drop of a few hundred feet into an open cultivated valley, that of the Tung Ho, flowing down from the south-western slopes of T'aipai Shan. This stream forms one of the headwaters of the great Szechuan River, the Chialing Chiang, which joins the Yangtzu at Chungking, so that though one has crossed the main range of the Ch'inling Shan and the Yangtzu Yellow River divide, one is not yet in the basin of the Han. The easiest line for the railway from here will probably be found to lie down the Chialing Chiang into Szechuan (though the latter flows mostly through precipitous gorges), thus not entering the

Han valley like the main road does. The trail runs S.W. down this valley through fields of wheat and maize past several villages, such as Huangniu P'u, Hunghua P'u, and Ts'aoliang Yi, in any of which a halt can be made. The Tung Ho is here, in summer, already a fair-sized mountain torrent, only just fordable, and is joined by several tributary torrents from the wooded mountains on either side. Between Ts'aoliang Yi and Feng Hsien, a distance of 70 li, the river runs mostly through winding gorges, with the path, a good mule-trail, ledged in the cliff over the water.

Feng Hsien, a third class district city, consists of one long street with a certain amount of life in it owing to the traffic on the high road. It lies hidden by poplars in a pretty cultivated valley. The confines of Kansu are not far off and there seem to be a good many Kansu Mahomedans in the district. There is plenty of loess in the Tung valley round Feng Hsien, though it is on the southern side of the Ch'inling watershed. There is not, so far as I know, any loess in the Han basin, but it may be noticed in the valleys of the headwater streams of the Chialing Chiang both here and above Li Hsien in Kansu, and doubtless in other places too. The presence of this loess south of the watershed range, which further east forms a barrier to and is the southern limit of this formation, seems to require a good deal of explaining; if the loess was deposited by water the fact that the relative height of the watershed above the ground north of it is so much lower in the west than in the east, may perhaps account for it.

We met a good deal of traffic on this road, in contrast to the empty trails of Northern Shensi, consisting of strings of coolies and pack-mules carrying tea, umbrellas, iron, etc., from Szechuan and the Han valley to Hsian and the towns of the Wei basin; when we got into Szechuan the contrast was still more marked, and the traffic was practically an endless procession of carrying coolies going both ways; and this in spite of the fact that Northern Szechuan abounds in brigands too, but apparently of a less formidable character than those of Northern Shensi.

At Feng Hsien the trail leaves the Tung River, which flows S.W. into Kansu, and turns up the mountain side to the south, reaching the pass, the Feng Ling (6300 feet) after a two to three hours' climb. My heights for these passes, obtained, like all the rest on my maps, from aneroid observations compared with an occasional boiling-point thermometer reading, are lower than those usually given; but in the most modern maps of China Hanchung is assigned a height of 2000 feet, which is probably 500 feet too much, and in one good map Mien Hsien further west is given as 1800 feet odd, thus causing the Han River to flow up hill between the two cities; so that there is room for argument on the subject all round. From the Feng Ling there is a fine view to the west over the cultivated slopes of the Tung valley backed by higher mountains on the Kansu border, and to the south-east over the wooded limestone ranges of the Ch'inling Shan. After running along the mountain side for a short distance the path drops steeply into a gorge which leads down to the village of Sanch'a Yi, an old posting stage, lying at the confluence of two streams some 2000 feet below the pass and 50 li from Feng Hsien, and following down this valley, where rice fields and some loess re-appear, for another hour's march, reaches the village of Liufeng Kuan. This stream is a tributary of the Tung Ho, so that one is still on the head-waters of the Chialing Chiang. Liufeng Kuan is the head-quarters of a deputy magistrate under Feng Hsien, and we passed the night comfortably in his yamen.

The trail, which has hitherto run S.W. all the way from the Wei valley, now turns S.E. up a winding ravine, leading into the heart of the Ch'inling Shan, the village of Nanhsing in Liupa district being reached after about two hours' march. This place is half-way between Feng Hsien and Liupa T'ing, and provides accommodation for the traveller who wants to cover the distance (180 li) in two stages. Four hours' march up the valley, which contracts to a gorge hemmed in by densely-wooded mountains, brings one to the pass, the Ch'aikuan Ling (5500 feet), which leads over the divide into the Han basin. The Ch'inling ranges are seen at their best round the Ch'aikuan Ling, where the rocky precipices and densely-wooded mountain slopes, clear mountain torrents, and narrow fertile ravines combine to form a landscape of great beauty. Though the ascent to the pass is by easy gradients the descent is precipitous, and a railway following the main road (which could avoid the more formidable Feng Ling by a détour down the Tung valley and up the tributary to Liufeng Kuan) would presumably require a long tunnel, and would meet with many more difficulties following down the gorge to Liupa and beyond. Some five li below the pass lies the Changliang Miao, beautifully situated at the junction of two wooded ravines, where we passed the night. This is one of the finest temples in China, built, I believe, in the Han Dynasty, and is well known amongst the Chinese; one would have liked to remain there a week.

From Changliang Miao (also known as Miao T'aitzu) the path runs down a winding gorge for the rest of the way to Liupa, a distance of 40 li. The latter, formerly a T'ing, and now a third class Hsien, is a picturesque little place, almost filling a narrow valley hidden away on the southern slopes of the Ch'inling Shan, its situation exactly resembling that of Huayang further east on the road to Fop'ing. The city is practically empty, the life of the place being concentrated in a suburb outside the south-east wall.

From Liupa to Paoch'eng in the Han valley plain is a distance of about 180 li, which can be covered in two long marches, the trail running all the way down a winding gorge, occasionally cutting off corners by crossing low spurs. The going is most of the way very rough and rocky. Some three hours' march below Liupa the stream joins another much larger one flowing down from the southern slopes of T'aipai Shan, called the Pao Shui; up this stream lies a very rough trail to Mei Hsien in the Wei valley, crossing a shoulder of T'aipai Shan by a high pass. Several villages living on the traffic of this great highway are passed in the gorge, T'ieh-fotien, Matao Yi (the half-way stage), Erhshihli P'u, and Ch'ingch'iao Yi, in any of which a halt can be made. As one approaches the plain, the gorge, instead of opening out, becomes narrower, the cliffs more precipitous, and the track more rocky; and just when the weary traveller is beginning to look forward to the end of the stage, the gorge becomes impassable, and the path ascends for several hundreds of . feet by flights of irregular stone steps, winds round the top of a spur, the Chit'ou Kuan, and drops straight down on to Paoch'eng Hsien, lying on the edge of the Han valley plain.

Paoch'eng, a second class district city, is the usual little Han valley town with much more life than the northern cities. It is memorable to us because it was there that telegrams were received reporting that General Chang Hsün had abolished the Republic by replacing the child Emperor, Hsuan T'ung, on the throne. One's first thought was that if China survived this supreme act of folly she would be lucky; and yet the next news we received of the situation a few days later was that it was all over, and the country again a Republic. Curiously enough it was the Northern Generals who squashed the incident so promptly and not the regular republicans. Discussing the matter with Chinese later on, one heard the opinion expressed in some quarters that the movement was not so mad as it seemed and that its prompt collapse was due to jealousy amongst the Northern military leaders; for, it was suggested, the Republic, though excellent in theory, is a hopeless proposition today and has proved itself unworkable. Others, on the other hand, maintained that the Republic has come to stay, and that the confusion and troubles of the past six years since the revolution are only its birth throes; in support of which theory the state of England during the years subsequent to the revolution against Charles the First may be adduced, which much resembles the condition of China today. In any case the believers in a constitutional monarchy have, it seems, got to look elsewhere for an Emperor than amongst the members of the Imperial Manchu family, against whom popular feeling is far too strong, and therein lies the great difficulty. It was a coincidence that we received the news of the restoration of the Manchu Emperor while we were in a distant part of Shensi, while the first intelligence regarding Yuan Shih-k'ai's ill-advised monarchical scheme of two years before reached us in the wilds of Kansu. In both cases it seemed that a catastrophe of the first magnitude was impending for the country, and in both cases things soon settled down after a certain amount of desultory fighting between the opposing parties. China is the land of compromise and it is perhaps this inability to settle any issue decisively one way or the other which has been the cause of the internal disturbances of the past six years. So far, whatever the row has been, the power has remained in the hands of Peking and the Northern Generals, when it was over; and the power of the North to retain in its hands the nominal government of the country, though it has so far proved itself incapable of subduing the South and the South West in a military sense, remains the only decisive and stable factor in the situation.

From Paoch'eng to Mien Hsien is a distance of 90 li by a good road up the Han valley plain, dotted with many prosperous hamlets and villages; at the time of our passage it was largely under cotton where the land did not permit of irrigation for rice. Fifty li out a tributary river from the north is crossed by an iron chain suspension bridge and the large village of Huangsha P'u on the banks of the Han is reached. Further on another river from the mountains to the north has to be crossed by a ford, and though it was now the rainy season, the magistrate of Mien Hsien, who was travelling with us, assured us that its passage would present no difficulties, as he had crossed it coming to meet us on the previous day. But it had been raining all day, and rivers in China are wont to increase and decrease in size with extraordinary rapidity. When we reached this particular stream we found, instead of the ford a foot deep, which we had been led to expect, a roaring torrent deeper than a man's height. A dilapidated little temple was discovered near by in which we made shift to camp for the night while waiting for the rain to stop and the waters to subside; but before darkness fell the magistrate's efforts resulted in a boat being secured, and we packed up again and started off to try and reach Mien Hsien that night. The passage of the river was a long business, but everything was got over in the end, and we continued our journey in the dark. The path seemed to run more or less along the banks of the Han, into which I nearly rode on more than one occasion, past the township of Ts'aiyuan Chen, which is a larger place than the district city and evidently a trading centre connected with the junk traffic on the river; and ten li further on the East Gate of Mien Hsien is reached, where we arrived about nine in the evening, wet through and tired out.

Mien Hsien, a second class district city, lies at the extreme western end of the cigar-shaped Hanchung plain, which extends eastwards to below Yang Hsien. The out-

PLATE XXI

CITY OF LIUPA T'ING, S.W. SHENSI

VALLEY IN S.W. SHENSI NEAR SZECHUAN BORDER

PLATE XXII

THE DIMINUTIVE SZECHUAN PONY

THE DIMINUTIVE SZECHUAN PONY

lying ranges of the Ch'inling Shan here meet the mountains which separate the Han valley from Szechuan and bring the plain abruptly to an end. There is some gold in the sands of the Han, as in almost all the rivers of Western China; but whereas the sources of many of the latter, and therefore the hills from which the gold comes, lie far off on the Tibetan plateau, those of the Han lie close at hand in these mountains, which ought, therefore, to be worth prospecting; they are said to be rich in other minerals as well.

The next regular stage on this road is one of 90 li to the village of Tai-an Yi. The trail runs west up the Han River, which here flows in a perfectly straight gorge, for 45 li to the village of Hsinwan P'u, which is of interest as the head of navigation for small boats; the Han is thus navigable for practically its entire course. The porterage west to the Chialing Chiang, which is also navigable, is only two or three marches over a low divide to the village of Yangp'ing Kuan, and the road is naturally a busy one, and carries much traffic between Shensi, Szechuan, and Kansu. At Hsinwan P'u the path leaves the Han for a time, passing through broken hills cultivated with maize and rice and dotted with the useful wood-oil tree, eventually returning to the river and following up its valley to reach Tai-an Yi, an old posting stage. The Han is remarkable for the suddenness with which it springs into existence as a navigable river. At Mien Hsien in the summer it is already a large stream; while one march further west, at Tai-an, it is a mere streamlet, and one is within a few hours of its source. At the other extreme are the two other chief rivers of Shensi, the Wei and the Lo, which, rising one in Central Kansu and the other on the Ordos border, are only navigable for short distances above their confluences with the Yellow River near T'ungkuan. The contrast is typical of China north and south of the Ch'inling Shan.

Above Tai-an the path turns south up the head-waters of the Han, now only a few inches deep. Beyond the hamlet of K'uanch'uan P'u, 30 li out, the valley narrows to a ravine, which leads an hour's march further on to a pass, the Wuting Kuan (about 4000 feet); whence the trail descends through a ravine in the jungle-clad mountains, past the hamlet of Tishih P'u, till it debouches into a larger valley and reaches the town of Ningchiang, formerly a Chou, and now a second class Hsien.

Ningchiang is a picturesque little place lying surrounded by rice fields in an isolated valley in the mountains near the Szechuan border. It is still in the basin of the Han, and a railway from Hanchung along the line of the main road into Szechuan could avoid the Wuting Pass by following the valley of its stream. There would be greater difficulties in crossing the divide into Szechuan, though these mountains are not in this neighbourhood to be compared with the Ch'inling Shan as a barrier to communication, being only about half as high.

From Ningchiang to Kuangyuan in Szechuan is a distance of 230 li, which is usually divided into three stages, 70 li to Chaoch'ang Pa, 70 li to Ch'aot'ien Chen, and 90 li to Kuangyuan; but as elsewhere along this road villages are numerous, and the traveller can make his own stages. Leaving Ningchiang the trail runs up the valley to the S.W., which ends 40 li out in an easy pass (3300 feet), being the divide between the Han and Chialing basins. From the pass there is a drop of a few hundred feet into a little rice valley enclosed by wooded hills which leads down to the village of Huangpa Yi, 50 li from Ningchiang. The path here leaves the stream, which flows south, and, crossing a spur, drops steeply into the gorge of a stream flowing down from a high range to the west. At the point where this gorge debouches on to a larger valley, 15 li from Huangpa Yi, there is a barrier wall and a gate, indicating the Shensi-Szechuan frontier, and a few li further down this valley the village of Chaoch'ang Pa is reached. Here we parted from our friends the Shensi officials, who had looked after us so well for the past four months, and with whom we had undergone many a hardship. One of these gentlemen, who acted as business manager of the expedition and who throughout displayed great powers of organization as well as capacity for enduring personal discomforts and hardships, is shown in the accompanying photograph trying a little Szechuan stallion[1]. Having served as district magistrate for

---

[1] These Szechuan ponies though very small are exceedingly well built and show a great deal of breeding; they are useful on the paved paths and stone steps of Szechuan to which they are accustomed, and which are fatal to the larger and heavier built ponies of Kansu and Mongolia.

many years in various parts of Shensi, his local knowledge and experience were of the greatest assistance, while his talents ranged from shooting mountain goat in the Ch'inling Shan to the writing of Chinese poetry.

Leaving Chaoch'ang Pa a spur is crossed to avoid a bend in the stream, and the path then runs down the open valley, good going at last after days of rocky scrambles, for 40 li to the village of Shenhsuan Yi, another old posting station and the head-quarters of a deputy magistrate under Kuangyuan. A little further on down the valley a curious natural phenomenon occurs, the valley coming suddenly to an end, and the stream flowing under a mountain spur through a tunnel in the limestone, to reappear in a deep gorge half a mile further on. The path ascends this spur by flights of stone steps, and then, crossing to the other side of the valley, runs along the mountain side several hundreds of feet above the gorge of the stream for the rest of the way to Ch'aot'ien Chen, a large village lying on the banks of the Chialing Chiang. The latter flows swiftly in a deep gorge in the mountains; and on the practicability of this gorge for railway construction appears to depend the possibility of finding a comparatively easy route for a railway into Szechuan from the Wei valley; for it is by this gorge that the Chialing Chiang pierces all those intricate ranges on the borders of Shensi, Kansu, and Szechuan, containing the head-waters of the Han, which are connected with the Ch'inling Shan in such a manner as to render their passage by a railway elsewhere extremely difficult.

From Ch'aot'ien to Kuangyuan, a distance of 90 li, the path is ledged in one of the cliffs of the gorges of the Chialing Chiang; but it is possible to do this stage by water, and as the magistrate had kindly prepared some boats, we were only too glad at this stage of our long journey to avail ourselves of so restful a method of travel. The river was high and the current very rapid, so that we covered the distance in less than four hours, instead of the nine or ten it would have taken us by road.

Kuangyuan, a second class district city, lies in a small plain formed by the junction of a tributary with the Chialing Chiang. It is considered an important place owing to its position at the point where the big road from the north debouches into Szechuan and where another road emerges from Kansu *via* P'ik'ou. Being a mountainous border district it is full of brigands, who do not, however, seem so formidable or so destructive to trade as their colleagues in Northern Shensi; at any rate much traffic continues on the big road.

We were now at the end of July, and as we emerged from the higher mountains of Shensi into Szechuan the heat became daily more terrific. Mosquitoes too, which are not noticeable in Kansu at all owing to the elevation, and which only begin to be bad in Shensi towards the autumn, became daily more voracious.

From Kuangyuan to Chaohua is a short march of 55 li down the left bank of the Chialing Chiang, which here winds a good deal between more open mountain slopes. The river is crossed by a ferry to reach Chaohua, a small third class district city, built on a point of land at the confluence of the Chialing Chiang and a large tributary called the Pai Ho from Kansu. These rivers have cut deep narrow valleys in the precipitous mountains, which seem to run in all directions.

Leaving Chaohua the road climbs to the top of a ridge between the two rivers and continues along the summit in a westerly direction for 40 li with finally a descent to the village of Tashumu, whence it ascends another ridge leading S.W. The trail is here a good paved path, ascending and descending where necessary by flights of stone steps, and the march along the summits of the ridges affords a series of fine views over the surrounding mountains. Seventy li from Chaohua the path drops steeply into the gorge of a stream flowing north, up which it continues for another hour, passing through a gate in a remarkable defile under steep precipices of conglomerate rock, to reach the large village of Chienmen Kuan, the seat of a deputy magistrate under Chien Chou.

On the next day's march the path follows up the valley for a short distance, and then climbs again on to a ridge which leads in a south-westerly direction. The paved path is much of the way bordered by venerable trees hundreds of years old, whose welcome shade accompanies one at intervals right through these mountains for several days'

march. The views from the ridge are again extensive. On
the right hand lies the peculiar range of mountains trending
from S.W. to N.E. which was crossed on the preceding
day by the defile of Chienmen Kuan; on their southern face
these mountains have an easy slope, but on the northern
side fall away in rock precipices, giving the impression of
having been tossed up by some internal convulsion. This
formation extends as far as one can see in either direction,
and may also be noted in the ranges south of Ningchiang.
On the left hand lies the much broken hill country of soft
red sandstone, sometimes called the red basin of Szechuan,
into which the defile of Chienmen Kuan gives access from
the N.W. Beyond the village of Hanyang P'u, 25 li out,
there is a descent and then an ascent on to another ridge,
which is followed southwards until it ends with a steep drop
to the city of Chien Chou, now called Chienko Hsien, a
picturesque little place lying at the bottom of the narrow
valley of the Chien Shui, a tributary of the Chialing Chiang,
65 li from Chienmen Kuan. The high ranges on one's right
now bear away to the west, and the mountains become
lower and flatter; but in this part of Szechuan, as elsewhere
outside of the Chengtu plain, there is scarcely any level
ground to be seen.

From Chien Chou to the next district city, Tzutung
Hsien, is two stages of 80 li each, through complicated hill
country intersected by a maze of little narrow valleys. The
road is the same paved path shaded with ancient trees, and
shows great engineering skill on the part of its designers,
whoever they may have been, in the manner it threads its
way through this difficult country. It is perhaps the most
famous road in China, and it certainly deserves such a
reputation. It was probably constructed by the Emperor
Shih Huangti about B.C. 200 to facilitate his conquest of
what is now Szechuan. Climbing out of the valley of the
Chien Shui and crossing a ridge, the trail drops into a gorge,
only to climb out again immediately, and winding round a
spur S. and S.W., descends to the village of Liukou, 40 li
from Chien Chou, at the junction of two streams flowing
south. Here it ascends again, and winding along a ridge
for 20 li reaches the head of a valley, crosses the divide, and
follows down another ridge, with finally a steep drop to

reach the large village of Wulien Yi, the end of the stage, lying at the junction of two valleys. From Wulien Yi there is a gradual ascent again until the top of another ridge is reached, along which the road winds, past the half-way village of Shangting P'u, and a fine temple in a grove of trees called Ta Miao, until it descends by a long easy gradient to Tzutung Hsien, lying in a rather more open valley sloping S.W. The hills, which grow steadily less formidable as one proceeds south on this road, are now quite low, and the mountains to the N.W. are almost out of sight.

The red basin of Szechuan appears to be an old plateau of red sandstone worn down by the action of water into a maze of hills and valleys in the same way as the loess. This formation is, however, by no means confined to Szechuan, for a vast extent of country, stretching all the way from Honan through Southern Shensi and Kansu to Hsining and the Kokonor, is composed of the same red sandstone, which in the west everywhere forms the southern limit to the loess.

At Tzutung we encountered the old joke of the North Gate closed to keep the rain out and had considerable difficulty in apprising the magistrate of our arrival and effecting an entrance.

Crossing the river outside Tzutung by a fine stone bridge, over which three motor cars might have been driven abreast, though the paved road leading to and from it is only a couple of feet wide, the trail winds westwards through the cultivated red hills to the township of Weich'eng, the end of the stage of 60 li; and on the following day continues through the same country, winding through the hills and following along undulating ridges for 65 li, to reach Mien Chou, now called Mienyang Hsien, a large and crowded first-class district city on the Fu River.

We were now practically out of the mountains and not far from the northern end of the Chengtu plain. From Mien Chou the road runs through low hills for 90 li to reach Lochiang Hsien, whence it descends to Têyang Hsien on the plain, and continues through Han Chou and Hsintu Hsien to Chengtu. These district cities, Lochiang, Têyang, Han Chou, and Hsintu are all rich and populous centres, the like of which are not to be found in the whole of Shensi and Kansu, situated short marches of 50 li one from the other. The Chengtu plain, notoriously one of the most fertile and thickly populated regions in the world, was one vast rice field, the grain nearly ripe, and promising, as usual, an enormous harvest. The most lucrative posts in the whole territorial administrative system of China are said to be the district magistracies on the Chengtu plain in Szechuan and in parts of Kuangtung, which are alleged to be more desirable from a monetary point of view than a Taoyinship.

Having left Chengtu five or six years previously shortly after it had been looted and partly burned during the troubles following on the Revolution of 1911, we now returned to find it once more in ruins, with street after street of wealthy shops and residences burnt down to heaps of rubble as the result of recent street-fighting between the Szechuanese and the Yunnan and Kueichou troops. Chengtu is incomparably the finest, richest, and most populous native city I know of in China, but it has known but little peace since the Revolution. Szechuan, the most fertile and thickly populated province in the Republic, lies in an unfortunate position between the North and the South, and has frequently been the bone of contention between the respective protagonists, the Peking Government and the Yunnanese, during the long drawn out and indecisive struggle of recent years. The Szechuanese themselves incline naturally towards the South and their fair province is in every respect a portion of the South-West; but the Yangtzu waterway and the overland road from Shensi render them very liable to invasion by the Northerners. Further the abundance of labour, rice, and all kinds of supplies make the province a most suitable battle ground, where both Yunnanese and Northerners can practise the latest Japanese manœuvres and test their newest foreign machine guns at a minimum cost to themselves. The Szechuanese are not a warlike race, and have not in the past played an important part in these civil wars; though recently signs have not been wanting that they propose to make a change in this respect in the future. As regards numbers they are in a position to swamp all the rest, while they also have the great advantage of a modern arsenal at Chengtu.

The Yunnanese have played a very large part in the

history of the past few years in China, and it has been they and not the Cantonese who have constituted the most formidable opposition to the North. When Yuan Shih-k'ai took steps to replace the post-revolution Governors of the various provinces by his own nominees, he omitted for some reason or other to do so in the case of Yunnan, and this omission cost him his throne. The Yunnanese are thus nowadays the champions of the Southern cause, but, unfortunately for the Szechuanese, their province is a poor one, and they have therefore always sought during recent years to finance and support their undertakings by means of the riches of Szechuan; for this reason it was highly desirable, if not absolutely essential, for them to control the government of Szechuan and occupy the province with their troops. Hence the trouble between Szechuan and Yunnan and the ruined streets of Chengtu[1]. The Yunnanese and the Szechuanese stand towards one another in much the same relation as the Japanese do to the Chinese, ambition, energy, and ability on one side, numbers and wealth on the other. Between them these two provinces number perhaps fifty millions of inhabitants and the weight of their influence, and that of the South West generally, on the rest of the country has recently increased from year to year, and that in spite of the extraordinary isolation of their geographical position.

[1] Chengtu has since changed hands on several occasions, and three years later, in the summer of 1920, civil war between the militarists of Yunnan and Szechuan was still ebbing and flowing round its walls.

PLATE XXIII

KANSU PONY

KANSU PONY

PLATE XXIV

TREE-LINED HIGHWAY THROUGH CENTRAL KANSU

TREE-LINED HIGHWAY THROUGH CENTRAL KANSU

CHAPTER VIII

FROM HSIAN FU IN SHENSI TO LANCHOU FU IN KANSU
BY THE GREAT WEST ROAD

The Great West Road—Hsienyang—Lich'uan—Ch'ienchou—Yungshou—
Pinchou — Ch'angwu—Kansu border — Chingchou — P'ingliang — Kansu
Mahomedans—Wat'ing—The late General T'ung Fu-hsiang—The Liupan
Shan—Lungtê—Chingning—Rest-houses and inns—Brackish water—Trail
of desolation left by Mahomedan campaigns—Huining—Disadvantages of
being a magistrate on the high road—Beacon towers—Anting—Kantsao
Tien—Lanchou—Kansu climate—Wool factory—The Governor of Kansu—
The C.P.O.—Missionaries—Recent events in Kansu.

FROM Hsian Fu in Shensi to Lanchou Fu in Kansu by
the Great West Road is a distance of about 1400 li (say
425 miles), which is covered in eighteen to twenty days.
If the road from Hsian to Chengtu and Lassa be considered
the most important overland route in China, this one, from
Hsian to Lanchou and Kashgar, has every claim to rank
next. Unlike the former, which is only a mule trail, it is a
cart track all the way. Passing from the coast into the
heart of North-Western China through a natural gap in the
mountains formed by the valley of the Wei River, it continues into Central Asia along the narrow strip of fertile
country occupied by the Chinese between the mountains of
Northern Tibet and the deserts of Mongolia. It is both one
of the longest and most ancient highways in the world.

The first stage, a short one of 50 li across the plain to
Hsienyang Hsien, crossing the Wei River by a cart ferry
just before getting in, is the same as the first march on the
Chengtu road. Outside Hsienyang the Szechuan and Kansu
roads bifurcate, the latter leading north-west across the
undulating loess plain for 70 li to Lich'uan Hsien, whence
it continues for another short march of 40 li across similar
country, ascending gradually, to Ch'ien Chou. During the
month of May these plains are covered as far as the eye
can reach with healthy-looking crops of wheat and lucerne;
the latter, a most useful crop in Western Shensi and Eastern
Kansu, is used for fodder; in the Han valley, however, a

sort of veitch or lucerne is grown in the dry rice fields in the winter and ploughed into the ground at the time of the spring flooding as manure for the rice crop.

Ch'ien Chou lies near the north-western edge of the Wei valley plains, and the road now ascends steadily over loess hills for 90 li to Yungshou Hsien, lying just under the summit of a loess clad range which here bars the way to the west. The corn fields in the neighbourhood were full of pheasants, though there was little or no cover apart from the standing crops. The times being at the moment fairly peaceful, we met a constant stream of the large carts which ply on this road, one animal in the shafts and three in front, mostly laden with the famous Lanchou water pipe tobacco, which is exported from Kansu to all parts of China. Leaving Yungshou, half an hour's walk uphill brings one to the top of the ridge (4500 feet), whence there is a steep descent into a stony valley leading down to a hamlet half-way to Pin Chou. Here the road ascends again through the loess to a plateau intersected by ravines, down one of which it descends steeply to reach the valley of the Ching Ho and the district city of Pin Chou, 70 li from Yungshou.

The Ching River is here a shallow mountain stream and quite different to the torrent of liquid mud met with lower down; apparently it assumes the latter character after its confluence with the Huan Ho, which flows down from the loess of N.E. Kansu. The road runs up the cultivated valley of the Ching Ho, here about a mile wide and bounded by cliffs of loess and sandstone dotted with caves. Twenty li out the temple of Tafo Ssu is passed on the left hand, where a number of cave temples have been cut out of the rock in one of which there is a huge figure of Buddha. Two hours' march further on the road leaves the valley and climbs up on to the loess plateau, across which it runs for the rest of the way to Ch'angwu Hsien, a little city floating in a sea of wheat, 80 li from Pin Chou.

From Ch'angwu Hsien to Ching Chou is a long day's march called 100 li, the Kansu border being crossed at a village 30 li out. The road runs across the plateau, winding to and fro to avoid the cracks and fissures in the loess, the beginnings of ravines, cañons and valleys. It is lined with trees much of the way, and often these are seen to lead to the edge of a precipitous cañon, which has engulfed the road during recent years, and to continue again on the further side, while the track now in use winds round the head of the ravine. All through the loess country of Shensi and Kansu it is the same story, the track winding about to avoid the rifts, which are ever widening and working backwards by the collapse of their vertical walls. We were met on the provincial border by some Kansu officials and a couple of dozen Mahomedan braves, picturesque looking warriors mounted on handsome Kansu ponies, from whose appearance it was evident we were entering a new country. All Chinese in the North can ride after a fashion; but a Kansu Mahomedan, a Mongol, or a Tibetan sits his pony as though born to the saddle. Thus escorted we dropped by a long descent of ten li through a gully in the loess to Ching Chou (now Chingch'uan Hsien), and found ourselves once more in the valley of the Ching Ho.

From Ching Chou to P'ingliang Fu is a distance of 130 li, which can be divided into two marches by halting at the village of Paishui Yi, 75 li out. The road, a broad tree-lined highway, runs up the valley of the Ching Ho, which is well cultivated and populated. The trees along this road, which extend on and off all the way from Hsian to Lanchou, are said to have been planted by the order of the great General Tso, the conqueror of the Mahomedans, and if so, all travellers in summer time have reason to be thankful to him for the welcome shade they afford. At Paishui Yi we were met by the P'ingliang magistrate, one of the very best district officers we came across in all our journeys, who proceeded that same evening to take advantage of his presence in the village to try a case in the courtyard of the rest-house in which we were stopping; no red tape or ceremony of any kind, but a quick, straightforward hearing. Kansu is an old-fashioned and conservative province, and at the time of our visit was jogging along in much the same way as under the Manchus, without having adopted many of the new methods of the Republic. This magistrate was a regular territorial official *de carrière*, the son of an official, and, though still quite young, had served for some years as a magistrate under the previous regime. Consequently he was thoroughly conversant with his work, and compared favourably with many of the young magistrates in Shensi, promoted to their posts straight from the schools or the army through revolutionary influence, and without administrative experience of any kind.

P'ingliang, lying near the head of the Ching Ho valley at an altitude of over 4000 feet, is an important place, an agricultural market town in a wheat-growing region, and the administrative centre of Eastern Kansu. Being the seat of a Taoyin and a General, we had as usual a festive time during our short stay. The town, like most Kansu cities, is half empty, but the east suburb, the Mahomedan quarter, is busy and full of well-stocked shops. It was there that we first noticed the white caps of the Kansu Mahomedans, of whom we were to see so much during the next few months. The prosperity of the suburb compared to the city and their presence there were connected by the fact that until recently no Mahomedan was permitted to reside inside the walls of an official city in Kansu (one of the suppressive measures taken against them after the great rebellion); with the arrival of the republic, however, and its watchword of equality for the five races (Chinese, Mahomedans, Manchus, Tibetans, and Mongols), this disability was allowed to lapse. Frequent reference to the Mahomedans of the North West will be made in the following chapters, but the subject of Islam in China is an obscure and contentious one, and it should be noted that the statements here made are not the product of scientific enquiries, but merely the results of conversations with Chinese, mostly of the official classes, who, though sometimes Moslems themselves, were only acquainted with the superficial facts and popular traditions relating to the Mahomedans and their religion.

I estimate the Mahomedans of Kansu to constitute from a quarter to a third of the total population. They are freely scattered throughout the districts of the province as merchants, especially dealers in horses, but they are settled on the land more especially in two regions, in the South and the North respectively, roughly separated by the Great West Road. In the South they form a kind of Mahomedan wedge between the Chinese and the Tibetans of the Kokonor, centring round Hochou and Hsunhua on the Yellow River; in the North they extend from P'ingliang through Kuyuan, and Haich'eng to Chinchi (Ningling) and Ninghsia. The Chinese consider those in the Southern area, who are of more recent Turki origin, to be the more dangerous and fanatical today. In a secluded valley near P'ingliang resides a sort of Mahomedan saint, who has great influence not only in Kansu but also in Yunnan, and who undoubtedly commands the services of thousands, or perhaps tens of thousands, of armed Mahomedans; he is not one of the regular Moslem leaders, who are referred to in later chapters; and there seems to be some sort of mystery about him, which it was not our business to enquire into.

The next stage from P'ingliang is one of 90 li to Wat'ing, a walled fort and posting stage at the foot of the Liupan pass. The road runs up the valley, which beyond a half-way village with inns contracts to a gorge, scrub-covered mountains of shale and sandstone taking the place of the cultivated loess hills. Pheasants were thick here, and so tame that one had to throw stones at them to make them fly. Wat'ing is rather an important point as the roads to Lanchou and Ninghsia here bifurcate (the latter *via* Kuyuan). We were met here by the magistrate of Kuyuan and also by a representative of the family of the late General T'ung Fu-hsiang, whose ancestral seat is in the neighbourhood. I have been told on more than one occasion by Chinese that T'ung Fu-hsiang was not a Mahomedan at all, but a Chinese General commanding Moslem troops; perhaps he was considered a Chinese because he fought against the Mahomedans in the great rebellion. The following is a sketch of the career of this celebrated individual, who came into contact with foreigners by leading his Mahomedan troops to the attacks on the Legations in Peking in 1900.

T'ung Fu-hsiang was a native of Kuyuan in Eastern Kansu. In the big rebellion of 1864–1873 he figured prominently as a military chief on the Chinese side under General Tso, and it was he who captured the rebel stronghold of Chinchi on the Yellow River near Ninghsia, an event which was the turning-point in the campaign. This was the foundation of his fortunes, as he was enriched with the confiscated estates of rebels, and from that time on counted as one of the most prominent and influential leaders in Kansu. Subsequently he fought in Central Asia against

Yakub Beg. In 1895 he had risen to be commander-in-chief of the Kansu forces and despatched troops to aid in the suppression of the Mahomedan rebellion near Sining in that year. In 1900 he commanded an army of Kansu braves in the attacks on the Legations, and subsequently arranged for the safety of the Imperial Court during its flight to Hsian Fu. Being proscribed by the Foreign Powers after the collapse of the Boxer movement he was cashiered and sent back to Kansu in disgrace, where he resided on his large estates in some state till his death about ten years ago. His rôle was loyalty to the Manchus through thick and thin, and his example in this respect has been followed more recently by the other Mahomedan leaders, who were ready to remain faithful to the cause of the fallen dynasty even after the abdication in 1912. Had Yuan Shih-k'ai not been at the head of affairs then, and had T'ung Fu-hsiang still been alive, the Mahomedan North West would perhaps have refused to accept the Republic, with disastrous results to the neighbouring provinces.

From Wat'ing the road runs up a ravine to the west, reaching the foot of the Liupan Shan after 15 li, whence it ascends by a series of zigzags to the summit of the pass, a grassy ridge about 9000 feet high. There were many big carts making the ascent, a most arduous business effected by relays of animals. Here again, as often on our journeys, we had reason to congratulate ourselves on having a caravan of good pack mules instead of carts. The Liupan Shan is a prominent range of mountains rising far above the loess, which crosses Kansu from N.W. to S.E.; it is probably a continuation of the chief range of the Nan Shan, which is crossed by the main road west of Lanchou at the Wushao Ling (10,000 feet) and through which the Yellow River breaks its way in a series of precipitous gorges between Lanchou and Chungwei. From the pass there is a steep drop of about a thousand feet, and the road then descends through a dreary barren valley to Lungtê Hsien, a most miserable little city almost entirely in ruins, 50 li from Wat'ing. The loess country west of the Liupan Shan is much more barren and desiccated than on the P'ingliang side, and round Lungtê the poor-looking wheat crops were only just showing above ground towards the end of May.

PLATE XXV

DEPARTURE FROM P'INGLIANG

APPROACH TO THE LIUPAN SHAN PASS

PLATE XXVI

THE LOESS COUNTRY OF CENTRAL KANSU

THE LOESS COUNTRY OF CENTRAL KANSU

Most of the magistrates' yamens throughout Northern and North-Eastern Kansu were dreadfully dilapidated, but the one here was about the worst we saw, being scarcely habitable, and in keeping with the rest of this ruined little city. The magistrate complained that the inhabitants of his district were poor to the verge of starvation.

I was told that the road across the Liupan Shan was made by General Tso to facilitate communications during the campaigns against the Mahomedans, the former route, which is still used to a limited extent, passing from Wat'ing to Kuyuan, and thence *via* Haich'eng and Chingyuan to Lanchou.

From Lungtê to Chingning Chou is a march of 90 li down the valley, which is cultivated but very arid-looking, and dotted with wretched farms and hamlets. There are no trees except those which line the road. The arid climate of North China is often ascribed to the destruction of the forests by the Chinese in ancient days, but it is doubtful whether the loess was ever covered by trees owing to its peculiar consistency; it is certainly quite unsuited for the growth of trees nowadays. Further on the valley becomes quite barren, the ground being covered with a white alkaline efflorescence, and 15 li from Chingning it narrows to a gorge with the path ledged in the hillside, eventually debouching on to a more fertile valley where irrigation is practised. Chingning, a considerable market town, lies in this valley.

On the following march the road turns up a side ravine, climbs a long steep hill to a pass in the loess, and descends through a maze of loess hills to a valley which leads down to the village of Kaochia P'u (45 li); it continues to follow this valley for another hour's march and then turns north-west up a long narrow defile in the loess, a weary trek with repeated little steep descents and ascents in and out of side nullahs, for the rest of the way to Ch'ingchia Yi, 90 li from Chingning, a walled village and former posting stage and fort. These posting stages, with which we became so familiar on the main roads of Kansu, are mostly provided with official rest-houses called *hsingt'ai*, in which we were usually quartered; though very dilapidated they provided quite good accommodation in the summer, being usually uninhabited and therefore free from smells. The inns of Shensi and Kansu, which we very seldom used, are also not bad, being large and roomy, and constructed mainly with a view to the accommodation of plenty of animals in the courtyard. I have a particular aversion to the Szechuan inn, usually considered, especially by the Chinese, as providing the height of luxury on the road; they are always crowded in between the other houses of a narrow street, and invariably have the defect of placing the *shang fang* (the chief guest room) next door to the *mao fang*, a revolting arrangement for a night's rest, which the Chinese do not seem to object to.

Ch'ingchia Yi was the first place where we struck brackish water, and from here on to within two days of Lanchou I found it scarcely potable. This is a very real trial in the dry season in Central Kansu, and though in the course of our journeys brackish water was of frequent occurrence, we never became accustomed to it, and found it a great hardship to be greeted with a cup of salted tea at the end of a hot day on the road. After the rains have fallen the water is said to sweeten. We were warned of this, of course, but were told that the Mahomedans collected sweet rainwater in specially prepared pits, called *chiao shui*; but owing to lack of rain most of these pits were dry, or contained only a little evil-looking liquid loess mud. I believe that water in pure loess is usually brackish, but in most parts streams or wells are available in the underlying rock; this portion of Central Shensi, however, is in the heart of the loess watershed between the Wei and Yellow rivers, lying mostly over 6000 feet above sea level, and it is the streams themselves which are the worst to drink. I thought I did not know what real thirst was till crossing Central Kansu at the driest season of the year, but later on, when traversing a portion of the Alashan desert further west in early August, we longed even for the salted tea of Huining.

From Ch'ingchia Yi the road continues to ascend the same defile for ten li, crosses a pass in the loess, and descends by a similar ravine leading west. Several hamlets mostly in ruins are passed, including the walled posting stage of Chaichia Tsui. These ruins, now more than fifty years old, which become increasingly frequent as one proceeds west, are part of the trail of desolation left by General Tso's victorious army all the way from Shensi to Turkestan, their method of dealing with the rebellion being to massacre the inhabitants and reduce to heaps of ruins every Mahomedan habitation they came across. As the male Mahomedans were mostly scouring the country in marauding bands, they met with little difficulty in doing so. Chinese rebellions have in the past of course always been suppressed in this manner, and indeed could probably not have been suppressed otherwise. Fifteen li from Huining the valley contracts into a gorge, and the road runs down the bed of the stream, a brackish trickle of water, for the rest of the way. Huining is a poor city lying in a region of arid valleys. Complaining of the hardships of life at his post, the magistrate informed us that in many parts of his district ordinary fuel was unobtainable, and the inhabitants were reduced to burning dried dung as in the deserts of Tibet and Mongolia. This arid region stretches away apparently to the north till it merges into the Ordos desert, a land of sand and camels. In addition to being such a miserably poor district, his post had the disadvantage of lying on this great road, and when an important personage, such as a Mongol prince or high Chinese functionary, passed by on his way to or from Turkestan, his passage would leave the unfortunate magistrate many hundreds of taels out of pocket, which he could ill afford. We were a very small party when travelling in Kansu and I hope we did not cost him anything; but I know that when we commenced our journeys in Shensi with a huge party we were a heavy burden on the people and officials of the districts through which we passed.

The next stage is a short one of 60 li to the walled posting stage of Hsikung Yi. The road runs down the Huining valley for 20 li, and then ascends a side ravine to the southwest for the rest of the way. The hamlets passed seemed more miserable and the country more desiccated than ever. All along this road, as on most of the bigger roads of Kansu, may be noticed groups of curious little towers every five to ten li. It was a long time before we could get a satisfactory explanation of what these towers were intended for; so far as I know they are only to be seen on the roads of Kansu. We now learned that they were beacon towers, another relic of the rebellion and its suppression, by means of which signals could be sent great distances in a very short space of time.

From Hsikung Yi to Anting, another short stage of 60 li, the road follows up the ravine for ten li, and then climbs a long steep hill by zigzags. On reaching the summit there is no immediate descent the other side, but the path winds along a high ridge with extensive views over the loess mountains all around, finally dropping steeply to Anting in a valley running north-west. Anting Hsien (now known as Tinghsi) is an important district city lying at the junction of three valleys, and, commanding several roads north, south, east and west, was formerly an important military centre. There is more water available here, and consequently the country is much more fertile and the people quite well off. Loess country in this rainless region is either a desert or a garden according to the amount of water available for irrigation, and from here on to Lanchou, though the hills become more and more sterile, the irrigated valleys are wonderfully green and fertile.

From Anting to Lanchou is a march of four short stages of about 60 li each. The road runs down the valley past several prosperous hamlets for 45 li to the village of Ts'ank'ou whence it strikes west up a side valley to the posting station of Ch'enk'ou Yi, the end of the stage. From here it ascends a gully for a few li and then climbs a steep loess hill to reach the summit of a ridge along which it winds for three to four hours' march, with finally a steep descent to the large market village of Kantsao Tien, lying amongst fertile irrigated fields at the junction of three valleys. To the south-west rises a high range of mountains, beyond which lie Titao and the T'ao River. From here on to Lanchou the irrigated valleys, bounded by desert hills, are highly productive, and the crops several weeks ahead of those in the barren region we had traversed since crossing the Liupan Shan.

From Kantsao Tien a good road runs down the cultivated valley for 70 li to Chinchia Yai, a large village and likin station, and the end of the stage. The district city of Chin Hsien lies just off the road, 25 li to the south. Leaving Chinchia Yai the valley soon contracts to a stony ravine, and after 20 li debouches suddenly on to the gorges of the Yellow River, which here rolls its turgid waters between precipitous granite walls. The path runs for a short distance along the river, and then enters a belt of sand hills from which it emerges on to the river again at the village of T'ungkuan P'o, lying at the entrance to the gorges. From here to Lanchou (20 li) the road is a broad highway up the open cultivated valley of the Yellow River.

Lanchou Fu, now officially known by the name of the district, Kaolan Hsien, is by far the most attractive of the provincial capitals of China I have visited. It is built along the right bank of the Yellow River at a point where the hills close in on the river, the valley expanding into small plains to the east and west. The greyish yellow city walls and towers blending with the yellow waters of the river and the desolate yellow grey hills all around, the whole relieved by the bright green of the irrigated fields in the valley, combine to form an attractive picture which will long remain with those on whom the deserts and mountains of the North West exercise their mysterious charm. The modern iron bridge across the Yellow River, constructed a few years ago by foreign engineers, is rather an eyesore, but its great utility more than makes up for its appearance. Across this bridge, which at the time of our visit was in a very decayed state as far as the woodwork was concerned, passes an almost incessant stream of traffic, carts, ponies, mules, camels, and sometimes yak, bound eastwards for China and westwards for Turkestan. So far as I know there are only three bridges across the Yellow River, this one, and the Peking-Hankow and Tientsin-Pukou railway bridges in Honan and Shantung; which is, however, a better record than the Yangtzu can show, the latter having no bridges across its course anywhere. The walls of Lanchou are well built and kept in good repair, and the whole city has an air of compact strength, comparative cleanliness, and prosperity. It was never taken by the Mahomedans during the rebellions of the past, and it was also one of the few provincial capitals to escape being looted by soldiers or mob during the revolution of 1911 and subsequent troubles, and its shops appear rich and well stocked. Owing to its situation at the junction of the Yellow River with the highway from China to Turkestan, as well as numerous other roads leading in various directions, it is by far the most important centre in the North West after Hsian Fu, and all the trade there is in the province converges upon it. Traders from Tientsin, Szechuan, Turkestan, Mongolia, Siberia, Tibet, and even India may be met with in its streets.

Kansu is considered by the Chinese of other provinces to be a dreadfully bitter place (*k'u ti hen*), nothing but wild Mahomedans and no rice to speak of; but for a European it is in many ways the pick of the eighteen provinces. Lanchou lies a little under 5000 feet above sea-level, which in that latitude means a white man's climate, no mosquitoes, and the wearing of European clothing all the year round. As regards food, excellent wheat flour, mutton, and milk are always obtainable, the two latter often scarce in other parts of China, and game is extraordinarily abundant in many regions. I have only one complaint to make against Kansu and that is the brackish water in certain parts. At Lanchou itself there are springs of sweet water at Wuch'uan Shan, a collection of temples on the hills immediately to the south of the city, and the Yellow River water is also good after it has been allowed to stand and clear itself.

Lanchou being situated near some of the best sheeps-wool producing regions of Asia, and the climate being essentially a northern one, common sense indicates it as a suitable centre for a cloth-making industry. This was recognized as long ago as the days of the great General Tso, who established a cloth factory, which was subsequently modernised during the comparatively progressive and constructive era preceding the Revolution by the introduction of modern foreign machinery and several Belgian instructors. But the Revolution put an end to progress in this enterprise as in so many others, and the foreigners have now all departed, and the factory does not flourish. All the same, on my departure from Lanchou, the Governor insisted on my taking away, as mementoes of progress in Kansu, two locally manufactured blankets, made, I think, of camels' hair, which were really first-class articles, and hard to beat anywhere for warmth and good wearing utility. There ought to be a large market for native-made cloth amongst the Kokonor Tibetans and beyond, but the trade seems never to have been developed successfully. There are also other so-called factories, for the manufacture of matches, soap, etc., but the products are wretched. In any case all these enterprises suffer from the blight of Chinese official management. Lanchou is also at a great disadvantage in this respect owing to the immense difficulties involved in transporting foreign machinery and all kinds of foreign goods across the many hundreds of miles of intervening mountains from the coast. The foreign resident can import a case of beer, drink the contents, and then sell the bottles for more than the original cost of the beer; but this does not represent a new method of getting rich quick, as the cost of transport is likely to be greatly in excess of the value of either the beer or the bottles. There is, however, one really flourishing native industry in Lanchou, independent of foreign machinery, and that is the cultivation and manufacture of water pipe tobacco, which is exported to all parts of China.

The time of our visit to Lanchou coincided with the period of Yuan Shih-k'ai's power, and the Governor was one of the latter's Northern Generals. He was an excellent representative of the type of Northern soldier, and was universally acknowledged to be one of the best rulers Kansu has ever enjoyed. Owing to the geographical isolation of the province and the conservative nature of its Mahomedan population, the rebellion of 1916 had but little effect locally, and the Governor maintained his position after the fall and death of Yuan Shih-k'ai; and had we again visited Lanchou two years later we should have found him still ruling only under a different title. After the Revolution the Governors of provinces were styled Tutu[1]; Yuan Shih-k'ai abolished this name with its republican associations, and revived the old title of Chiangchün[2]; after the compromise which followed the rebellion and Yuan Shih-k'ai's death, the title of Governor was also compromised in true Chinese style into Tuchün[3]. The Governor was a native of Hofei Hsien in Anhui, and consequently not a few civil and military officials throughout the province at the time of our visit wrote Hofei on their cards. It is extraordinary what a number of prominent Chinese in recent years have been natives of this obscure little district in Anhui, ever since

[1] Literally "General Manager," i.e. Governor.
[2] Literally "Army Leader," i.e. Marshal.
[3] Literally "Army Manager," i.e. Military Governor.

the days of the great Li Hung-ch'ang, himself a native of that place. All these officials are, of course, more or less members of the Anhui military party, whose influence in the government of the country has been so great in recent years[1].

The foreign community of Lanchou at the time of our visit consisted of the China Inland Mission, a Catholic priest, and the British Postmaster, who, like his colleague in Hsian Fu, and indeed the foreign postal officials through-out the country, is doing splendid work for the Chinese. The efficiency of the Chinese Postal Service, under a French Director-General in Peking working with a staff of French, British, and other nationals, is truly remarkable, when one takes into consideration the many difficulties there are to contend with. Especially has this been the case during the constant rebellions and civil wars of the past few years, in spite of which steady progress has been made. On the whole the warring factions, whether government troops, revolution-aries, rebels, or brigands, respect the C.P.O. in a remarkable manner, due apparently to their genuine admiration for the one really sound institution in the interior; and the postal couriers are often able to pass backwards and forwards through districts where no other Chinese dare venture. Occasionally, but not often considering the numbers carried, a mail is lost through the action of brigands.

There are not a great many missionaries in Kansu com-pared to some of the other provinces, at the time we were there only about ten or a dozen stations altogether, and only one doctor. It would probably surprise many people not well acquainted with missionary work in China to find how few ordained clergymen there are amongst the ranks of the Protestant missionaries; I do not think we met any in Kansu. This puzzles the Catholics very much with their strict system of training. Of course there is no particular reason why a missionary should be a clergyman, though the uninitiated are apt to look upon him as such; except that ordained clergymen are usually well-read men of superior

[1] This influence has since steadily increased until in 1920 a group of rival Northern Generals challenged the Anhui military party (on the usual pretext of defending democratic principles) and overthrew them in a series of battles round Peking in the summer of that year.

education, and one seldom finds amongst them the type of corybantic missionary of little education familiar to most travellers in the interior of China. In Kansu the missionaries are mostly veterans of the C.I.M., who have spent the best part of their lives in isolated posts where they seldom see another white face for months or years on end, and whose steady work during a generation of time, though possibly not richly productive in converts, cannot but have accomplished an enormous amount of good for the Chinese. Protestant missionaries in China have been subject to many attacks, which they often invite, from their own countrymen; but after all, mankind must apparently have a religion of some kind, and would the critics of Christianity in China contend that the teachings of Christ are inferior to those of Buddha or Mahomed? Only, to be fair to the Chinese, the missionaries should surely propagate an up-to-date form of Christianity, as modified by modern scientific research, instead of teaching, as seems usually to be the case, old literal beliefs which have ceased to hold good in Europe. Also Christianity, a westernised oriental religion, is being taught back to orientals, and for that reason should in China be stripped as far as possible of its Western exterior. It is difficult to imagine anything more utterly absurd than the construction of a foreign style church, with steeple, etc., in the interior of China as a place of worship for Christian Chinese; and there are many other respects in which the missionary often endeavours to impose purely European methods of worship, which have nothing to do with original Christianity, on the Chinese. All this merely emphasises the foreign nature of the Christian Church in China, which is one of the greatest obstacles to its real establishment. When we were in Kansu we learned that a new mission composed of believers in the gift of tongues (known to the vulgar as the "Holy Rollers") was about to open in Kansu with the object of working amongst the Tibetan tribesmen of the Kokonor border. The experts in this sect are in the habit of working themselves up into a sort of fit, when they are said to roll on the ground and speak in strange and unknown tongues; apparently the promoters of this mission in Kansu are banking on the unknown tongue being in this case the Amdo dialect of North-Eastern Tibetan. That missionaries holding these strange beliefs should be the only vehicle for the propagation of Christianity amongst the Kokonor tribesmen does not seem to be fair either to Christianity or to the tribesmen.

Having outlined the history of recent events in Shensi since the Revolution in a preceding chapter, with the Ko Lao Hui in the leading rôle, it may be of interest to recount the history of the same period in Kansu, assigning the principal part to the Mahomedans.

Kansu only played a small part in the Revolution of 1911, and, as was to be expected in so backward and isolated a province, there was little sympathy with the republican cause. The troops in the province at that time consisted still of the old style *Hsün Fang Tui* who were in the course of being modernised into the new regular army known as *Lu Chün*, and of Mahomedan soldiers peculiar to the province called *Hsi Chün*. After the Revolution the *Hsün Fang Tui* and the *Lu Chün* melted away together with the provincial government, and the attitude of the province towards things in general was governed by the action of the Mahomedan leaders and the Mahomedan troops, who, true to their recent traditions, remained loyal to the Manchu throne. Ma An-liang, the famous leader of the Kansu Mahomedans, who thus found himself at the head of the province, together with Sheng Yün, ex-Viceroy of the North West and one of the Manchu die-hards, despatched Moslem troops across the border into Shensi to fight the revolutionary forces of the Ko Lao Hui, but were eventually induced by the wise statesmanship of Yuan Shih-k'ai to withdraw them and accept the republic in name. Had Yuan Shih-k'ai not been at the head of affairs at that time, and had the Manchus been able to rally themselves to the Mahomedans of the North West, the settlement of 1912 might have been much delayed.

The result of the Revolution was therefore to give the Mahomedans what they had failed to obtain by rebellion in the past, namely complete autonomy and control of the province under General Ma An-liang, who moved into Lanchou from his residence near Hochou. There was a republican Tutu at the same time, but he seems to have been a mere figure-head. General Ma's management of the

affairs of the province during those critical times appears
to have been admirable, and Kansu was spared many of the
troubles which were afflicting the rest of China during that
period. Early in 1914, however, Yuan Shih-k'ai, who was
then engaged in centralising his power by replacing the
republican Tutus by his own nominees, sent one of his
Northern Generals to Lanchou as Governor, accompanied
by a bodyguard of a couple of thousand good Northern
soldiers. To avoid friction the latter travelled up to Kansu
as Commissioner for the Kokonor, his appointment as
Governor only being announced by telegraph when he was
within a few days of the capital. For some months there
was a period of great tension between the Mahomedans and
the new Governor, but the latter was a true Northern
soldier, strong and reliable, and the Mahomedans, under
wise leadership, eventually accepted the situation, and
General Ma retired again to Hochou.

In the summer of 1914 the southern portion of the
province suffered greatly from the incursion made by the
so-called White Wolf rebels, who, after ravaging parts of
Anhui, Honan and Shensi, made a sudden raid into Kansu
by the Ch'inchou road, being attracted probably by the
stocks of opium in those parts. A year after their passage
we could trace their route by ruined towns and villages
and burnt out yamens. After looting the rich cities of
Ch'inchou and Fuchiang and other towns in that neighbourhood, they struck west through the mountains to Minchou
and T'aochou on the Kokonor border. At Old T'aochou
they encountered the Mahomedans for the first time and
met with a fierce resistance from the Moslem population of
that district. This so infuriated the rebels that when, by
sheer weight of numbers, they eventually captured the city
they massacred the inhabitants and literally razed the town
to the ground. At the time of our visit a year later the four
walls of the city enclosed a mass of ruins, not a single house
being left intact. The destruction of T'aochou proved,
however, the turning-point in the career of that terrible
horde. So far they had ranged, pillaging, murdering, and
burning, right across China practically unchecked. But
here they had been severely handled by the Mahomedans,
who were not accustomed to take that kind of thing lying

down; and in that wild and out of the way country there soon arose a shortage of supplies for so many thousands. Northwards towards Lanchou the way was barred by the Moslem troops of Ma An-liang, and southwards towards the rich province of Szechuan the intervening country was wilder and even more desolate; and so the rebels started back the way they had come, through towns and villages already laid waste. The mountain tracks were bad, the stages long, and food and fodder scarce. The bridge across the T'ao at Minchou had been destroyed, and many were drowned in the fierce waters of this Tibetan torrent. At Fuchiang and other places on the road the local people wreaked a terrible revenge for what they had suffered, and many hundreds of rebels hiding in the cornfields and scrub were beaten to death with sticks and agricultural implements. Many straggled back through Shensi with their silver and opium to their homes in Honan, but this was really the end of the White Wolf rebels whom 30,000 picked troops of China's modern army had completely failed to destroy in the central provinces six months previously.

With the disappearance of the White Wolf rebels and the surrender of the nominal government by the Mahomedans to Yuan Shih-k'ai's Governor, peace returned to the province. During the anti-monarchical rebellion of 1916 there was a renewal of unrest, especially after Shensi had joined the rebels, and influence was brought to bear on the Governor from various quarters, urging him to resign or secede from Peking. But a declaration of independence was successfully staved off until Yuan Shih-k'ai's death relieved the situation, perhaps largely owing to the attitude of Ma An-liang, who prepared his troops for action, and let the republicans know that if anyone was to succeed the Governor it would be himself, and that he and his Mahomedans would stick by Yuan to the last.

The shadow of another Mahomedan rebellion is always over the Chinese in Kansu, who stand in great fear of the Moslems and have passed through some anxious times during recent years. But the general opinion we heard expressed was that there was no need for alarm as long as the Mahomedans continue to be guided by the wise and statesmanlike leadership of their present chiefs.

CHAPTER IX

FROM LANCHOU FU SOUTH TO CH'INCHOU AND THENCE WEST TO T'AOCHOU ON THE KOKONOR BORDER

Shani—Titao—Weiyuan—Kungch'ang—Ningyuan—Fuchiang—Ch'inchou —Schools, government and missionary—Li Hsien—Western end of Ch'inling Shan—Profusion of pheasants—Grass plateau—Modern maps of China— Min Chou—T'ao river valley—New T'aochou—Mahomedans on Kokonor border—Choni—Old T'aochou—Tibetan trade—The Min Shan—Mission work amongst Tibetans—Pneumonic plague.

WE finally left Lanchou on June 9 for Ch'inchou, Minchou, and T'aochou. The road runs due south, ascending a narrow stony valley, for 40 li to reach the village of Akan Chen, picturesquely situated in a wooded gorge. Most of the coal consumed in Lanchou comes from this neighbourhood, and the manufacture of pottery seems to be quite a local industry. We passed the night here, though the village was hard put to it to accommodate our moderate-sized party. On the following day the road ascends through a wooded ravine where pheasants are numerous for some 15 li to the top of the pass, and then descends for three hours' march through a barren rocky gorge to the hamlet of Chungpu, which is an alternative halting-place to Akan for breaking the 120 li from Lanchou to Shani into two stages. From here the road threads its way through barren hills of sandy loess for about 35 li to Shani, a wretched walled village recently promoted to the rank of district city under the new name of T'aosha Hsien. It is suitably named for the surroundings are almost desert, which is characteristic of the T'ao valley from here down to its junction with the Yellow River, and form a curious contrast to the thickly wooded slopes round Akan Chen.

From Shani to Titao Chou is a march of 90 li up the T'ao River valley, which is here about a mile broad and converted by irrigation from a desert into a market garden. Numerous villages are passed, the largest being Hsintientzu and Hsink'ai P'u, 30 and 50 li out. Titao Chou, now Titao

Hsien, surrounded by rich irrigated lands, is a city of some importance, occupying a strategic position between Lanchou Fu and the Mahomedan strongholds round Ho Chou. It is also a centre of the water pipe tobacco industry and of the trade in lumber, the latter rafted down the T'ao River from the forests of the Kokonor.

From Titao to Weiyuan Hsien is a distance of 110 li across the watershed between the T'ao and Wei rivers, which can be divided into two marches by halting at the hamlets of Yaotien or Ch'ingp'ing, where there are inns, 50 and 80 li out respectively. Leaving Titao the road runs up a shallow cultivated valley bounded by hills of red clay in an easterly and then a southerly direction for 80 li to the hamlet of Ch'ingp'ing, where the valley is a mere ravine. From here it ascends a grassy ridge which is followed for two hours' march to gain the watershed pass, and then drops steeply to Weiyuan Hsien. The railway from Hsian to Lanchou which, it is proposed, shall follow up the Wei valley, will here presumably require a tunnel through this watershed to reach the valley of the T'ao. Weiyuan is of some interest to the Chinese as lying on the headwaters of their historical river the Wei. We found it a small but well-kept city, rejoicing in a particularly progressive young magistrate. The river is here quite small and easily fordable, and its valley though narrow is cultivated and has a prosperous appearance.

From Weiyuan to Kungch'ang is a march of 90 li by a good road down the valley, generally a mile or two wide, well cultivated, and bounded by bare hills. Numerous villages are passed, the largest being Shouyang Ch'eng, half way. Kungch'ang Fu, now known as Lunghsi Hsien, is a large city in extent, but having been destroyed during the Mahomedan rebellion is still half in ruins. Another march of 90 li, still down the valley, brings one to Ningyuan. Forty li out the hills close in on the valley which becomes barren and stony. The Wei River is forded twice on this stage and also the Nan Ho, a large tributary from the south. The latter was in flood and gave us some trouble. Immediately after crossing the Nan Ho there is a steep ascent and descent over a ridge which blocks the valley at this point, followed by an hour's march down the open valley to Ningyuan.

Many villages are passed on this stage, the largest being Ssushihli P'u and Chaochiakengtzu, 40 and 50 li out respectively. Ningyuan (new name Wushan Hsien) is a pleasant little city lying in the irrigated valley of the Wei River producing heavy crops of corn and hemp.

From Ningyuan to Fuchiang is a long stage called 100 li. The road continues down the valley, crossing a loess ridge just before getting to the large market village of Lomen Chen, 30 li out. The valley on this stretch of the road is very fertile, thickly populated, and well timbered. Fuchiang is quite a wealthy town, and this part of Kansu is probably the richest in the province, with the exception perhaps of the Ninghsia plains. It used to be a centre for the opium trade, now more or less extinct. The poppy was formerly cultivated extensively in all the irrigated areas in Kansu, and the product was considered the best native-grown opium in China and was in great demand in Peking, Tientsin, and North China generally.

At Fuchiang the road leaves the Wei valley and ascending a gorge in the loess hills, crosses a steep little pass and descends to the large village of Kuantzu Chen, 40 li out. From here it continues down this valley, that of a tributary of the Wei, passes through a stony gorge, and emerges at the village of Liushihli P'u, 60 li from Fuchiang, whence there is a good road through cultivated fields down the valley for the remaining 60 li to Ch'in Chou. The latter, now known as T'ienshui Hsien, consists of no less than five cities built one alongside the other, and is one of the largest and most important towns in the province. A considerable trade is carried on with Shensi and Szechuan, the exports consisting of the regular products of Kansu, such as wool, hides, deer's horns, furs, musk, rhubarb, mountain medicines, tobacco, and opium, and the imports of silk, tea, piece goods, etc. The Szechuanese element in the population is considerable, and the proximity of that province is in many ways noticeable. It is not a Mahomedan centre, but there is a small community of Moslem merchants engaged as usual in the horse and cattle trade and in the export of hides to Hankow. Two roads lead from here into Shensi, one *via* Hui Hsien to Hanchung, and the other *via* Ch'ingshui to Fenghsiang; two roads also lead into Szechuan, one *via*

Hui Hsien to the Chialing Chiang, and the other *via* Hsiho Hsien, Chieh Chou, and P'ik'ou; these are all mule trails.

Ch'in Chou is the seat of a Taoyin, a General, and a magistrate, by whom we were most hospitably entertained, being lodged in the local middle school. The latter provided quite luxurious accommodation, consisting of remarkably fine spacious buildings. There were plenty of students too, and the popularity of the government schools was here, as elsewhere in this remote province, very apparent. English, nowadays the official foreign language of China, is taught. I am not in a position to give any opinion as to the standard of the work done in these middle schools in Kansu but it is evident that they are more popular than the missionary schools, which is perhaps hardly to be wondered at. Immensely beneficial as the educational work of the missionaries is to the Chinese, it has the disadvantage, from the Chinese point of view, of being adulterated with evangelistic effort; so that the student, athirst for Western knowledge, has to swallow the Christian powder skilfully hidden between layers of scientific jam. Then there is always the underlying feeling against the alien institution, and also the fact that all the missionaries who engage in educational work in China are not always well qualified to lead their pupils very far. In Kansu missionary schools exist in only a very small way; but in some provinces, notably Szechuan, large institutions have been established, including a university. These remain, however, like the Christian Church in China, purely foreign institutions for the Chinese under foreign management, and for that reason are not always appreciated by the Chinese as they doubtless deserve to be; the latter would probably prefer that the foreign teachers should offer their services in the government schools.

From Lanchou Fu we had so far been following one of the main trade routes of Kansu, but we now turned westwards *en route* for T'ao Chou on the Kokonor border, following a very rough mountain trail through the heart of the western extremity of the Ch'inling Shan. Our first objective was the little district city of Li Hsien, distant two days' march, lying on the headwaters of the Chialing Chiang and therefore in the basin of the Yangtzu.

Leaving Ch'in Chou the path runs up a bare valley

due south for 15 li and then branches off up a side ravine to the S.W., another road continuing south up the main valley towards Hui Hsien. After an hour or two's march up this ravine the trail ascends a low pass, crosses a small valley, and immediately rises again to cross another low pass, whence it descends to the village of Kaomo Chen in the valley of a streamlet flowing from west to east. We were delayed in Kaomo Chen for half a day by our mule train following the wrong path, and its poverty was evidenced by the fact that we could get nothing but unleavened cakes of maize to eat, the most unpalatable form of nourishment I have ever had to put up with in China, though very often the only food of the people in mountainous country. From here the trail ascends by easy gradients to a pass in the Yangtzu-Yellow River divide, a climb of less than an hour over grassy slopes devoid of trees, and then descends steeply to a valley running south-west. The track follows down this stream for 20 li to the village of Lochia P'u, where it debouches into a broad and fertile valley, bounded by low cultivated hills of loess, the stream flowing from east to west. This stream is one of the headwaters of the Chialing Chiang, which flows through Szechuan to Chungking, and it is remarkable to find so much loess south of the divide. The latter formation may also be seen on the headwaters of the Shensi branch of the Chialing Chiang round Feng Hsien on the Hsian Chengtu road.

From Lochia P'u there is a remarkably good road down the open loess valley for two hours' march to the walled village of Yen Kuan, where there are said to be salt wells. The magistrate of Hsiho Hsien met us here, as we had entered his district; he said that a road branches off at this point to Hsiho and Chieh Chou and so to Szechuan. From Yen Kuan the road continues down the valley until within 20 li of Li Hsien, where it crosses a spur to avoid some gorges, and the loess formation comes to an end. Li Hsien is a picturesque little city lying hidden away on the southern slopes of the Ch'inling Shan in a country of narrow fertile valleys, whose streams all go to form the headwaters of the Kansu branch of the Chialing Chiang. From here to Min Chou our route followed an unfrequented trail which penetrated the Ch'inling Shan in the most curious way, passing and repassing from one to the other side of the watershed. In this neighbourhood the Ch'inling ranges do not appear such a formidable barrier between the Yellow River and the Yangtzu as in the places where we had crossed them further east in Shensi, perhaps owing to the greater elevation of the country on either side; unfortunately my aneroids were temporarily out of action owing to an accident on this portion of the journey, so that we could not follow the heights. West of Min Chou the Yangtzu-Yellow River divide is continued by the magnificent Min Shan, a rocky and almost impassable barrier reaching in places above the line of perpetual snow; but there does not seem to be any well-defined barrier ridge joining this range to the Ch'inling Shan, and if railways ever reach this part of Kansu it should not prove very difficult to connect them up with the future lines of Northern Szechuan.

Leaving Li Hsien the trail leads up a narrow valley to the north-west for 40 li to the hamlet of Wuch'uanli, a most picturesque spot surrounded by wooded mountains, where we passed the night in a temple. An hour's march further on the path turns up a side ravine, crosses a low pass, and descends into another narrow valley trending from north to south. Ten li up this valley a few huts called Chiutientzu are reached, beyond which the trail turns up a side gorge and climbs steeply to reach the summit of the Fenshui Ling ("Watershed Pass"). The scenery in these mountains is very fine, and the country wild and uninhabited. From the pass the trail descends through a flat grassy valley and then through cornfields to reach the market village of Mawu Chen 60 li from Wuch'uanli. Here one is apparently again on the northern side of the Ch'inling Shan, the stream flowing north to join the Wei.

From Mawu Chen the path turns west up a narrow valley, which for profusion of pheasants beat every other locality we traversed in all our long journeys. The sides of the ravine were clothed in dense jungle while in the bottom were patches of cultivation with the corn ripening for harvest. These fields were literally alive with pheasants, which blundered up in flocks as one moved up the valley through the corn. Here, as often before in Shensi and Kansu, we could not fail to be struck by the absurdity of all this game being untouched by the natives who not only neglect all this excellent food lying to their hands, but also presumably lose quite a lot of corn eaten by the pheasants. In the eastern provinces where there is a foreign market and also the demand created by the companies which export frozen game (a demand which is a serious danger to the stocks of game in those parts) the Chinese wage an unceasing war against the pheasants with gun, net, and even poison. I have known Chinese hunters in the mountains of Northern Chihli who used to make good shooting with the prehistoric looking Chinese gun with its pistol stock, which discharges a stream of bits of old iron and gives the shooter a severe blow on the cheek-bone when it is fired; and I have also been out with Chinese hunting pheasants with a native dog and hawk. But I have never come across a native in the mountains of Kansu who took the least interest in the pheasants picking grain on his threshing floor.

Following up this ravine from Mawu Chen for some 30 li the trail crosses a small pass and descends to a few huts called Shachin Kou, where one is apparently again on the southern side of the watershed with the stream flowing south towards the Chialing Chiang. From here it turns west again up another wooded gorge, where we startled a couple of deer, too big, I think, to be roe, leading to an easy pass over grass-covered mountains. Here there is a sudden and complete change in the scenery, and the trail descends into a broad shallow valley, devoid of trees, and dotted with farmsteads and patches of cultivation. Crossing this valley, which slopes north and is apparently once more on the northern side of the watershed, past the village of Suluk'o (60 li from Mawu Chen), the track engages itself in another grassy valley leading west. At the head of this valley one emerges on to a treeless marshy plateau dotted with herds of cattle. We were here assailed by a rain storm, and though the season was the end of June it was bitterly cold; my aneroids being out of action I can only guess the height, which was perhaps 9000 feet. An hour's march across this plateau brought us to our destination for the night, the hamlet of Tachuangtzu, 80 li from Mawu Chen, where the black peaty soil was under cultivation to a limited extent.

As we rode into this little place, cold, tired, and generally rather miserable, the entire visible population fell on their faces, since republican principles had not yet penetrated to this out-of-the-way spot, and they thought they were prostrating themselves before an "Imperial Mission." The headman had, however, prepared the best of the mud cabins for our accommodation, and we were soon warm and dry again, and engaged in disposing of some of the cock pheasants picked up *en route*.

A few li beyond Tachuangtzu the trail drops over the edge of the plateau to reach the considerable village of Ch'enchiachi, lying in a flat cultivated valley sloping north and surrounded by grassy mountains. We halted here for the night owing to the rain, only having made ten li; quite good accommodation was secured in a farm house, but it was miserably cold. From here the road runs westwards across rolling grass country intersected by shallow cultivated valleys sloping north with sheep and cattle grazing on the hill slopes. This curious grass-covered plateau, the presence of which is entirely unexpected in a region of steep mountains, appears to be the westernmost end of the Ch'inling Shan, a range which we had come to know so well in the course of our journeys. After about three hours' march there is a slight rise to a pass, and then a precipitous drop for ten li to reach a village called Panchi Chuang, lying in a narrow valley. Another two hours' march down this valley brings one to the large walled village of Lich'uan, 60 li from Ch'enchiachi and 70 li from Min Chou. Here the stream flows south towards Szechuan and one is again on the southern side of the watershed.

From Lich'uan the track runs N.W. up a side valley ending in a grassy pass. For the next five li or so it keeps to the top of the mountain, whence there are truly magnificent views over the rocky snow-patched Min Shan to the south-west, and then descends steeply through a ravine to the valley of the T'ao River. Two tributary torrents are forded before the city of Min Chou is reached. Being now again in the valley of the T'ao we were once more on the northern side of the Yangtzu-Yellow River watershed. Since leaving Ch'in Chou a few days previously we had crossed this divide no less than six times, which is sufficient to show the interesting nature of this mountain trail. A proper survey of this region would be sure to bring many interesting facts to light. Unfortunately the prospects of accurate map-making in China are not very bright at present. The Chinese, not unnaturally, have recently taken to objecting to the wandering foreigner who used to roam across the country making a map, and they profess to be compiling an accurate survey of the whole country themselves. The results of the work done in this connection in the north-east provinces has not been published, however, and at the present rate of progress it does not seem likely that the more remote parts in the west will be reached for generations. In the meantime existing maps of China are most unsatisfactory. Some of the coast provinces have been fairly thoroughly mapped by foreign military officers after 1900; there is also a very good British map of Szechuan, though where its authors have relied on the work of previous travellers, as in the case of the important Hsian-Chengtu road, it contains many errors. In the case of a remote province like Kansu, however, the best existing foreign maps are merely compilations of the route surveys of various foreign travellers, with the result that one gets an accurate representation of certain roads intersected by spaces which are practically blank, or filled in more or less at haphazard with names from old Chinese maps. In the case of Kansu many of these route surveys were compiled by Russian travellers long ago, more interested in Tibet and Mongolia than in China, so that one finds names like Mount Konkyr, Donkyr, Ugambu, etc. (to mention a few in the neighbourhood of Hsining) reappearing on the most modern maps; some of these names are nowadays quite untraceable amongst the Chinese; others are curious corruptions of well-known Chinese centres, like the two last mentioned, which represent Tanko and Weiyuan P'u respectively. Thus, although the interior of China is nowadays so well known, it is likely to remain for long one of the worst mapped parts of the world. For travelling purposes we found modern Chinese maps, compiled from the rough charts of the various districts (Hsien), though geographically very inaccurate, more useful than the foreign maps, as one could at any rate rely on the place-names.

9—2

It is suggested that the Chinese might with advantage borrow the services of some officers from the Survey of India and proceed to the triangulation of the whole country. The results, at any rate in Kansu and parts of Shensi, would be surprising. Amongst many other interesting facts which would be brought to light are the actual heights of the snow-clad mountains on the western borders of Kansu and Szechuan, some of which probably equal or surpass all but the highest giants of the Himalayas.

Min Chou (now Min Hsien) is a small city with busy suburbs situated on the right bank of the T'ao River at the point where the latter, flowing down from the Kokonor mountains in the west, makes a sharp right-angle turn to the north. The altitude is about 7500 feet. The T'ao River valley, here nearly a mile wide in places, is very fertile, and produces wheat, barley, beans, hemp, etc. Like T'ao Chou and Hsiku, Min Chou is a centre for the Chinese trade with the Tibetan inhabitants of the Kokonor country further west. A rough cart built entirely of wood with remarkably high wheels and drawn by the half-bred yak is used round Min Chou, on the roads to T'ao Chou, on the grasslands round the latter, and in other border parts of the province. I mention this cart because it is obviously very useful and because it is quite unusual to find wheeled traffic of any kind in such mountainous country in China; its introduction into the Tibetan inhabited plateau west of Tachienlu in Szechuan would revolutionise transport in that region.

Leaving Min Chou the road runs along the right bank of the T'ao River for ten li, and then crosses to the left bank by a ferry, the bridge having been destroyed at the time of the White Wolf raid. The river is here in the summer about 80 yards wide, six to eight feet deep, and very rapid. Navigation is confined to rafts of lumber down stream. From the ferry the path continues up the valley for three to four hours' march to the village of Hsitachai. The T'ao River valley is in this neighbourhood one of the most attractive regions in Kansu, or perhaps in China, being fertile and well cultivated, and bounded on the southern side by forest-clad mountains, the foothills of the great Min Shan. The river flows much of the way in a narrow trough below the surrounding level of the valley. Just beyond Hsitachai the path leaves the T'ao River, along which another track runs direct to Choni, and turns up a side valley to the north to reach a semi-Tibetan hamlet called Shanch'a, 80 li from Min Chou, where we passed the night in the house of the headman. Pheasants were abundant in this picturesque and well-wooded valley.

At Shanch'a the path turns up a side ravine leading after an hour's march to an easy pass, whence there is a descent for another hour into a bare valley, followed by a rise over a second low pass, and a descent to New T'ao Chou in another bare open valley, a march of 40 li in all. New T'ao Chou (now called Lintan Hsien) is the official town, as opposed to Old T'ao Chou, distant 60 li, the commercial town, and is an empty shell of a city of no importance. About half the few buildings inside the walls had been destroyed by the White Wolf rebels the year previously. We were accommodated in a temple which the magistrate had fitted up temporarily as his yamen. The city lies in a bare open valley some 20 li or so north of the T'ao River in a region of treeless hills of loess, red clay, and red sandstone. This somewhat dreary belt of bare red hills intervenes practically all along this border between the loess of Kansu proper and the pine forests and grass lands of the Kokonor country, and corresponds roughly to a similar Mahomedan wedge between Chinese and Tibetans. The red hills round New T'ao Chou are cultivated and dotted with villages, mostly Mahomedan. The Moslems extend from here along the border to their real strongholds round Ho Chou and Hsünhua, and thence north of the Yellow River to beyond Hsining. We were travelling round the two T'ao Chous during the season of summer thunderstorms (early July), and usually experienced several daily, some very severe and rather alarming in this elevated region. On one occasion hurrying into a Mahomedan farmhouse for shelter we found the inhabitants at prayer as though in a mosque; this custom of using private houses for prayer is, I was told, confined to the followers of the "New Sect," which is very extended and influential in Kansu. Our sudden intrusion was not resented in the least, and on this, as on every other occasion when I met Mahomedans in Kansu, we were treated with every courtesy. The Mahomedans of Kansu still consider themselves to a certain extent as foreigners sojourning in a strange land, and greet travellers from the west as fellow-wanderers.

From New T'ao Chou to Choni, a march of 30 li, the track runs south-west over a low pass in the red clay hills, crosses a valley trending south, ascends another low pass, and descends through a grassy ravine to the T'ao River. Choni, the residence of a T'ussu, or native chief, ruling several Tibetan tribes in the neighbourhood, is a picturesque little place, a walled village built round the chief's residence on the banks of the T'ao, and overlooked by a lamasery containing some 500 monks. We were received by the usual cannon shots (an old-fashioned Chinese custom still surviving in most parts of Kansu which is terrifying to one's pony unless accustomed to it) and really sumptuously lodged in the chief's residence. The Choni T'ussu is by far the most important native chief in Kansu and exercises jurisdiction over an extensive territory. Some of his tribes, especially those living to the south of the Min Shan, are turbulent and not easy to control. The chief is under the authority of the Governor at Lanchou, but unlike his colleagues in Szechuan west of Tachienlu, he retains his power unimpaired over his Tibetans. On the east his jurisdiction is bounded by Chinese territory; on the west it fades away amongst the lawless nomads of the grass-lands. His authority, like that of most native chiefs in China, extends rather over tribes and families than fixed territory, and its limits are therefore vague.

The T'ao River is here the dividing line between Tibetans and Chinese (Mahomedans), the forest-clad mountains to the south being inhabited by the former, and red hills to the north by the latter. There is good big game shooting to be had in these forests, wapiti, sheep, goral, serow, bear, etc. The elevation of the valley seems to be about 8000 feet at Choni.

Leaving Choni the road runs up the beautiful T'ao valley for about ten li, and then turns north-west up a small ravine leading to an easy pass. From here it runs along the top of the mountain for a few li, descends into a valley, crosses another low pass, and drops down to Old T'ao Chou, 45 li from Choni.

PLATE XXVII

TIBETAN VILLAGERS AND MAHOMEDAN SOLDIERS

TIBETAN VILLAGERS AND MAHOMEDAN SOLDIERS

PLATE XXVIII

APPROACH TO TIBETAN COUNTRY WEST OF T'AOCHOU

HALT IN A TIBETAN VILLAGE WEST OF T'AOCHOU

Old T'ao Chou lies in a valley about ten li north of the T'ao River at an elevation of about 9000 feet in the same region of bare red hills with cultivated valleys as the New City. At the time of our visit its chief feature was the fact that the four walls enclosed nothing but a mass of ruins, the town having been completely burnt out by the White Wolf rebels the year before; we saw many a ruined city in Kansu in the course of our travels—indeed in that province ruins are the rule rather than the exception—but nothing so utterly and completely destroyed as Old T'ao Chou. Outside the city, however, there was a suburb which did not seem to have suffered much, and here we were well lodged in a large Tibetan inn. T'ao Chou is the Kansu counterpart of Tachienlu and Sungp'an in Szechuan, a centre for the exchange of the products of China and Tibet, where barley meal, piece goods, tea, tobacco, and Chinese wares such as saddlery, boots, guns, felt, etc., are exchanged for wool, skins, furs, gold dust, medicines, deer's horns, Tibetan incense, and other produce of the highlands, a lucrative trade here largely in the hands of the Mahomedans. There are, however, certain marked differences in the conditions ruling at T'ao Chou and Tachienlu. For instance in the latter place trade during recent years has been greatly interfered with by the hostilities which have been carried on intermittently between Chinese and Tibetans during the past few years, whereas at T'ao Chou the traffic has been uninterrupted; secondly at Tachienlu the lamas and native tribesmen have been completely cowed by the Chinese and are not allowed to carry arms, whereas at T'ao Chou the wild-looking nomads swagger about the streets armed to the teeth, and have so far only been bested by the Chinese in commercial transactions.

A road leads from T'ao Chou through the grass country of the independent Golok to Jyekundo and Central Tibet. Though this route is little known, it is said to pass through good grass country most of the way, and is perhaps the easiest road from China into Tibet. Another road leads south to Sungp'an in Szechuan, passing over the Min Shan by a peculiar looking square gap in this rocky barrier range, called the "Shih Men" (Stone Gate), but it is little used as it traverses the territory of one of the most lawless tribes under the Choni chief. From the neighbourhood of T'ao Chou fine views are obtainable over this great Min Shan range, rising like a gigantic wall of snow-patched rock immediately to the south of the river, its serrated peaks being, I should say, 16,000 to 17,000 feet in height. It here forms the divide between the Yangtzu and the Yellow River, and from it the Ch'inling Shan continues eastwards right across China to the plains of Honan, separating the rice-eating peoples of Central China from the wheat-eating inhabitants of the north. Should such a catastrophe ever occur as a temporary separation of Northern from Southern China, this great barrier range would form an ideal political boundary between the two States.

There is a station of an American mission at T'ao Chou (as also at Min Chou, Choni, and Titao) designed for work amongst the Tibetans of the Kokonor border. But as has been the case with missionary work on the Szechuan Tibet frontier, their efforts to influence the Tibetan tribesmen have been practically without result owing to the immense power of the lama church and its monasteries. This mysterious Sino-Tibetan borderland and the prospect of attacking lamaism in its native strongholds have attracted some of the finest missionaries in the East, who, however, find after years of strenuous work and self-denial, that they have only succeeded in influencing a few of the Chinese. In Tibetan Yunnan the Catholics, and on the Indo-Tibetan frontier the Moravians, have been working for the past 50 years or so, I believe with the same lack of success as far as the Tibetans are concerned; and in the case of the China Inland Mission, which worked for years amongst the Tibetans of the Szechuan marches, the only converts obtained were amongst the Chinese settlers of that region. Viewed from a missionary point of view, it therefore seems a doubtful policy to waste so much money and energy in attempting the impossible on the sparsely populated Tibetan borderland, when there are still many great centres, at any rate in the north-west, of the more receptive and friendly Chinese untouched.

The year after our visit there was an outbreak of pneumonic plague round T'ao Chou, which appears to have originated in the same kind of grass country inhabited by nomads and marmots as the Manchurian outbreak of 1911.

It seems to have been checked by the energetic action of the Chinese authorities acting under the advice of a British missionary doctor from Lanchou. The terrible thing about pneumonic plague in North China is that a patient once afflicted seems bound to die, which accounts for the amount of attention it attracts. But the ravages even of such an outbreak as the Manchurian one of 1911 seem small when compared with those of bubonic plague in India. The outbreak of 1911 caused a panic in North China amongst Chinese and foreigners alike, and the Legation Quarter in Peking barricaded itself behind its defences as though to repel another Boxer rising, though only a case or two occurred in the city; one does not hear of similar measures being taken in India.

From Lanchou Fu to Old T'ao Chou by the route we followed is a distance of about 1450 li and occupied some 24 day's travel.

CHAPTER X

FROM T'AOCHOU ACROSS THE GRASS-LANDS TO LABRANG MONASTERY, AND THENCE *VIA* HOCHOU BACK TO LANCHOU FU

Difficulties of travel west of T'aochou—Tibetan houses—Grass-lands of the Kokonor border—Tibetan nomads—Heitso Monastery—Tibetans of Amdo—Labrang—Reception by Lamas—Hochou—Mahomedans in Kansu—Mahomedans and Christian missionaries—Return to Lanchou.

THE journey from Old T'ao Chou to Labrang monastery is usually made in four days, the distance being called 250 li. The track is little used and a local guide is essential, inasmuch as once on the grass-lands faint trails lead in all directions; a Tibetan interpreter is also useful, since few or no Chinese are met with *en route*. The Choni chief had very kindly deputed one of his own headmen to accompany us, since his jurisdiction extended some way towards Labrang, and the services of this man, as interpreter, guide, and sponsor were invaluable and cleared away all difficulties. We were also accompanied by half a dozen of the chief's Tibetan soldiers and as many Mahomedan braves, the latter being useful owing to the peculiar influence exercised at present by the Mahomedan leaders over the Tibetans; indeed it is commonly said locally that Labrang, formerly so bitterly hostile to the Chinese and strangers generally, is now entirely under the thumb of General Ma An-liang. It should be noted that the Kansu borderland differs at present from the same country in Western Szechuan in that the latter has been largely taken over by the Chinese, whereas the former has not. While in Szechuan, therefore, it may only be necessary to make arrangements with the Chinese officials for travel on the border, in Kansu it is necessary to arrange matters with the local native chiefs and the Mahomedans; otherwise travel west of T'ao Chou and Labrang is by no means safe. From Labrang to Ho Chou there is a mule trail much frequented by Mahomedan merchants, and no special arrangements are necessary.

PLATE XXIX

NOMAD TIBETANS ON THE GRASS-LANDS NEAR LABRANG

NOMAD TIBETANS ON THE GRASS-LANDS NEAR LABRANG

PLATE XXX

GRASS COUNTRY (11,000 FEET) ON THE ROAD TO LABRANG

TIBETAN ENCAMPMENTS NEAR LABRANG

Leaving T'ao Chou the trail runs north-west over a low pass in the red clay hills, traverses a cultivated valley trending south, and ascends by easy gradients to another pass, whence there is a particularly fine view over the Min Shan to the south of the T'ao River. Beyond this point Chinese cease to be seen. From this pass the track descends steeply to another stream flowing south and then continues north-west up a flat shallow valley bounded by bare grassy hills. In this valley and its neighbourhood there are several Tibetan villages, in one of which, about 50 li from T'ao Chou, we passed the night; its name has escaped me, if I ever heard it. These villages are under the control of the Choni chief, and preparations had been made to receive us in the headman's house. The Tibetans are usually considered to live under the hardest and most filthy conditions, which is certainly so in the case of these Amdowa where they are nomads on the grass-lands. But the houses of the headmen of the agricultural Tibetan villages, both here and elsewhere where we rested in them, showed an astonishingly high standard of comfort and were superior to any Chinese house I have seen. These houses are solidly built of wood and stone of two stories, and the rooms of the one in which we were lodged here were spotlessly clean and panelled with stained wood.

An hour's march beyond this village the trail emerged from the valley after topping an easy pass, where marmots were very abundant, sitting up in front of their holes and dodging in as one approached them. This pass is here the boundary of the real grass-lands, and apparently the border of the Choni chief's territory in this direction. Beyond it all cultivation ceases, there are no more houses, and one enters a region of shallow valleys and low mountains (elevation about 11,000 feet) dotted with large herds of yak, sheep, and ponies grazing round the black rectangular tents of the Tibetan nomads, here, as elsewhere, called Drokba. These grassy steppes, always referred to by the Chinese as *Ts'ao Ti*, bound China everywhere on the north and west, and always one ascends to them through a region of broken mountains, whether it be from Szechuan or Kansu up to the highlands of the Tibetan plateau, or from Chihli or Shansi up to the highlands of Mongolia; and always it is the same land of nomads and lamas, whether Tibetan or Mongol. In past centuries the Chinese were ever engaged, with varying success, in defending their fertile plains and valleys against the incursions of Tartar hordes from these tablelands; now the nomads are impotent outside their own territories, reduced in numbers and virility perhaps by the lama religion, and these vast empty spaces serve as buffers protecting China from the rest of Asia. Undoubtedly her wisest policy is to leave the scattered inhabitants to manage their own affairs as hitherto under her vague suzerainty.

The trail runs north-west across these grass-lands, passing continually from one shallow valley to another; at first these valleys slope S.E. towards the T'ao River, but after 20 li or so they slope N.W. towards the Ho Chou River. The pasturage is excellent and there are many nomad encampments; the latter are only to be approached with care, as they are guarded by huge Tibetan mastiffs, I should think easily the most formidable breed of dog in the world, and the nomads themselves are not friendly to strangers. Indeed the Amdo Tibetan of the Kokonor grass country is about the last kind of individual one would choose to meet alone on a dark night, and a wilder or more picturesque looking lot of ruffians it would be difficult to imagine. They always go heavily armed, and are robbers by nature. Once properly introduced to them, however, one can count on friendly treatment, and we had nothing to complain of in this respect. After six or seven hour's march from the village where we had passed the night the trail descended from the plateau into an open and partly cultivated valley with the temples and barrack-like buildings of the monastery of Heitso Ssu at the end of it, a most striking sight in this land of tent-living nomads.

Heitso Ssu (the Chinese name) is a large and wealthy monastery, containing, we were told, some thousand lamas. It is quite a little town in itself, with, as is usually the case on this border, a small Chinese village or bazaar of one street, run mostly by Mahomedans, attached to it. It lies at the junction of two small valleys below the level of the grass country, and the neighbouring slopes are well cultivated with barley and peas and dotted with Tibetan farms. We were badly housed in a kind of inn in the Chinese bazaar, which is separated from the lamasery by a stream, and as the lamas did not appear particularly friendly, and we were only passing through, we left them alone. This was really the only place on all our long journeys where we were not well received. Heitso is called 120 li from T'ao Chou. To the south are forest-clad hills and to the north and north-west are high rocky mountains patched with snow. My amateur map led me to take these to be the divide between the sources of the T'ao and Tahsia rivers and the upper Yellow River, and therefore probably the true boundary between Kansu and Kokonor territory in this direction. The boundaries of Western Kansu are extremely vague, owing to the practice of the native chiefs exercising jurisdiction over tribes and families of nomads rather than fixed areas.

The Amdo Tibetans we met round Heitso and on our road from T'ao Chou to Labrang, whether nomads or agriculturists, were just like the tribesmen who come into Tachienlu in Szechuan from the uplands of Kham, except that the latter have been partly disarmed while the Kansu Tibetans all carry swords thrust crosswise through their belts and often the long Tibetan gun with prong attachment in addition. Their dress is of the simplest description, consisting usually of a sheepskin robe worn winter and summer with the wool inside, often no trousers, and long leather boots. The hilts and sheathes of their swords and knives are often handsomely inlaid with silver and decorated with turquoise and coral, and probably come from Kham. The head dress of the women is peculiar, the hair being braided into a number of small plaits, which hang down below the waist and are bound together at their extremities by a piece of cloth ornamented with silver and stones. On the grass-lands they live by cattle-raising and robbing, becoming more and more lawless as one proceeds west, till the Golok and similar tribes are reached living round the upper Yellow River and thence southwards towards the Szechuan marches, who are entirely masterless and acknowledge the authority of neither China nor Tibet. As a result their territory is about the least known portion of Asia.

The Chinese call the Amdo Tibetans Hsifan, a wide term meaning Western Barbarians applied to all the non-Chinese tribesmen from Sungp'an to Hsining. Some

European scholars have maintained that the Hsifan are not Tibetans and suggested that they represent a northern branch of one of the non-Chinese races of S.W. China, like the Lolos or Mosos. Granting that there is no such thing as a homogeneous Tibetan race, the Hsifan of the country west of T'ao Chou speak the Tibetan language and are as much Tibetans as the inhabitants of any other portion of the Tibetan plateau. A little further north they come into contact with the Kokonor Mongols, whom they bully and plunder. Unlike the Mongols, who are everywhere being pushed back by the encroaching Chinese agriculturist along the northern borders of Shansi and Chihli, the Tibetans of the Kansu border hold their own against the Chinese colonist; partly perhaps because the country is too elevated to suit the latter, but also because the N. Eastern Tibetan is truculent and independent compared to the Mongol and further takes readily and successfully to agriculture. Their food is the buttered tea and tsamba (parched barley meal) of the Tibetans everywhere. Tsamba is a palatable food for people fond of porridge, and the buttered tea is not at all bad when regarded as gruel or soup instead of tea; it is for this reason that the bitter teas of India are unsuited to the Tibetans. It is often said that the Chinese sell the merest refuse of their tea bushes to the Tibetans; but it happens to be what the latter want to make their gruel with. There is little or no resemblance between the tea drunk by the Tibetans and that consumed in Europe.

There appear to be two racial types in Tibet, the short round-faced Mongoloid type, and the tall prominent-featured Aryan type; the latter is common among the Tibetans of Amdo as amongst those of Kham. A peculiar feature of the eastern Tibetan, by which he could in nine cases out of ten be recognised in Chinese or foreign dress, is his habit of standing with his feet turned out at right angles to his body.

From Heitso Ssu the trail runs north over low grass-covered hills for a few li and then descends through a rocky gorge to a small monastery called K'achia Ssu (all our names are Chinese) lying in a narrow wooded valley trending N.W. In this neighbourhood there grows a plant poisonous to ponies and mules. From here the track runs down the valley, at first through cultivated fields and then through a densely wooded gorge. This is a difficult march in the summer, as the trail constantly crosses and recrosses the stream, which is rapid, obstructed by boulders, and only just fordable. Several of us got a wetting, but we were lucky in keeping the pack-mules on their feet and our bedding dry. The mountains in the neighbourhood are covered with fine forest, but mostly on the slopes facing north only, a peculiarity which may be noticed all along the Kokonor border; I have observed the same thing in the forests of Northern Shansi; whether it is that the sun is too hot on the southern slopes, or that the northern slopes alone receive sufficient moisture, I am unable to say. Four to five hours' march down this gorge, past several small lamaseries, brings one to the junction of this stream with the Tahsia River, a torrent flowing from Labrang to Ho Chou. The Labrang road turns up this valley and runs for a few li through cultivated fields to the small monastery of Shakou Ssu, which lies on the north side of the stream, with a Mahomedan hamlet, Sasuma, opposite, where we passed the night in an inn. There are pine forests all around, and the Tahsia River, though only a mountain torrent, is used for rafting the cut timber down to the Yellow River and Lanchou. The timber is made up into narrow sections, fastened one behind the other, and the jointed raft which results is navigated down the rapids and through the rocks with extraordinary skill by Mahomedan raftmen.

From Heitso to Labrang is a distance of some 120 li, and Sasuma lies about half way, the track running for the rest of the way up the valley of the Tahsia River. For the first 30 li the path is very bad and rocky, the valley being a gorge hemmed in by wooded mountains; there is no more fording to be done, however, as the river is spanned by good cantilever bridges, this being a portion of the Labrang-Ho Chou road, which is much used by the mule trains of Mahomedan merchants. In this neighbourhood we saw some *ma chi*, the large and handsome silver pheasant with red legs (*Crossoptilon auritum*, probably). For the second 30 li the valley opens out and the road becomes a good highway. The first intimation we received of the approach to Labrang were the white and blue tents dotted over the mountain slopes, and then a sudden bend of the valley reveals the gilt-roofed temples and huge barrack-like constructions of the great monastery. The buildings are, I should say, without parallel in the whole of China for magnificence, solidity, and size, and present a most startling appearance in that wild and sparsely populated region of mountains and grass-lands.

Labrang (Chinese Labalang Ssu) lies at an altitude of about 9000 feet in the valley of the Tahsia River just below the level of the grass-lands which commence immediately to the west. It is a regular town in itself containing over 3000 monks as well as a considerable floating population of visiting Tibetans, hundreds of whom were at the time of our visit encamped in the neighbourhood. The monastery is the most important religious centre between Lassa and Urga, not excluding the better known establishment of Kumbum (T'a-erh Ssu) near Hsining. It contains a university which attracts students from all parts of Tibet and Mongolia, and even Siberia. The monastic authorities exercise control over the neighbouring Tibetans and until recently over Chinese as well. Of late, however, the chief lama, a Re-incarnation (referred to as a Hutukotu by the Chinese), has fallen much under the influence of the Mahomedans of Ho Chou, and the monks are no longer as unruly and hostile to foreigners as formerly; at the time of our visit they had even applied for the establishment of an agency of the Chinese Post Office at Labrang. All the same it is advisable for foreign visitors to be provided with an introduction from some Tibetan or Mahomedan authority. A li or two from the monastery is the usual Chinese, or rather Mahomedan, bazaar. These large monasteries on the Kokonor border are commercial as well as religious centres, and the Chinese trading villages attached to them resemble in a way the foreign settlements attached to Chinese cities opened to foreign trade. This border trade is almost entirely in the hands of the Mahomedans, and even where the Chinese take a hand in it, it is through the agency of Mahomedan middlemen, called *Hsiehchia*, who travel amongst the Tibetans further west, and barter Chinese wares for their produce, especially wool. There are many queer tales about Labrang to be heard locally.

PLATE XXXI

A MIDDAY HALT ON THE ROAD TO LABRANG

VIEW OF THE MONASTERY OF HEITSO SSU

PLATE XXXII

PORTION OF HEITSO MONASTERY

PORTION OF HEITSO MONASTERY

We were well accommodated by the Mahomedans in their village. The Hutukotu was away "saying prayers in the grass-country" (*Ts'ao Ti Nien Ching*—as we were told), but the second lama in charge, an aged monk of refined and intelligent appearance, received us most amicably in a gorgeous apartment glittering with gold images and other signs of wealth, and gave instructions for us to be shown round the monastery. I am not sufficiently acquainted with Lamaism to be able to give an intelligent description of what we saw, but the temples were the finest and richest I have visited in China, and the residences of the monks the usual gloomy buildings common to all lamaseries. At our interview with the lama we were presented with the usual silk scarves (*Khata*), and it may be noted that the Chinese and Tibetans with us attached these in a prominent manner to their persons to show all and sundry that they had been received by the authorities of the monastery; I do not know whether this is a usual use to which to put the *Khata*, but it seemed a good idea here. After getting back to our quarters we found a present consisting of half a sheep for ourselves and several bushels of peas for our animals from the lama, which was very welcome in a country of scanty supplies.

From Labrang to Ho Chou is a distance of about 200 li, which is usually made in three stages. The first day's march took us back down the valley of the Tahsia River to Sasuma. From here the trail continues down the valley, which is here cultivated, past several small lamaseries, for 40 li to the village of Ch'aokou. Here gorges are entered through which the river winds for another 20 li to the village of Ch'ingshui (these villages are Chinese, or rather Mahomedan, with nothing Tibetan about them). The path ledged in the rock and supported by wooden stagings high above the torrent is very dangerous in places. There is an idea that mules and ponies accustomed to the mountains never fall, but this is by no means the case, and I have on more than one occasion seen an animal plunge to his death over the edge of one of these precipices, though fortunately we never lost one ourselves; it is always wise to dismount in such places. In spite of the dangerous nature of the road we met large numbers of mule caravans going up to Labrang with the goods of the Mahomedan merchants of Ho Chou.

We passed the night at Ch'ingshui, where we met a military officer sent up to escort us down into China Proper who calmly informed us with little apparent interest that China and Japan were at war. This news afterwards turned out to be a local echo of the crisis existing between the two countries two months previously, and the incident shows that even today momentous events on the coast have comparatively little interest for the inhabitants of the far interior. Below Ch'ingshui the path continues through winding gorges with the foaming torrent hemmed in by forest-clad mountains for 20 li to the likin barrier of T'ungmen Kuan, where the gorges debouch on to an open cultivated valley. This is one of the numerous "Gates" leading into and out of China Proper on her western and northern frontiers. There is a bit of an old wall to be seen, perhaps a portion of the Kokonor loop of the Great Wall. From here to Ho Chou, a distance of 60 li, a good highway runs down the fertile valley past numerous Mahomedan villages. We did not see the valley at its best, because it poured with rain during the whole march, and the clay soil was turned into a slippery morass; at one place, crossing a nullah by a narrow causeway, one of our mule litters containing a cook was overturned into the ditch, and remained literally upside down with the eight legs of the two mules pointing skywards for some time, till they were hauled out in that position, no damage being done.

Ho Chou (new name T'aoho Hsien) is a pleasant little city lying in a most delightful valley plain, from five to six thousand feet above the sea, sheltered by high mountains, and as fertile as a garden. The mountains to the west and south-west (T'aitzu Shan) are very bold and rocky, and carried a good deal of snow at the time of our visit (middle of July). Ho Chou itself consists of a small Chinese town with large and busy Mahomedan suburbs, containing many fine mosques and seminaries. It is the centre of Mahomedan power and influence in the province, and General Ma Anliang, who actually lives a day's journey or so away near the Yellow River, has a fine residence in the suburb. The Chinese magistrate in the city seems to have little to do

PLATE XXXIII

TIBETAN VILLAGERS NEAR KACHIA SSU

A PORTION OF THE MONASTERY OF KACHIA SSU

PLATE XXXIV

MONASTERY OF SHAKOU SSU

CANTILEVER BRIDGE ON THE ROAD TO LABRANG

with the Mahomedan population of the district. At the
time of our visit there was also a Chinese General with a
few hundred old-fashioned Chinese troops in the city, the
Mahomedan troops, of whom there are many thousands in
the neighbourhood, being quartered in the surrounding
Mahomedan districts. We spent a day in Ho Chou, which
I thought a delightful place, feasting and receiving callers.

The Chinese differentiate between two kinds of Mahomedans in Kansu, the Sala, the descendants of a Turkish
tribe which came from the neighbourhood of Samarcand
some five or six hundred years ago and settled on the upper
Yellow River round Ho Chou and Hsünhua, and the
original Mahomedan population of the province, which also
came from Turkestan, but at a much earlier period. The
former are really Chinese Turks, while the latter are probably
so mixed with early Chinese colonists who adopted Islam
as to merit the title of Mahomedan Chinese. The Chinese
look upon all the Moslems as being of a different race to
themselves, and they are assigned one of the five colours of
the republican flag, which symbolises the union of the five
Mongoloid races of the former Chinese Empire. They are
locally known as Hui Hui, or Hsiao Chiao Jen; the origin
of the former name is still occupying the attention of
scholars, and has been explained in various far-fetched and
unsatisfactory ways; the latter means People of the Lesser
Religion. The Mahomedan religion itself is known as
Ch'ing Chen Chiao (Pure and True Religion). The Sala,
who are considered by the Chinese to be the more fanatical
and dangerous, show their comparatively recent Turkish
origin in their long narrow faces, large eyes, and strong
beards, and a Turkish dialect of some kind still survives
amongst them.

There are two large sects amongst the Mahomedans of
Kansu, those who follow the Lao Chiao (Old Religion) and
those who follow the Hsin Chiao (New Religion), which I
have heard compared by the Chinese to the Catholic and
Protestant Churches of Christianity. These two sects are
bitterly hostile to one another, and generally speaking the
Mahomedans are always quarrelling amongst themselves
about religious matters. But, in spite of these apparent
internal dissensions, they present on the whole a united

front towards the Chinese and the rest of the world, and in this unity (as also in the case of the unity of the Catholic Church) lies their amazing strength today. I have heard the Chinese compare both Islam and the Catholic Church to vast world-wide secret societies bound together for purposes of mutual benefit and protection against the rest of mankind. At present the Moslems of North West China, though unsupported by the Treaties of any Foreign Powers, and in spite of the terrible set back after the rebellion, have acquired by their own efforts a privileged and independent position, and indeed are now the principal power in the province.

The various sects and classes seem to differ a good deal in the strictness of their observance of the tenets of their religion. Abstention from pork seems universal, and many abstain also from wine, opium, and even tobacco. The Ramadan fast is carefully kept by the upper classes, but not so strictly by the lower. Every Moslem appears to have an Arabic as well as a Chinese name, but a knowledge of the former language is confined to a few Ahongs and scholars. The Koran is read in Arabic. All classes hold keenly to their religion, and their religious centres are visited from time to time by priests from Turkey, Arabia, and Central Asia. They keep aloof from the Chinese, whom they consider unclean, and do not usually frequent the Government schools. They occasionally take Chinese wives, but the latter have to be cleansed before marriage externally and internally by a course of baths and water drinking. The veiling of their women is not, I believe, practised in other parts of China, but in Kansu we saw veiled women on two or three occasions, each time travelling on the road. The superiority of the Moslems over the Chinese in regard to housing, food, personal cleanliness, and general standard of living is marked, and their spotlessly clean and well-kept mosques (*Lipai Ssu*) are in striking contrast to the dirty and dilapidated temples of the Chinese. These mosques are Chinese-style buildings, and in this respect as in most others they have created a Chinese Mahomedan Church. Though the magistrates in the Mahomedan districts are Chinese, they usually refrain from any interference with the Mahomedans, who appear to manage their own affairs through a sort of local government. In other parts of China the Mahomedans are mostly indistinguishable externally from the rest of the Chinese population; but in Kansu, apart from the Salas, who are of a distinctly Central Asiatic type, my experience was that the faces of most of the Mahomedans are somehow different from the Chinese; they are in any case usually rendered noticeable by their white caps. Foreign scholars attach importance to the early Arab intercourse by sea, but all the Chinese with whom I discussed the question of Islam in China agreed that it came overland from Central Asia, and this is probably true of the North and North West at any rate, which, apart from Yunnan, are the regions where Mahomedanism counts.

The Mahomedan population of Kansu, decimated by the great rebellion, is now recovering and increasing again as the result of many years of comparative peace. Apart from natural increase by births and, after the Chinese fashion, by adoptions, there are a certain number of conversions; these are due rather to expediency than to religious conviction, but the converts having once adopted Islam, appear usually to become good and zealous Moslems. The Chinese as a race seem to require stiffening by a virile religion of some kind, and the effects of Mahomedanism on the characters of those among them who embrace it appear remarkable, and give rise to curious speculations.

It may briefly be stated here that the Mahomedans of North West China, in spite of their religious connection with Turkey and the intrigues of enemy agents, have throughout the War remained absolutely loyal to the Chinese Government.

The relations between the Moslems and the foreign missionaries are comparatively good, so long as religious questions are not concerned. Even in religious matters they agree with the foreigner up to a certain point, since they consider that both they and the missionaries worship the only true God, in contrast to the idolatrous Chinese. It is only when the divinity of Jesus, whom they regard as a prophet but not divine, is raised that they join issue with the foreigner, and then they become inexorably hostile. The early history of Protestant missions in China contains many references to assistance received from the Mahomedans during the first difficult days. But evangelistic work amongst the Moslems of Kansu appears hopeless. A hospital is now being erected in Lanchou under the auspices of the China Inland Mission with the special object of converting the Mahomedans; it remains to be seen whether it will meet with any success.

Some remarkable facts are brought to light if the history and progress of Islam and Christianity in China are compared, the Chinese authorities having been equally tolerant to both religions, as to all others, until in recent years rebellions caused them to mistrust the former, and political considerations rendered them suspicious of the latter; but in both cases only to a limited extent, for in the past and in the present China holds a record for religious tolerance hard to beat anywhere amongst the nations of the world.

Christianity was propagated in China by Nestorian missionaries during the 7th century and later for an unknown number of centuries (they appear to have still existed in Marco Polo's time); Catholic missionaries flourished under the Mongol dynasty in the 14th century, and from the 16th century on penetrated to all parts of China; Protestant missionaries have been working actively in China during the past half century, during which period vast sums have been expended and great activity shown in the attempt to convert the Chinese. Islam was introduced into China by immigrants from Central Asia, who in most parts became entirely merged in the Chinese, and now exists in all the provinces of the Republic. Practically speaking, there are not now, and never have been, any active Mahomedan missionaries at work amongst the Chinese. And yet today there are perhaps a million and a half nominal Chinese Catholic Christians, a third or a quarter as many Protestants, and at least ten times as many Moslems.

It is difficult at first sight to account for this state of things. The explanation lies perhaps partly in the fact that Islam has become, so to speak, naturalised amongst the Chinese and is firmly rooted as a native faith, without retaining, as far as its believers are concerned, any alien character; while Protestant Christianity remains in most cases a foreign institution supported by foreign energy, brains, and money. Many missionaries appear to the un-

PLATE XXXV

VIEW OF LABRANG MONASTERY

VIEW OF LABRANG MONASTERY
(The two views join to form a panorama)

PLATE XXXVI

CANTILEVER BRIDGE BETWEEN LABRANG AND HOCHOU

T'AO RIVER VALLEY BETWEEN HOCHOU AND LANCHOU FU

prejudiced observer to aim at Europeanising the Chinese in the course of converting them, which may be an excellent object, but is fatal to the establishment of a native Christian Church. Christianity, an oriental religion, is now being offered to the oriental Chinese in all its Western trappings. Foreign-style churches are erected in which the Chinese attend services after the foreign fashion, and are even taught to sing translations of the Western hymns, all of which seems to have little connection with the original teachings of Christ, and which often appears absurd and grotesque in the interior of China. Even the hierarchy of the Western Church is imposed upon the Chinese by the appointment of foreign bishops. It is submitted therefore that if Christianity is ever to take root in China as a native Church it must be divested of all its European trappings; and if it is to reach the educated classes it must be taught in a modern and liberal spirit, dropping the belief in miracles and a material hell, and compromising with ancestor worship and the ethics of Laocius and Confucius.

The vast sums of money expended by the European Churches on missionary work in China have been productive of an enormous amount of good in improving the material lot of the Chinese, but the religious results have been small in comparison to the efforts put forth. In one respect, however, large sums have been expended without producing any good results either material or spiritual. Every year millions of copies of translated Scriptures are distributed in China by the native colporteurs of the great Bible Societies, not more than ten or twenty per cent. of which are ever read by anyone. One often hears of statistics of the large numbers of copies disposed of, not given away, but sold; but it is not stated in explanation that the books are disposed of so cheaply that they are sometimes bought for the paper they contain and used in the manufacture of the soles of Chinese shoes (which, curiously enough, is also the use to which the Chinese are said to have put the sacred books of the lamas when campaigning amongst the monasteries of Eastern Tibet). Further, even where the Bibles are read, it is now widely recognized, even by many missionaries, that the wholesale distribution of obsolete tracts and translated Scriptures, in their less objectionable parts often but a meaningless jargon of transliterated Chinese characters, does more harm than good to the cause of Christianity. A translation of the Old Testament, distributed, in accordance with the declared policy of the Bible Societies, without notes or comment, cannot but compare unfavourably with the austerely pure classics of Confucius. In striking contrast to the work of the Bible Societies is that carried on by the Christian Literature Society in its dissemination of wholesome modern literature.

From Ho Chou to Lanchou Fu is a three days' journey called 210 li. The road runs in a north-westerly direction across the fertile valley to reach the Tahsia River, which is crossed by a well-built wooden bridge. From here it ascends steeply over hills of loess and red clay for a few hundred feet, and then runs along a ridge between two deep narrow valleys for 35 li to the village of Sonanpa. The divide between the T'ao and Tahsia rivers is crossed just before reaching Sonanpa, a village with inns perched up on the top of the ridge, where we passed the night.

On the following day's march the road continues along an undulating ridge, gradually descending, for four hours' march to the village of Tawant'ou, lying on the edge of the loess mountains overlooking the T'ao River valley, into which the road drops by a long and very steep descent to reach the township of T'angwanch'uan. This place is about half-way between Ho Chou and Lanchou Fu and is the largest centre passed on the way. The T'ao valley in the neighbourhood is irrigated and fertile, but the surrounding hills are bare of all vegetation, and the country is absolute desert where irrigation ceases. The geological formation of the hills, loess superimposed on red sandstone weathered into pinnacles and pillars of all kinds of shapes and designs, presents a most curious sight. In the valley the noonday heat of the midsummer sun reflected off the desert rocks was terrific. The T'ao River, here about 80 yards wide, deep and rapid, is crossed by a ferry, and the road continues north-east through desolate sandy hills to Manp'ing, a miserable village, the end of the stage and 80 li from Lanchou. This place is in the district of Shani, which is mostly desert.

From Manp'ing the road ascends through a desolate

rocky gorge and then by steep zigzags to reach the pass over the divide between the T'ao and Yellow Rivers, on the further side of which there is a complete change of scenery, green hills and fertile terraces taking the place of the desert mountain sides. From the pass the trail descends into a ravine, climbs over a mountain spur, and drops steeply to the village of Chiangchia Wan, whence it descends gradually for three hours' march through the loess to reach Lanchou and the valley of the Yellow River. Our tour of South Western Kansu had occupied us about five weeks, during which period we had covered some six to seven hundred miles.

CHAPTER XI

Through the desert hills to P'ingfan—The Wushao Ling—Kulang—How
to raise a mule—Liangchou—Opium suppression—Chenfan—Trails from
Mongolia to the Kokonor—Crossing a corner of the Alashan desert—
Yungch'ang—The Pien Tu K'ou passage—Êpo—Wool, deer horns, and
musk.

WE left Lanchou on the 17th of July bound for Chenfan,
an oasis in the Alashan desert lying ten to eleven days'
journey almost due north. For the first week, as far as
Liangchou Fu, we followed the Great West Road leading
to Turkestan, most of the way a good cart track with
accommodation and supplies every 40 to 50 li. From
Liangchou to Chenfan the road ran through a string of
little oases in the desert.

Leaving Lanchou by the iron bridge the road runs for
30 li westwards up the Yellow River valley, which here opens
out into a small cultivated plain, and then turns north up a
narrow gorge in the hills for ten li to reach Chuchia Yingtzu,
a small village in a desolate region of bare stony hills. From
here the track continues to ascend gradually through barren
hills of sandy loess, crosses a small pass, and descends to the
miserable hamlet of Yuchia Wan, the end of the first stage
of 70 li. The surrounding country is nearly desert and the
water brackish. From Yuchia Wan the track undulates
north-westwards through a maze of bare loess hills, treeless
and waterless, for 45 li to the village of Hsienshui Ho,
where, as the name implies, a brackish streamlet enables
some poor crops to be grown. In Kansu the Yellow River
is roughly speaking the boundary between China and the
wastes of Central Asia, all the country north-west of it being
desert where there is no irrigation. The road continues for
another two to three hours' march through these barren
hills until it suddenly emerges on to the fertile valley of

the P'ingfan River a few li south of Hung Ch'engtzu, a small walled town and the end of the second stage from Lanchou.

From Hung Ch'engtzu to the district city of P'ingfan is a pleasant march of 70 li up the fertile valley, past several villages, including the township of Nan Tatung about half-way. A mile before getting in the old Manchu garrison town of Chuang-lang T'ing is passed, imposing in appearance with its well-built walls, but nowadays an empty shell. The remnants of these old Manchu garrisons in Western Kansu are now, as elsewhere, in extreme poverty. But their existence at any rate gives the province the distinction of being, so far as I know, the only one of the eighteen provinces which contains a resident population of the five races, symbolised by the new five coloured national flag, which go to make up the Republic, Chinese, Manchus, Mongols, Tibetans, and Mahomedans. The Union of Races represented by this flag has hardly become a reality yet; and is perhaps not likely to materialise until the Chinese cease fighting the Tibetans and grant them autonomy as a self-governing dominion of the Chinese commonwealth on the lines of the relationship between Canada or Australia and the rest of the British Empire. P'ingfan is a prosperous little place, the centre of a rich irrigated valley, and is of some importance as the junction of roads to Lanchou, Hsining, Liangchou, and Ninghsia, the four largest towns of Western Kansu.

From P'ingfan the road continues up the valley with the ruins of the Great Wall on the right hand, the scenery becoming wilder and cultivation and habitations less as one proceeds. Thirty li out the mountains close in on the valley to form a gorge, and shortly afterwards the river is forded to reach the village and former posting stage of Wusheng Yi, 40 li from P'ingfan. Beyond this place the valley becomes flat and open and assumes a plateau-like character, with patches of cultivation here and there. Another 40 li brings one to the village and ruined fort of Ch'ak'ou Yi, the end of a stage of 80 li. General desolation and ruins are the features of this part of Kansu, intensified to us perhaps by the fact that we rode during the afternoon through a succession of bitterly cold hailstorms, the elevation being close on 9000 feet. The remains of the Great Wall, the ruins of farms, villages, and forts, the abandoned fields in the marshy valley, and the background of bare snow-sprinkled mountains, made up a wild and desolate landscape, the scene of uncounted contests between Chinese, Tartars, and Mahomedans in the past.

The trail continues up the valley, which is here a mile or two wide and slopes gently up to grassy downs on either side, for four to five hours' march to an old military post called Chench'iang Yi. Here the river is crossed by a ford, which must be difficult in rainy weather, and the road, leaving the P'ingfan valley, runs due north over easy grassy slopes for 15 li to gain the Wushao Ling (10,000 feet), the divide between the waters which flow east to join the Yellow River and those which flow north into the desert and fail to reach the sea. Immediately to the west some rocky peaks patched with snow rise to a height of 14,000 to 15,000 feet. From the pass the road descends, at first over grassy downs alive with marmots, and then by a steep stony track, to the ruined village of Anyuan P'u in the narrow valley of the Kulang River. The Wushao Ling will prove the principal engineering obstacle to the railway which is projected as an extension of the Lung Hai line along the main road towards Central Asia, and will presumably necessitate a considerable tunnel. Otherwise the construction of this extension will be easy compared to the section from Hsian to Lanchou. Fifteen li down the valley brings one to the village of Lungk'ou P'u. This is a long day's march called 90 li (which means 30 miles in Western Kansu) and the track beyond the pass is bad and rocky.

On the following day a short march of 45 li by a rough road down the valley brought us to the district city of Kulang, a small town three-parts in ruins situated at the point where the stream debouches from the mountains on to the plain. Here we were given a typical instance of Chinese administrative methods. One of our mules having fallen lame, we asked the magistrate to be good enough to procure us another animal, which he said could easily be done. We were accommodated in a small yamen and our mules in an inn, and that evening the head muleteer came round in a great state and said that one of our mules had been seized by the underlings from the magistrate's yamen. Explanations were of course immediately forthcoming and the misunderstanding cleared up. The magistrate had instructed his underlings that a mule must be found, and the latter had gone round to the inn as the most likely place to find a suitable animal, and had simply walked off with the best one they could lay hands on.

At Kulang one is 120 li, two short marches, from Liangchou. The road runs at first across a loess plain dotted with fortified farms past the village of Shuangt'a to the old posting station of Chingpien Yi, a short stage of 50 li. The villages and post stations on this side of the divide are even more dilapidated than those further east, and are mostly nothing but a heap of ruins round an inn or two. The people here seem to have given up living in villages, so prominent a feature of Chinese life in most provinces, and occupy the fortress farms with which the plains are dotted. From Chingpien Yi to Liangchou the road continues across the level plain which is in places almost entirely covered with loose stones, rendering the going very slow and tiring. On the left hand the view is bounded by the snow-capped Nan Shan; on the right the plain extends to the horizon. The twin pagodas of Liangchou form a prominent landmark denoting the approach to the city.

Liangchou Fu, now known as Wuwei Hsien, is about the most important city, commercially and politically, in Western Kansu. It lies in an irrigated plain dotted with fertile oases between the Nan Shan mountains and the desert of Alashan. This plain is traversed by numerous streams and irrigation channels flowing down from the snows of the mountains to lose themselves eventually in the sands of the desert, and owing to this never failing supply of water for irrigation purposes is a very fertile and productive region. The inhabitants of Liangchou and the surrounding plains are mostly Chinese; the whole region was devastated during the big rebellion, and was again laid waste by marauding bands of Mahomedans from the Hsining neighbourhood during the rebellion of 1895. The interior of the city is very poor-looking and dilapidated, like most Kansu towns, and the streets are almost entirely covered with the same loose stones found outside; riding being the only method of getting about, these stones are a great drawback to the place. There is a station of the China Inland Mission at Liangchou which can compete with those at Hsining and Ninghsia for being the most isolated post occupied by the mission; Ninghsia is probably the worst off in this respect; but in any of them years may go by without the resident missionary seeing a strange European face. The Catholics are strong in the neighbourhood, having a large establishment with a bishop at a village called Chenchia Chuang, 20 li to the west.

The Liangchou neighbourhood used to be famous for its poppies, the opium being considered the best native drug produced in China. The success of China's measures for the suppression of poppy cultivation has been one of the most striking events in her recent history. In 1907 the policy of total suppression within ten years was adopted amidst general scepticism on the part of most foreigners and many Chinese. It was generally felt that this policy would be but another instance of the maxim *Yu Ming Wu Shih* (Theory but not Practice), so deeply engrained in Chinese official life. The ten years have now elapsed, and though cultivation may not be completely extinct in wild mountain districts and amongst the semi-independent tribes of the west and south-west, yet one may travel for months through the plains and valleys of provinces such as Szechuan, Shensi, and Kansu, where most of the native opium consumed in North China used to be produced, and never see a single poppy plant. Conclusive evidence of the success of the suppressive measures is to be found in the fact that in the former poppy-growing areas of Shensi and Kansu, where opium could be bought locally ten years ago for 100 cash an ounce, the price has now risen to about 12,000 cash an ounce. Further the success which has been attained, has been accomplished in face of great obstacles, such as the revolution, after which there was a general recrudescence of cultivation, and the subsequent rebellions; in every case where there was a general collapse of local government and law and order the people immediately returned to their poppy cultivation. Yunnan and Shensi have probably been the worst offenders and the slowest to achieve comparatively complete suppression, owing in the first case to the tribes, and in the second to the brigands. The stimulus exercised by the Treaties with Great Britain of 1907 and 1911, under which the import of Indian opium was to cease if China could succeed in putting her own house in order with regard to cultivation, has of course had a great effect on the good results obtained. It now remains to be seen whether suppression can be maintained after the withdrawal of this foreign stimulus. In the eastern provinces where the upper and middle classes are more or less in contact with the West a strong native public opinion now exists against opium; the same cannot be said of the backward North West; and it is there that the authorities will have to watch for recrudescence of cultivation. As regards the suppression of smoking and consumption generally, the same success has by no means been attained, and in out of the way parts it appears to be indulged in much as formerly. In view of the increasing scarcity of the drug, however, and the rising price, this cannot really be the case, and if suppression of cultivation is strictly adhered to, the existing stocks will gradually be exhausted, and the rising generation will grow up without contracting the opium habit.

We rested at Liangchou for a day, being entertained by the officials, and then left for Chenfan, distant three marches. The first stage was 65 li to a group of farms called Chungchia Ta Men lying on the edge of the desert. For the first three hours the road, a good cart-track, lies through rich irrigated country, and for the rest of the way belts of sandy desert alternate with irrigated fields. The water, where it is not obtainable from irrigation channels, is very brackish. From Chungchia Ta Men the road continues north across a sandy plain between the desert on the right hand and cultivated lands on the left. Farms with wells are passed 20 and 40 li out. Hsiangchia Wan, the end of another stage of 65 li, is a thickly populated oasis on the edge of the desert, lying just east of a range of barren hills which form a prominent landmark from afar. The snow mountains behind Liangchou now fade out of sight. From here to Chenfan Hsien is a distance of 70 li. The trail still runs north over a sandy plain covered with scrub and rough grass with a river on the left hand, the latter formed by the junction of various streams and irrigation channels, and flowing north to water the Chenfan oasis and beyond to lose itself in the sands of the desert. Branches of this stream have to be forded at various points; though quite shallow, they contain dangerous quicksands and should be approached with care. Thirty-five li out cultivation and houses are reached at Kaochia Ta Men, the beginning of the large Chenfan oasis, and for the rest of the stage the road runs through rich irrigated lands with occasional excursions into sand dunes.

Chenfan Hsien is a prosperous little district city in a highly fertile oasis. Immediately round the town is a belt of rich cultivation, and patches of irrigated land occur in the desert for 200 li to the north. There are no villages in these oases, the people living entirely in walled farms. Wheat is the main crop raised, and the abundant water supply from the snow-fed streams for irrigation purposes, combined with an almost rainless climate, appears to assure good crops with machine-like regularity. Chenfan compares favourably with most towns in Kansu, the streets are clean and well kept, there is a noticeable absence of ruins, and the shops display a surprising variety of goods. At the time of our visit the district enjoyed the services of one of the best territorial officials we met throughout the North West, a young man who really appeared to have the interests of the people at heart, and to devote himself as far as lay in his power to improve their lot. He remarked that the post, though so isolated, was pleasant enough in the summer, but that in the winter the north winds from the Alashan desert were terrible, much worse than the severest winter sand-storms ever experienced at Peking. The inhabitants of the surrounding oases seem entirely cut off from the rest of China, and form little self-supporting communities. Chenfan itself, however, is, strange to say, in direct communication with Tientsin and the coast by means of a much frequented camel route from Kueihua Ch'eng to Liangchou across the Mongolian grass country and the Alashan desert. This road, which debouches from the desert at Chenfan, enables the Mahomedans of the Ho Chou and Hsining neighbourhood to communicate with the coast without passing through Chinese Kansu at all.

From Chenfan we had to proceed to Hsining, the frontier town on the high road to the Kokonor and Tibet. Enquiries showed that we had the choice of two roads, to the north or south of the snow mountains behind Liangchou respectively. As the latter would have meant retracing our steps to Kulang, we decided to follow the former, which entailed going due west until we had got behind the Liangchou mountains, and then dropping south to Hsining along the Kokonor border. There is a shorter trail south-west from Liangchou, passing apparently more or less directly over the snow-range, but we were told that it was very difficult, seldom used, and probably impassable for loaded mules. There are only a limited number of trails leading up from the plains of Mongolia through the Nan Shan to the Kokonor plateau, and the route we followed, though little known to foreigners, is probably one of the most important of these tracks. It reaches the plateau by means of a famous gorge known as the Pien Tu K'ou (meaning Passage across the Frontier), and the section of our route from Chenfan, in the Alashan desert, to Êpo, in the Kokonor, is probably a portion of an important trail connecting Urga with Lassa, placing these two capitals of Lamaism in communication without the necessity of passing through settled Chinese territory. Our first few days' march lay across a portion of the Alashan desert to regain the Great West Road at Yungch'ang, a very trying experience, since the season of the year was the end of July, when nobody travels in the desert if he can possibly avoid it.

The first stage on this road being a very long one of 100 li across the desert, the magistrate had kindly arranged for us to break it into two by sending on tents to some wells 30 li out. Leaving Chenfan the road runs south through the oasis for 15 li, crosses the main branch of the Chenfan River by a ford, and then turns west into the desert. Two hours' march further on we reached the wells of Sha Ching, where we found a luxurious camp established for us by the forethought of the magistrate. The water from the wells is evil-looking and very brackish, but we had arranged to bring sweet water with us. The contrast between these rich oases, such as Chenfan, and the absolutely lifeless desert, lying side by side so that one passes in one stride from the one to the other, is most striking. The great wealth of the irrigated land is evidenced by the fact that the district of Chenfan, though containing so much desert, offers a highly lucrative post to its magistrate; that is to say the land-tax receipts, consisting of grain, are large; the grain collected in this fashion by the magistrate is remitted by him to the provincial treasury in silver at an old-established rate much below the market price, permitting a considerable profit to be made on the transaction. The productiveness of the land is of course entirely dependent on the irrigation streams from the snows of the Nan Shan, the magistrate informing us that he had been nine months at his post and only seen rain fall on two occasions.

The following day's march of 70 li to the oasis of Shehsia Kou would have been easy enough had we not lost our way. We started at 3 a.m. in order to try and reach the wells of T'ou Ching, 40 li out, before the sun got too hot. The trail led across a waste of sand hills and soon ceased to exist. The desert is devoid of all vegetation and lifeless except for antelope, which were constantly in view; what they find to eat I cannot imagine. After we had been marching for some hours the soldier from Chenfan who was acting as guide announced that he had lost the way. Looking for the wells where we were to have our midday halt was like searching for a needle in a haystack, and the position was unpleasant enough. Altogether we wandered round, steering more or less west, for some seven or eight hours, suffering greatly from thirst, with the sand often over the ponies fetlocks. Our only landmark was an ancient ruined tower, the remains of some old fortification in this region, perhaps a part of the Great Wall. At last one of the soldiers sent out to reconnoitre from a rise descried the tents pitched at the wells in pretty well the opposite direction to that in which we were then trekking, and an hour later men and animals were satisfying their thirst. Another three hours' march across the desert brought us to the oasis of Shehsia Kou, where we were comfortably lodged in the interior of one of the fortified farms so common in this region.

The next stage is another desert march of 80 li to the village of Ningyuan P'u, but there is an oasis, Tung Wan, half-way, the going is better, and we took care not to lose our way. Ningyuan P'u is a walled village at the mouth of an irrigated gorge where the mountains meet the desert plain. From here to Yungch'ang is a distance of 75 li. The trail follows up the irrigated valley for 35 li to the hamlet of Tsungchia Chai, where it turns up a barren stony ravine, crosses a low pass, and descends across an arid sloping

CAMP IN THE ALASHAN DESERT, NEAR CHENFAN

CHINESE SETTLER'S CATTLE-FARM ON THE GRASS-LANDS

PLATE XXXVIII

LOWER END OF PIEN TU K'OU GORGE, LEADING TO THE KOKONOR

TRAVELLING UP THE PIEN TU K'OU GORGE

plain to Yungch'ang Hsien, a small district city on the mainroad.

Leaving Yungch'ang the trail runs west up a cultivated valley for 25 li to the ruined village of Shuimo Kuan. Here the stream is forded, and the trail, leaving the high road to Kanchou and Suchou on the right hand, continues up the valley due west, ascending very gradually, for 50 li to Kaoku Ch'eng, an old walled military post surrounded by a ruined village, where we passed the night in the dilapidated yamen of the *Yu Chi*, or Major in the old army of the Green Standard, who still survived in this remote corner of the Republic, though about eight years out of date. Kaoku Ch'eng lies in a broad shallow valley sloping up to the mountains on either side, with very little cultivation. Ruined farms and abandoned fields are numerous, and signs of former prosperity and present depopulation are not wanting. A huge snow mountain is visible lying ten to twenty miles away to the south, apparently part of the snow range behind Liangchou.

Beyond Kaoku Ch'eng the flat valley merges imperceptibly into a rolling grassy plain, bounded north and south by mountains, and uninhabited save for flocks of sheep and occasional antelope. The road undulates due west across this plain, running more or less parallel to the main range of the Nan Shan, a high rocky barrier bounding the Kokonor plateau. For the last ten li there is a descent through cultivated fields to Tama Ying, another old walled military post mostly in ruins, lying on the head-waters of a stream flowing N.W. towards Shantan Hsien. There are several farms of settlers in the neighbourhood, and the barley looked well, though still green in early August (elevation between 8000 and 9000 feet). On this day's march we noticed the ruins of some of the old beacon towers common to the high roads of Kansu, and these ruins, with those of the old military posts, show that this was once an important military road. At Tama Ying we were again quartered in the yamen of the *Yu Chi*, the latter an aged veteran of the Mahomedan campaigns, who was spending the evening of his no doubt active and adventurous life in this remote spot, with only the vaguest ideas of the momentous changes which had come to pass with the disappearance of the Manchu dynasty.

From Tama Ying the trail runs south-west across rolling grassy downs, on which cattle and sheep are pastured, gradually approaching the main range of the Nan Shan on the left front. We saw large numbers of antelope on this march and in places the pasturage was extraordinarily luxuriant and the grass up to the ponies' knees. The stage is a short one of only some 50 li and for the last hour the trail runs through fields of barley to reach Maying Tung, another of the old walled forts with which this region is dotted, surrounded by farms and patches of cultivation. It lies close under the Nan Shan, whose rocky peaks rise above the snow-line, and a few li from the mouth of the gorge leading up to the Kokonor plateau. This is the well-known passage through the Nan Shan called the Pien Tu K'ou, and is a remarkable cleft in the huge wall of rock presented by the main range, from which there issues a torrent flowing north towards Kanchou.

From Maying Tung to Êpo on the Kokonor plateau is a long march, called 100 li, which took us over twelve hours. The trail runs across the plain for an hour or two to reach the foot of the mountains and then enters the Pien Tu K'ou, a narrow gorge hemmed in by precipitous mountains. The trail up the gorge is very bad, and is made more difficult by its constantly crossing and recrossing the torrent, which descends in a succession of cascades and, in the summer, is only just fordable. We were told that camels negotiate this road in the winter, when it is probably much easier. Every time we forded the stream I expected our mules to come to grief, the donkeys, which accompanied us in the capacity of grain carriers for the mules, being in places nearly sub-merged. At length the inevitable happened, and one of the mule litters turned turtle in mid-stream owing to the mules being swept off their feet by the current; all the contents were washed down stream and the occupant, one of the servants, nearly drowned. This incident, and the subsequent collection of as much flotsam and jetsam as we could recover down stream, delayed us for an hour or so. The gorge is uninhabited except for two likin huts which seem to have gone out of business. After some five hours' march the going improves and the precipitous mountains give way to grassy slopes dotted with herds of yak and flocks of sheep and the black rectangular tents of nomad Tibetans, the usual hinterland of *Ts'ao Ti* (Grass Lands), which everywhere in the north and west lie behind the border ranges of China. Apart from the nomads and their ponies, yak, and cattle, the only sign of life were the huge vultures, which were extraordinarily abundant. The final ascent to the pass is by easy gradients, and a similar descent of about 10 li brings one to Êpo, a dot of a place lying in a sea of grass.

Êpo (this is the regular romanisation of the Chinese characters, pronounced Ôbaw) is a small walled village and former fort situated in a shallow valley sloping from east to west, surrounded by grassy downs and backed by rocky snow capped mountains. The elevation is probably between 11,000 and 12,000 feet, and there is no cultivation, the necessary grain being brought up from below. The entire community, composed of a few Mahomedan Chinese, seemed to be engaged in the collection of wool, with occasional purchases of musk and deer horns. The latter (wapiti antlers) when old are quite cheap and are collected and sent down to China for the manufacture of glue; when n velvet they are extremely valuable and are ground up to form the well-known Chinese medicine for revivifying the old. This medicine is said to be very powerful, and I was informed by a member of our party, who here purchased a pair for a friend, that care must be exercised in taking a dose to see that the powder comes equally from both antlers, otherwise there is a grave danger that the patient may be revivified on one side only! Musk may also be profitably purchased at Êpo, and for some days afterwards our caravan was redolent with it. Wherever one may pack a pod of musk it is guaranteed to make its presence widely known. The advantage of buying musk at a place like Êpo, apart from its cheapness, is that one is pretty certain to get the genuine article, adulteration being widely practised in the trade in China.

Êpo appears to lie actually on the Kansu-Kokonor border (though boundaries are vague in those parts), and its position is of some strategic importance as commanding one of the few routes from Kansu and Mongolia up to the Kokonor, north of Hsining. We were met here by some Mahomedan braves sent up from the Hsining and Tatung neighbourhood to escort us down to those parts, for we had now again entered the Mahomedan sphere. Life in Êpo must be a trifle monotonous for the wool buyers. It was about the most distant and isolated spot we reached on all our travels, lying some forty to fifty days' journey from the coast or the nearest railway.

CHAPTER XII

FROM ÊPO SOUTH ACROSS THE KOKONOR GRASS COUNTRY TO HSINING, AND THENCE BACK TO LANCHOU FU

Grass lands and snow mountains—Gold washing—Kokonor Mongols—Yungan—Pei Tatung—Passage of Tatung River and Tapan Shan—Tatung or Maopeisheng—Chinese place-names in foreign guise—Hsinch'eng and a loop of the Great Wall—Hsining—Chinese control over the Kokonor territory—Kansu wool trade—Kansu ponies—Hsining to Lanchou Fu—Aborigines—Defile of Laoya—Sandstone and loess—Copper—Lanchou water melons.

FROM Êpo the trail runs south for three very long stages, each one probably well over 30 miles in length, across the grass country on the Kokonor border. Along this border stretches an old line of walled military posts, Êpo, Yungan, and Pei Tatung, which make up the stages, and the grass lands being otherwise uninhabited except by a few nomads, it is necessary for the traveller unprovided with tents to cover each of these long marches in the day.

Leaving Êpo the track runs south-east up the flat grassy valley, which is dotted with the black tents of Tibetan nomads and countless flocks of sheep. After some hours' march the stream is left on the right hand and the path rises gradually to an easy pass 40 li from Êpo. The view from the summit (between 12,000 and 13,000 feet) is the same on both sides, treeless grassy downs and rocky mountains streaked with snow. Immediately to the south-east rises a gigantic snow mountain, being apparently another view of the snow range which we saw south of Kaoku Ch'eng, and which seems to lie immediately behind Liangchou. There appeared to be thousands of feet of snow on this mountain in early August, and its height must be some 18,000 feet or more. This pass, like the Wushao Ling, is the watershed between the Yellow River and the Central Asian basins, and we also gathered from the soldiers who accompanied us that in crossing it we passed again from the Kokonor territory into Kansu.

From the pass the track drops steeply into a rough stony ravine, the stream in which is followed in a south-easterly direction for the remaining 70 li to Yungan Ch'eng. For the first half of the way the track is very bad, lying down the bed of a stream which is apt to rise in wet weather and render the road impassable; further on the going improves, the gorge opening out on to a flat grassy valley, and the last hour's march is over prairie, spoilt for riding, however, by the countless holes of a small rat-like rodent; in places the ground is alive with these little animals, dodging in and out of their holes like miniature marmots. The bed of the stream flowing down from the pass is apparently rich in gold, and Mahomedan gold washers were at work at various points when we passed. They live in tiny tents and appear to pass a very hard life for small returns. The industry is under the patronage of the leading Mahomedan Generals. We followed the washing in several spots and always saw a few grains of gold dust produced; nuggets are, we were told, occasionally found. We had descended this stream almost from its source, so that in this case the gold-bearing rocks from which the gold has been washed cannot be far off. Very large profits can be made in ordinary times by buying this gold on the Kokonor and selling it in Shanghai.

Just before reaching Yungan we passed some Mongol tents, identical in appearance with the felt yurts to be seen in the grass country north of Kalgan, and it seemed strange to come across these people here, whom one associates with summer trips to the north of Peking. The Kokonor territory is the meeting-point of the Tibetan and Mongol races, and here, as elsewhere, the black rectangular tents of the former may be seen almost side by side with the round grey tents of the latter. It appears that the Mongols, who originally occupied the country far to the south, are gradually retreating northwards before the encroachments of the more virile Tibetans. Unlike the Tibetans, who are in these parts all robbers by nature, the Mongols are peaceful and inoffensive herdsmen, who give the Chinese authorities no trouble. They are organized into Banners under their own Princes,

nominally responsible to the Chinese officials at Hsining.
Mongol tribes are found living in the bend of the Yellow
River, near the Golok country, and even as far south as
the country between Jyekundo and Nagchuka towards
Lassa, but appear to have become completely Tibetanised,
and to retain only the tradition of their origin.

Yungan is a replica of Êpo, only poorer, an old walled
post with the interior almost entirely in ruins. It lies not
far from the Tatung River, surrounded by grassy downs
and overlooked by rocky snow-capped ranges. One is here
on the reverse side of the outer barrier range of the Nan
Shan, the snows of which provide the water for the streams
which fertilize the Liangchou oases. This portion of the
Kokonor border is the meeting-point of the four widely-
spread races of High Asia, Chinese, Mahomedans, Tibetans,
and Mongols.

From Yungan to Pei Tatung is another long march of
over 100 li. The trail runs east and then south-east across
undulating grass prairies dotted with herds of yak for 45 li
to a solitary inn or ranch known as Paishui Ho, whence
it continues across a plain, gradually approaching the
Tatung River, to reach Pei Tatung. The going is excellent
across grass all the way. Pei Tatung, lying on the left bank
of the Tatung River, is another walled village mostly in
ruins. Barley is grown in the neighbourhood, the first
cultivation met with since entering the Pien Tu K'ou from
Maying Tung. The valley of the Tatung River in this neighbourhood consists of a rich grass prairie bounded on either
side by rocky snow-capped ranges; to the south the mountains
approach close to the river; to the north they rise on the
other side of the plain. Between Kueitê on the Yellow
River and Kanchou in Western Kansu the Nan Shan
consist of three huge parallel ranges, dividing off the valleys
of the Tatung, Hsining, and Yellow rivers. We were now
between the two highest and most northern of these ranges.

The following day's march occupied us from dawn till
eight o'clock at night, the distance being called 100 li but
entailing the passage of the Tatung River and of a high
pass known as the Tapan Shan. The river, some eighty
yards wide (in August), deep, and very rapid, has to be
crossed immediately on leaving Pei Tatung. Men and loads

are ferried across on a small raft of inflated skins (called
p'ifatzu), but the animals have to swim. Owing to the
rapidity of the current and the frail nature of the skin-raft
(a light wooden platform resting on nine blown-out yak
hides) the passage is rather exciting. Inducing the animals
to swim across was a long and tedious business, and not
without danger for them, but all our mules and ponies were
eventually got across with no worse damage than one pony
lamed. The water was icy, and the wretched animals were
shivering with cold when they emerged, notwithstanding
the season of the year, which was mid-August. Leaving the
river the path enters a narrow gorge in the mountains and
almost immediately commences to rise steeply. From the
river to the top of the pass (between 13,000 and 14,000 feet)
is a hard climb of four hours or so by a bad rocky trail. The
summit is a narrow ridge of bare rock composed of bright
green and red slabs of shale. We missed the view as we
reached the pass in a bitterly cold snowstorm, through
which I caught a glimpse near the top of some animals
which looked like wild sheep. This range is known locally
as the Tapan Shan, and is a most formidable barrier. It
is noted amongst the Chinese for its noxious vapours, which
are supposed to rise from the ground on the higher slopes,
and most of our party crossed it with scarves wound round
their faces; it is a waste of time trying to explain even to
educated Chinese that the air is not noxious, but only
rarified; they have not the least objection to your believing
in the rarified air theory, but intimate that they know better.
My experience of high passes on the borders of Kansu
and Szechuan is that the effects of rarified air are much
worse on the razor-backed passes, like the Tapan Shan,
than on even higher divides which are approached by easy
slopes.

The ascent of the Tapan Shan is steep enough, but the
descent on the other side is much worse, and the trail
very rough and rocky. Eventually a gorge is reached,
which is followed for three hours' march to a solitary
Mahomedan inn called Tuchia T'ai. By the time we reached
this spot, although the snow had turned into rain as we
descended, and then ceased altogether, everyone was pretty
well tired out; but the accommodation was limited, and the

PLATE XXXIX

GRASS PRAIRIE (11,000 FEET) NEAR YUNGAN

MONGOL TENT

PLATE XL

TIBETAN NOMADS ON THE KOKONOR BORDER

TIBETAN PRAYER FLAGS

canny Mahomedan innkeeper, seeing such a large party of officials and soldiers (everywhere unwelcome guests owing to their custom of helping themselves to what they want and not always paying for it), assured us it was only 30 or 40 li to Tatung Hsien by a good road; so we took the road again after a rest, and had another weary six hours' march before getting in. The road lies down a narrow picturesque valley, in which trees, farms, and cultivation make their appearance again, and finally debouches on to a broad and fertile valley, closely cultivated and thickly populated, which is crossed to reach Tatung Hsien. I have but the vaguest idea of the latter part of this long march, which was finished by the light of lanterns in the dark, beyond remembering that we forded a stream running in various branches just before getting in, and narrowly missed taking an evening bath on more than one occasion.

Tatung Hsien is a prosperous city, the centre of a fertile corn-growing valley populated largely by Mahomedans. The elevation is about 8000 feet and the wheat was ripening for harvest during the middle of August. It reminded us somewhat of Ho Chou. Being comfortably quartered here in an old military yamen, we enjoyed a welcome day's rest. Tatung Hsien is also known locally by its old name of Maopeisheng, and usually appears on foreign maps under that name in various guises. If a traveller in China, unacquainted with Chinese characters and their usual romanisation, writes down the names of places as they sound to his ear, the results are often unrecognizable; further confusion is entailed by the varying forms of romanisation in use in different European languages. There are several townships called Tatung in Western Kansu; they are sometimes distinguished by being referred to as Tatung Hsien, Nan Tatung, Pei Tatung, and Hsi Tatung, but confusion often results.

From Tatung to Hsining is a distance of 110 li by a good cart track down a fertile and well-cultivated valley past numerous farms and villages. The march may be divided into two by halting at the walled township of Hsin Ch'eng, 40 li out, where the valley narrows to a defile and is barred by an old wall with a gate and the inevitable likin barrier. This is considered by some to be a branch of the Great

Wall; if this is so, the old gate and wall at T'ungmen Kuan, between Labrang and Ho Chou, is probably a portion of the same loop, which must have been constructed to protect the Hsining region against the incursions of Tibetans or Mongols from the Kokonor, and the course and history of which it would be interesting to trace. The road eventually debouches on to the city of Hsining, lying in a small cultivated plain of loess formed by the junction of three valleys, the Pei Ch'uan from Tatung Hsien, the Hsi Ch'uan from Tanko T'ing, and the Nan Ch'uan from T'a-erh Ssu (Kumbum), the combined streams going to make up the Hsining River.

Hsining is one of the chief cities of Kansu, being the centre of a region of fertile corn-growing valleys, producing wheat, barley, and particularly beans. Its commercial importance arises from its position near the Kokonor border, and together with Tanko T'ing, a day's journey further west, it commands the bulk of the valuable Kokonor trade in skins, furs, deer horns, musk, gold, and particularly wool. A state of passive hostility has reigned between China and Tibet since the collapse of Chinese power in Lassa consequent on the revolution, and the Szechuan-Tibetan trade through Tachienlu has suffered greatly thereby; the Hsining and Tanko trade, on the other hand, has continued uninterruptedly throughout these troubles, and has perhaps even increased. As elsewhere on this border this trade is largely in the hands of the Mahomedans. Before the Mahomedan rebellion of 1860–70 the Hsining-Kokonor road to Lassa was the most frequented route between China and Tibet, but was then replaced by the Szechuan road through Tachienlu; now it is coming into its own again. The interior of the city is fairly prosperous in appearance as far as Kansu towns go, but by no means indicative of the commercial and political importance of the place. The east suburb, the former Mahomedan quarter, is still completely in ruins, a relic of the last Mahomedan rebellion in 1895, when the city successfully withstood a siege by the rebels. The walls are particularly formidable and well built.

Hsining, as well as being the seat of a Taoyin and a Mahomedan General, has always been the residence of the high Chinese official controlling the immense territory of the Kokonor (in Chinese Ch'ing Hai, meaning, like the Mongol name, "Azure Lake"), who used to be known by the Tibetan or Mongol term of "Amban," but who at the time of our visit was styled in the republican manner *Ch'ing Hai Pan Shih Chang Kuan* ("Chief Authority in charge of the Affairs of the Kokonor Territory"). Soon afterwards the post and its occupant, an old Manchu, were abolished by Yüan Shih-k'ai's Government, and the control of the Kokonor territory handed over to the Mahomedan General of Hsining. This control is of the usual vague and shadowy nature, such as has been exercised for so long by China over her outlying dependencies. The Mongol inhabitants are ruled by their own princes under China's overlordship; the Tibetans wander pretty well at will over the territory, robbing one another, the Mongols, and the Chinese, and generally pay but little respect to their nominal Chinese masters. It is possible that the Mahomedans will now take measures to bring them more under control[1].

We remained some days at Hsining, but unfortunately had no leisure to visit either the Kokonor Lake or the famous monastery of T'a-erh Ssu. In the intervals of official business we were hospitably entertained by the Mahomedan General, the Manchu Amban, the Taoyin, and other officials. The former, like most of the Mahomedan leaders we met, was a bluff, hearty soldier and a delightful companion; he had served under T'ung Fu-hsiang at Peking in 1900.

Tanko and Hsining are the headquarters of the great Kokonor wool trade, which has been going on for twenty years or more and has now reached very large dimensions. This wool is produced on the grass lands of the Kokonor border, and is carried by raft and boat down the Yellow River and by camel caravan across the desert to Tientsin, whence it is exported to America. The trade is largely in the hands of the foreign export firms in Tientsin who, through their compradores, maintain buying agencies at various collecting centres such as Hsining, Tanko, Kueitê, Hochow, Hsünhua, Tatung, Yungan, and Êpo on the

---

[1] Such measures have since been taken, with the result that the Tibetans, and more especially the lamas, have on several occasions risen in arms against the Mahomedans, and the peace of the Kokonor border has been seriously disturbed.

Kokonor border. The wool is usually bought by Mahomedan middlemen, called *Hsiehchia*, and passed on by them to the Chinese agents. A similar, but smaller trade, is carried on at collecting centres such as Chungwei, Ninghsia, Shihtsuitzu, Wufang Ssu, and Huamach'ih on the borders of Mongolia in the north of the province, but this Mongolian wool is inferior in quality to the Kokonor produce.

The immense journey made by this wool from the Kokonor to Tientsin is only rendered commercially possible by the Treaty right exercised by foreigners of bringing produce down to the coast from the interior under transit pass, which exempts the goods from taxation by the likin barriers *en route*, a fixed transit duty being paid to the Customs at the coast. This arrangement is all right when the provinces are knit together under a strong central government and when the finances of the country are national rather than provincial; under a loose federal system of semi-independent provinces, however, into which China appears at times to be drifting, the authorities of a distant interior province like Kansu can scarcely be expected to look with favour on an arrangement by which the most valuable trade in the province is in theory immune from all local taxation.

We purchased ponies at various places during our long journeys as we required them; one of the best I secured was acquired at Hsining. These Kansu ponies are bred on the grass-country of the Kokonor, and the two chief collecting centres for horse flesh are Hsining and T'aochou, especially the latter. They are of an entirely different breed to the East Mongolian pony so well known in the Treaty ports. The Kansu pony is much finer in appearance though not so strongly built or as good a weight carrier at fast paces as the Kalgan pony; and being usually handled at an earlier age he is generally more civilized. For the purposes for which they are required, that is to say long road journeys at four miles an hour or so, the Kansu ponies would be difficult to beat anywhere, doing twenty to thirty miles a day for weeks or months on end, with the roughest of stabling, and on a diet of chopped straw, bran, and peas. A *Pei K'ou Ma* (pony from the Northern Passes, i.e. from Kalgan) is considered of little account in Kansu, and similarly on the grass lands north of Peking a *Hsi K'ou Ma* (pony from the Western Passes, i.e. Kansu) is a drug in the market; and both are useless on the stone paved paths south of the Ch'inling Shan, where the diminutive stallions of Szechuan, Yunnan, and Kueichou alone are employed. Small horses from Turkestan are also often seen in Kansu, but they are not as satisfactory to use as the native ponies. A *sine qua non* of all travelling ponies is that they should be able to *tsou*, which means the smooth amble or pace of four to five miles an hour always used by the travelling horseman in Eastern Asia; a pony that cannot *tsou* is practically worthless as a mount in Chinese eyes, and the reason will be apparent to anyone who has tried to do a long journey on a pony which has no pace between a slow walk and a slow trot.

From Hsining to Lanchou there are two roads, a cart track *via* P'ingfan in eight stages, and a mule road down the Hsining River in six stages; we followed the latter. The first day's march is one of 75 li down the valley, which is most of the way a mile or so wide and bounded by bare dreary hills of loess and red sandstone patched with a white alkaline efflorescence, to the village of Changch'i Chai. Twenty-five li out at the hamlet of Hsiaohsia K'ou the hills close in to form a short defile, and the road crosses the river by a good bridge. Much of the valley is an arid waste like the hills, as the river runs part of the way in a trough at a lower level, thus rendering irrigation impossible. The next stage is one of 80 li to the village of Kao Miaotzu. The trail runs down the valley, fertile where irrigation can be practised; it passes through a rocky defile 15 li out and reaches the small district city of Nienpo 50 li out. Occasional glimpses are caught of the high range to the south separating the Hsining River from the Yellow River. There is a curious mixture of races in this neighbourhood, including some people locally called *T'u Jen*, who were described to us as "tame" aborigines, and some Mahomedans who are said to speak a Mongolian dialect. There is plenty of subject matter for the ethnologist's study in Western Kansu, as in Western Szechuan and Yunnan.

From Kao Miaotzu the road continues down the cultivated valley for 20 li to the village of Laoya. Here the valley narrows to a rocky gorge, and the cart track branches off towards P'ingfan. The mule trail through this defile, which is some 40 li in length, is a nightmare of a path, especially in wet weather, being very rough and narrow, ledged in the cliff side above the roaring waters of the Hsining River; two-thirds of the way through there is an opening and an inn, Yangchia Tientzu, where we had a welcome rest. From the eastern end of this gorge to Hsiang-t'ang, the end of the stage, is a distance of ten li. The peculiarity of the valley in this neighbourhood is that the cultivated fields are entirely covered with large stones which are placed there on purpose, in order, we were told, to preserve the moisture in the ground. These stone-covered fields produce most excellent melons of various kinds, and the sight of the huge juicy fruit apparently growing out of bare stones is a remarkable one.

Just below Hsiangt'ang the Tatung River is crossed by a good wooden bridge at the point where it debouches from a defile in the mountains on to the valley of the Hsining River; it is here less than twenty yards wide, but very deep and rapid, and flows between almost perpendicular cliffs of rock; though it contains much the greater volume of water, it joins the Hsining River in the form of a tributary, issuing from a cleft in the mountains on to the open valley of the latter. From here the trail continues down the arid valley, being rough and stony most of the way, especially where it climbs in and out of side nullahs or ascends the face of the cliff. Fifty li out a ruined wall and fort are passed, barring the valley at a narrow point, and just before reaching the village of Hotsuitzu, the end of a stage of 75 li, the river washes the left-hand side of the valley, and the weary traveller is forced to follow a narrow footpath high up the face of the sandstone cliff; here a block of sandstone, becoming detached from higher up on the cliff and hurling itself into the torrent below, only missed by a few feet bringing the career of the principal member of the expedition to an abrupt termination. The valley round the village of Hotsuitzu is desolate in the extreme, bare red sandstone with a layer of yellow loess superimposed like icing on a cake. It is difficult to persuade oneself that this loess was not laid down by water. One of the arguments in favour of the aerial origin of the loess is the absence in it of fossil shells of water animals; but so far as I know such fossils are equally absent in re-deposited loess obviously laid down by water. If the great rivers of South America have deposited the soils of the Argentine pampas, there seems little reason to doubt that the Yellow River has done the same for North China. The desert mountains round the lower end of the Hsining River valley are rich in copper, and before the Revolution a mine was being worked in the neighbourhood with the assistance of a foreign engineer and foreign machinery; it appears to have suffered the fate common to all Chinese official enterprises of this nature, but its failure was not, so far as I am aware, due to any deficiency in the quality or quantity of the ore.

From Hotsuitzu the road continues down the valley which debouches on to the Yellow River 55 li further on. The latter can be crossed by a ferry here, but the path usually followed ascends through a desolate defile past a number of salt pans to a loess plateau, whence it descends to a ferry. The Yellow River is here some 200 yards wide and is crossed by means of a large ferry-boat taking animals. A further hour's march down the Yellow River valley through irrigated fields brings one to the township of Hsin Ch'eng, the end of a stage of 75 li.

From Hsin Ch'eng to Lanchou Fu is a march of 70 li by a good road down the valley through fertile irrigated fields backed by desert hills. This stage can be accomplished rapidly and easily by taking passage on one of the small skin rafts, numbers of which descend the river in the month of August laden with water melons for the Lanchou market. These rafts, composed of a light framework resting on a few inflated skins, are usually small enough and light enough to be carried back up stream on the shoulders of their owners. We were fortunate in striking the valleys above Lanchou during the height of the melon season. The dry heat in these arid valleys at that time of the year was at times truly terrific, and the melons, of which we consumed large quantities on the road, were delicious. The best melons in China are grown in this neighbourhood. We found four varieties; the *tsui kua* and the *hsiang kua*, small and very fragrant sweet melons; the *hsi kua*, the ordinary water melon, here grown to perfection, not the insipid watery pulp it is in many provinces, but a huge mass of juicy fruit of the most delicate flavour; and the *ta kua*, a tasteless variety fed to sheep and goats, and grown for its seeds. We were told that there is only one other melon which can compete with those of Lanchou for juiciness and delicacy of flavour, and that is the *Hami kua*, from Hami in Turkestan.

Our round tour of North-Western Kansu, *via* Liangchou, Chenfan, Êpo, and Hsining, a distance of about 700 miles, had occupied a little more than a month.

CHAPTER XIII

FROM LANCHOU FU DOWN THE YELLOW RIVER TO NINGHSIA AND PAOT'OU, AND THENCE OVERLAND TO KUEIHUA CH'ENG AND RAILHEAD

Yellow River rafts—Currency in the North West—Through the desert hills to Powan—Kansu mules—Sandstone caves on the Yellow River—Chingyuan—Gorges and rapids—Goral—Wufang Ssu—Chungwei—Rafts abandoned for boats—Kuangwu gorge—Irrigation works—Chinch'i and Mahomedan rebellion—Steam and motor navigation on the Yellow River—Ninghsia—Yuan Shih-k'ai's attempt to become Emperor—Wool boats for journey to Paot'ou—Shihchu Shan (Shihtsuitzu)—The Ordos—Mongol brigands—Liquorice root—Paot'ou—Tibetan lamaism in Mongolia—Kueihua Ch'eng—Feng Chen and railhead.

AFTER returning to Lanchou from Hsining we had finished our work in Kansu and were free to choose the easiest way back to the coast. Needless to say after so many months on the road we decided to return by the Yellow River. For some distance below Lanchou the river breaks its way through a series of mountain ranges, flowing in alternate gorges and rapids, and Chinese travellers taking this route usually go overland to Chungwei, about eight days' march, and take boat from there. The prospect of another long desert journey was not attractive, however, and at first we decided to start on the river from Lanchou itself and chance the rapids; but were eventually persuaded to go overland for three days' march to a village called Powan, thus avoiding the most dangerous rapids which occur immediately below Lanchou. From all I heard on the subject I gather that these rapids really are very dangerous; certainly the ones between Powan and Chungwei are quite exciting enough.

The safest way of descending the rapids of the upper Yellow River is by large rafts, which stand a great deal of knocking about amongst the rocks and rapids without breaking up, and the officials had very kindly arranged for four of these rafts to be placed at our disposal, two for the ponies and two for ourselves. These rafts were thirty to forty feet in length by ten to fifteen in breadth, with the lumber piled up in the centre to form a platform a foot or so above the water, on which we pitched our tents; I have seldom struck a pleasanter method of travel in China, the only objection being the floor of pine logs, which meant that if one dropped any small article it was irrecoverable except by taking the raft to pieces. We subsequently learned that we had been lucky in securing particularly fine rafts, as they consisted of a flotilla of telegraph poles *en route* from the Kokonor forests above Hsining to Ninghsia for the construction of a new telegraph line from that place across the Ordos desert to Paot'ou.

We were delayed a few days in Lanchou while our rafts were being got ready and various other preparations being made. It is as well to put a few days' provisions on board to last till one gets to Chungwei; all kinds of presents were thrust upon us in the way of supplies by our hospitable hosts, the Governor and his staff, including a skin bag of the famous dried apricots which are thus exported from Central Tibet—or perhaps they even come from India. A new supply of silver had also to be secured, for at the time we were in Kansu the old-fashioned lumps of silver and strings of cash were still the only currency available; two years later travelling in Shensi and Szechuan we were able to use silver dollars and copper cents even in the most out of the way parts, a great convenience; the buying up of the cash for the export of the copper they contain, which is now going on so extensively throughout China, may be illegal, but it is hardly to be regretted by the tourist in the interior, if it means the gradual disappearance of this dirty and cumbersome form of currency.

We finally left Lanchou on August 26 on our overland march to Powan, distant three marches of 65, 80, and 70 li respectively. The road runs down the left bank of the Yellow River for about 15 li, and then, turning north up a gully, winds through a maze of low waterless hills of loess for the rest of the way to the walled village of Ch'ang Ch'uantzu in the valley of a brackish rivulet, the end of the first stage. The second day's march is through similar desert hills to the hamlet of Hsikou. In places the small shallow valleys are cultivated and produce millet and inferior melons, but

PLATE XLI

OUR RAFTS ON THE UPPER YELLOW RIVER

OUR RAFTS ON THE UPPER YELLOW RIVER

PLATE XLII

SANDSTONE CLIFFS OF UPPER YELLOW RIVER

SANDSTONE CLIFFS OF UPPER YELLOW RIVER

the landscape is dreary in the extreme, the population scanty and miserably poor, supplies non-existent, and the water, where it is found, brackish. The third day's march is through similar country until, 50 li from Hsikou, the trail debouches from these barren hills on to a small irrigated plain alongside the Yellow River, which here issues from a cleft in the mountains; at the further end of the plain lies the long straggling village of Powan. To the north and south are bare desolate mountains.

At Powan we abandoned our train of Kansu pack-mules. These particular mules, each carrying between two and three hundred pounds, had accompanied us for three to four months, during which period they had covered over 2000 miles without a hitch, with never a sore back, and never one sick or lame. The Kansu mule is perhaps the finest in the world; his only drawback is that he requires a lot of grain and does not do well in the grass country. The muleteers, Kansu men, walked the entire distance and never gave us any trouble whatsoever; both they and their animals seemed capable of going on for ever as long as they both got plenty to eat. The Kansu pack-mules are all entires, and their strength and endurance are simply astounding; the mares are worked in carts.

We found our rafts waiting for us, having accomplished safely in a few hours the journey which had taken us three days. Two of them were fitted out to take our ten ponies, and two others had tents pitched for our accommodation; another carried the soldiers of our escort, and two more were laden with odds and ends of merchandize belonging apparently to the owner of the lumber. By midday the whole flotilla of seven were swirling down the river under the autumn sun, and as we reclined in front of our tents and watched the sandstone cliffs shoot by after so many months of mountain and desert we felt thoroughly at peace with things generally. The river flowed between low hills of red sandstone with loess superimposed, grass covered on the right bank and desert on the left. In places small plains, like that in which Powan lies, opened out on either side; they were always irrigated by huge water wheels, of exactly the same type as those so common in Szechuan, and their green trees and fertile fields formed a striking contrast to the background of desert hills. The red sandstone cliffs bordering the river are pocked with square caves similar to those on the Min River and other streams in Szechuan. The origin and use of these caves, whether they are old tombs or the former dwelling-places of an aboriginal race, are, I believe, still unknown. Here on the Yellow River several of them were inhabited and provided with ropes and ladders as means of access. I should have liked to have visited the inhabitants, but it was quite impossible to stop the heavy rafts in the swift current under the base of a perpendicular cliff of rock; it is very strange that anyone should want to live in a cave half-way up a sandstone cliff overhanging the Yellow River, with no other means of access but a rope or ladder up or down the rock, unless it be the inherited custom to do so, or as a refuge against robbers. In my experience these square-faced caves, which are of an entirely different style of architecture to the round-arched caves in the loess in which millions of Chinese still dwell, are only found in the faces of sandstone cliffs overlooking rivers.

Three hours below Powan we reached the district city of Chingyuan Hsien on the right bank of the river; it lies on an old main road from Shensi to Lanchou *via* Haich'eng which was in general use before the construction of the present road across the Liupan Shan, and appears still to carry a certain amount of traffic, mostly camel caravans. The valley opens out in this neighbourhood and there are cultivated strips along both banks for a space. Four hours below Chingyuan the river, hitherto flowing north-east, is running north-west between sandstone cliffs owing to the incidence of a range of mountains on the right front; this range appears to me to connect the main Nan Shan range with the Liupan Shan, which itself seems to run S.E. to join the Ch'inling Shan near Paochi, thus forming one continuous barrier trending across North West China from N.W. to S.E.; but this is only a guess. Near here we tied up for the night to some rocks on a shelving sand-bank.

Two hours further on the mountains are reached and the river enters a series of bare rocky gorges hemmed in by precipitous cliffs of red sandstone and shale, opening out in places to reveal a desolate wilderness of reddish mountains without a scrap of vegetation. A little gold-washing is carried on in this neighbourhood. There were numerous rapids, over which our rafts rode triumphantly. Navigation, carried out by sweeps at the bow and stern, consists in avoiding the rocks and sand-banks and keeping the raft clear of the cliffs where the river swirls round a corner. Unless engaged in a particularly fierce rapid but little attention is paid to these cliffs, and on several occasions my raft crashed against the perpendicular wall of rock in a way which would have smashed a boat to pieces, but without doing any damage beyond shifting a few telegraph poles. In the bad rapids, however, where the water is heaped up into the centre of the river in a tongue like the big rapids on the Upper Yangtzu, great care is taken, since the pace is so tremendous that the raft could scarcely survive the impact with a large rock. Towards evening we noticed large numbers of goral (or wild goat of some kind) in these gorges, clambering about the precipitous cliffs in tens and twenties; one could have shot any number from the raft, but it would have been impossible to stop and retrieve them.

These gorges last for six or seven hours, until finally a picturesque temple on a bluff overlooking the river marks the exit from the gorge and the approach to Wufang Ssu, a boating village in a small plain on the left bank of the river. Sheep are grazed extensively on the semi-desert hills in the neighbourhood, and wool is collected here and shipped down river for the Tientsin trade.

From Wufang Ssu the river flows east and north-east again. Two hours further on another long gloomy gorge, with many rapids and whirlpools, is entered, the passage through which takes seven to eight hours; coal is exposed in the cliffs in places. At length the mountain walls give way to huge sand-hills and then to an irrigated alluvial plain, and two hours further on Chungwei Hsien is reached. Chungwei, lying inland about five li from the left bank of the river, is quite an important town, the centre of a rich fertile region where the desert is irrigated by canals from the Yellow River, and also a market for the wool trade.

Below Chungwei the Yellow River becomes a broad stream obstructed by sand-banks and shallows, flowing through an immense plain dotted with low hills and irrigated stretches. So far our river journey had been a complete success; but now things began to go wrong, and we spent three days making a few miles owing to the rafts constantly running aground, when, owing to their unwieldy weight, it was an extremely difficult matter to move them. The culminating misfortune was a tremendous storm of rain and wind one night, which blew our rafts adrift and scattered them over various sand-banks miles apart in impossible positions. We decided therefore to abandon them, and an appeal to the Chungwei magistrate having produced a couple of small boats, we transhipped our effects, sending the ponies overland to Ninghsia, distant a few days' journey. To be on board a raft stuck on a sand-bank in the middle of the Yellow River for two or three days is a good test of one's patience. I at first passed the time by shooting geese, which here began to appear in some numbers, but had to desist as no one would eat them; the Chinese goose, though a magnificent bird to shoot, is very tough and stringy to eat, and is only palatable if carefully cooked and stuffed. Fortunately the banks were here irrigated and inhabited and one could buy grain and vegetables. Our water supply, as all the way down, was the river; we had no filters, but a pinch of alum in a bucket soon changes the yellow pea-soupy liquid into clear water; another method of eliminating the yellow mud is to scoop a small hole in a pebbly bit of beach, which immediately fills with clear filtered water.

Making a fresh start in our small boats we floated down stream rapidly past several villages for some twelve hours to the walled township of Kuangwu, where the cultivated strips on both banks come to an end, and the large irrigation canal, which commences above Chungwei, rejoins the river. The abrupt cessation of these irrigated lands is due to a range of low mountains through which the Yellow River here breaks its way, and which separate the irrigated plains of Chungwei and Ningan from those of Ninghsia and Chinch'i. The desert everywhere begins where irrigation ceases. The passage through the gorge in these hills below Kuangwu takes about an hour, the exit being marked by temples on either side, and the river emerging on to a vast plain. A couple of hours further down we tied up at a village on the right bank not far from the district city of

Chinch'i, where we were able to examine some of the wonderful irrigation works which render these huge plains, otherwise desert, so fertile. There are similar works on the other bank near the village of Tapa. Their destruction would turn one of the richest plains in North China into a desert. In the North West irrigation is the key to agricultural prosperity, and though the ancient Chinese have done so much in this region, modern engineers could probably accomplish wonders in turning immense areas of what is still desert into fertile lands. Especially lower down, where the river makes its great bend round the Ordos, there would seem to be great openings for modern irrigation works.

Chinch'i Hsien, formerly known as Chinch'i P'u or Ningling T''ing, is a Mahomedan centre, and was the chief rebel stronghold in the great rebellion. The Mahomedans are still very powerful in this region, where their settlements extend south through Haich'eng and Kuyuan to P'ingliang in Eastern Kansu. T'ung Fu-hsiang's family own large estates in the neighbourhood, which they appear to have acquired after the capture of Chinch'i in 1871 by the latter. This event was the beginning of the end of the rebellion in Kansu, which led to the eventual defeat of Yakub Beg and the recovery of Chinese Turkestan; had the Kansu Mahomedans held out, the reconquest of Central Asia would have been rendered impossible, and the fall of Chinch'i constitutes therefore an event of the first importance in Chinese history.

Shortly before reaching the neighbourhood of Chinch'i we noticed, much to our amazement, a small stern-wheel steamer tied up to the right bank. An examination through glasses showed her to be a mere rusty skeleton, and our boatmen said she had lain there for years. From subsequent enquiries in Ninghsia we learned that this vessel represented an attempt, made just before the revolution, by the Kansu Viceroy with the assistance of a Belgian gentleman to establish steam navigation on the upper Yellow River. A small river steamer was purchased, transported in sections at great expense overland and put together at Paot'ou. She seems to have made one trip up river, reaching with great difficulty the spot where she is now, and where she is likely to remain until she falls to pieces. The Revolution was probably partly the cause of the abandonment of this progressive enterprise, as has been the case in so many others.

The shifting channel is said to be the chief obstacle to steam navigation on the upper Yellow River. There should, however, be a profitable opening for motor boats between Ninghsia and the important mart of Paot'ou, or even from Chungwei down to Hok'ou where the river takes its southerly bend and enters the Shansi mountains. Above Chungwei, to Lanchou, a special type of high-powered shallow draft vessel, similar to that in use on the upper Yangtzu, would be required to overcome the rapids, and the volume of trade and traffic is not likely to justify such an enterprise for many years, if ever. But with the Kalgan-Kueihuach'eng railway pushing on towards the Yellow River and Paot'ou, a motor boat service from that place to Ninghsia would revolutionise the existing means of communication between the coast and Kansu and the North West. Paot'ou is an entrepôt of increasing importance for the import and export trade of the North West and there would be no lack of traffic; the one great objection would be the suspension of the service in the winter. It usually takes months nowadays to reach Ninghsia from the coast going up stream; with a combined motor boat and railway service, even if the latter stopped short at Kueihua, it could be reached in a few days. Below Hok'ou and the southern bend of the river steam or motor navigation is out of the question owing to the many gorges and rapids, one of which, we were told, near the Yümen K'ou, amounts to a small waterfall. Below Yümen K'ou (Lung Men) the gorges come to an end, but beyond T'ungkuan, where the river turns east, more rapids occur, including those at Sanmen, which are said to be impassable for upward bound boats. The navigable section of the upper Yellow River is therefore confined to the Hok'ou-Paot'ou-Ninghsia-Chungwei section, which, however, forms the necessary link between Kansu and the Kalgan railway extension leading to the coast.

Below Chinch'i the river is a broad and placid stream flowing between irrigated and densely populated plains. Beyond Ling Chou the land on the right bank rises, irriga-

PLATE XLIII

RAFTING DOWN THE GORGES OF THE UPPER YELLOW RIVER

RAFTING DOWN THE GORGES OF THE UPPER YELLOW RIVER

PLATE XLIV

OUR PONIES RAFTING DOWN THE UPPER YELLOW RIVER

RAFTS OF INFLATED SKINS ON THE YELLOW RIVER

tion comes to an end, and the fertile plain gives way to a sandy waste. Eventually, after some twenty-seven to thirty hours of actual drifting down stream from Chungwei, exclusive of halts, we reached the walled fort of Hung Ch'eng, which is, so to speak, the port of Ninghsia, lying on the right bank at the point where the Great Wall and the main trail from T'aiyuan *via* Suitê to Ninghsia strike the Yellow River. Behind it the land rises in sandy uninhabited downs, the beginning of the Ordos desert. The river is here about three-quarters of a mile wide and is crossed by a ferry. Ninghsia lies 40 li inland on the opposite side.

As our ponies had not yet turned up on their overland journey from Chungwei we found ourselves stranded on the river bank opposite Hung Ch'eng, until the Ninghsia authorities, learning of our arrival, sent some animals down to meet us. The trail to Ninghsia leads across a strip of waste land five li in extent stretching along the river, and then runs for the rest of the way through irrigated fields, mostly under rice, traversing several large irrigation channels. There is probably more rice (though of an inferior kind) grown on the Yellow River plains between Ninghsia and Chungwei than anywhere else in China north of the Ch'inling Shan; but also this was the only region in Kansu where we were troubled by mosquitoes, the elevation being under 4000 feet. We spent a few days in Ninghsia, being hospitably entertained by the Mahomedan General and other officials. It is a large town, and a political and commercial centre of some importance, but the interior is very dilapidated and poor-looking. It is the centre of trade with the Mongols of the Ordos and the Alashan (the latter really the name of a Mongol state rather than a mountain range), chiefly in wool and sheep and goat skins; a particularly fine lamb-skin, called *t'anyang p'i* is a noted local product, as well as felts and carpets. An old Ninghsia rug is of considerable value anywhere. The local Mahomedan General, Ma Fu-hsiang, who is also a sort of Military Governor of North-Eastern Kansu, is one of the leading Mahomedans of the Province, and represents a fine soldierly type of Chinese Moslem. He served under T'ung Fu-hsiang in Peking in 1900 and commanded the Dowager Empress' escort on the retreat to Hsian. The Manchus had no more loyal servants than the Mahomedan leaders of Kansu. But, unlike some of the Manchu irreconcilables, General Ma Fu-hsiang moves with the times, and was later on one of the staunchest supporters of Yuan Shih-k'ai and the Peking Government. He is looked upon in some quarters as a likely successor to General Ma An-liang as leader of the Kansu Mahomedans, a position which it is generally agreed he is well qualified to fill.

Ninghsia was one of the few places in Kansu which had a rough time during the Revolution of 1911 owing to the city being seized by the Ko Lao Hui, and matters seem to have been very bad until the arrival of Mahomedan troops under one of Ma An-liang's Generals, when many Ko Lao Hui heads rolled in the dust and order was speedily restored. It is only in the extreme north and south of Kansu, for instance at Ninghsia and Chieh Chou (Kai Chou), where there is a considerable extra-provincial element in the population, that the Ko Lao Hui are formidable, owing apparently to the counter-influence of the Mahomedans, who will never have any dealings with secret societies.

Immediately west of the Ninghsia plains rises the barrier range usually known to foreigners as the Alashan, and three days' distant in these mountains lies Tingyuan Ying, or Wangyeh Fu, the residence of the Mongol Prince of the State of Alashan. It was to this place that Prince Tuan, the Boxer leader and father of the then Heir Apparent, retired after the events of 1900, though he was supposed to have been exiled to Turkestan. After the Mahomedans had occupied Ninghsia during the Revolution of 1911, he came down and lived there for some time awaiting the issue, but on the abdication of the Manchus he appears to have retired west into Turkestan, together with the famous old Manchu die-hard, Sheng Yün.

At Ninghsia we received what then seemed the incredible news of Yuan Shih-k'ai's intention to make himself Emperor. Kansu and its Mahomedans probably welcomed the event, since they were never particularly enthusiastic about the Republic, but it was a terrible blow to the young men of the student class who believed in the *Min Kuo*[1]. I have heard Yuan Shih-k'ai's opponents allege that his ambition was always fixed on the Throne, and that in the days when

[1] "People's Country," i.e. Republic.

he was living in retirement in Honan after the death of the Empress Dowager he was in secret communication with many of the military chiefs of the new army of his own creation and plotting a *coup d'état*; then followed the revolution, and he was able to advance with consummate skill, under the pretence of trying to keep the Manchus on the Throne, to the positions of Provisional President, Dictator, and Emperor. Other Chinese assure one that he was a faithful servant of the Republic led astray by the ambitions of his family and entourage. Whatever the facts may have been, there is no doubt that Yuan Shih-k'ai would have made a splendid Emperor, and subsequent events have proved that he was then the only man capable of ruling China. The Kansu officials, like those of all the other provinces, were instructed to make preparations for the holding of popular elections for or against a monarchy, which were to follow a joint memorial from the provincial Military Governors, all with one or two important exceptions Yuan's own men, begging their master to ascend the Throne. These instructions were, however, accompanied by secret telegrams regarding the working of the elections, and so successful were these arrangements that Yuan Shih-k'ai was elected Emperor practically unanimously by all the provinces. Everyone throughout the length and breadth of China knew that these elections were a sham and a fraud from beginning to end; but the Chinese are a race of actors, and make-belief enters largely into most phases of their private and public lives, and the farce was solemnly completed. Yet when the standard of rebellion was raised by General Tsai Ao in Yunnan on Christmas Day, 1916, the fraud was soon apparent, and the whole monarchical scheme came tumbling to the ground as province after province, all of which had supposedly announced themselves as unanimously in its favour, deserted the Imperial cause. As an instance of Chinese make-belief (*yu ming wu shih*) the monarchical elections of the autumn of 1916 are hard to beat.

The officials of Ninghsia had kindly prepared two of the large wool boats for our accommodation and smaller craft for the ponies for the journey down river to Paot'ou. Our craft were broad flat-bottomed scows with high sides, and when roofed over with our tents made quite comfortable

house-boats; they are used for the conveyance of the wool
down stream, and are as often as not tracked up empty.
For the convenience of future travellers on this route, it
may be stated that the hire of one of these large boats from
Ninghsia to Paot'ou should be about 35 taels, and of a small
boat or raft from Lanchou to Ninghsia about 25 taels; but
with a limited amount of baggage the journey can be
accomplished very much more cheaply by hiring accommodation on a laden wool boat. The rapidity of the journey
depends on the amount of wind met with, as with high
winds, which are frequent in the Ordos, the clumsy scows
are blown ashore or on to sand-banks, and have to tie up
till the weather calms. Night travel is possible part of the
way round the Ordos. It is a peaceful journey, navigation
consisting in keeping the boat more or less in the middle
of the current and watching the banks drift by. The boatmen
are mostly Mahomedans, and thoroughly up to their job.
We were much delayed by wind and other causes and took
ten days to get to Paot'ou, the actual floating time being
about 100 hours.

We finally left Ninghsia, or rather Hung Ch'eng, on
September 9th and reached Shihchu Shan in the evening
of the following day. The weather, as all the way down
the river, was beautiful, cold in the early mornings, but
brilliant sun during the middle of the day. Between
Ninghsia and Shihchu Shan the river is a broad and placid
stream with many shallows and islands. On the right hand
is sandy desert, the Ordos, now included in the "Special
Territory" of Suiyuan; on the left hand the land is still a
part of Kansu province, a strip of waste land along the river,
behind which lies the irrigated belt, with cultivation, trees,
and houses, backed by the Alashan mountains. In places
the sands were grey with geese. Shihchu Shan, locally
known as Shihtsuitzu, is an unwalled township built of
mud, which appears to owe its existence to the wool trade.
It is a weird and desolate little place, lying on the left bank
at a point where the Alashan mountains and a low range
in the Ordos converge on the river, which narrows to a few
hundred yards in width. All around are desert hills. The
community, consisting of the native agents of the foreign
wool exporters of Tientsin, is engaged in drying and re-

packing the wool which comes down from Western Kansu by boat on the river and by camel overland, and in collecting local produce from the Mongols. The overland trail from Paot'ou, eight to ten marches from well to well across the Ordos desert, here strikes the Yellow River, crosses by a ferry, and continues up the plain to Ninghsia. Supplies must be laid in at Shihchu Shan to last to Paot'ou, little or nothing being obtainable in the Ordos *en route*.

Leaving Shihchu Shan we passed finally out of Kansu into the Ordos. The river runs for some hours with a rapid current between bare mountains, which gradually recede and give way to sandy desert. After about twelve hours drifting down stream Tengk'ou, a desolate little village in the desert on the left bank, is reached, and some eight hours further on the township of Santaohotzu is passed, where there is a Catholic Mission and a considerable Chinese population engaged in agriculture round the old branches of the Yellow River. The river banks on either side are lined much of the way with a belt of willow scrub, which furnishes a most useful supply of fuel to the boats going up and down. The current is fairly strong through the Ordos, considering the level nature of the country, but we were frequently compelled to tie up to the bank to wait for the wind to drop. On one of these occasions my five ponies, which were being exercised on the bank, took alarm at something and galloped off into the desert. We followed them for miles and then lost their tracks on some hard stony ground. The country was desert without a sign of life except for numerous antelope and an occasional camel turned out for the summer, and the boatmen expressed the opinion that we should never see the ponies again unless we chanced on them further down stream, as though they had galloped off inland they would be bound to return to the river for water. On the following day after having drifted many miles further down we fortunately spied a Mongol watering his camels on the bank, who turned out to have met the ponies inland, and they were soon recovered, very hungry, thirsty, and tame.

Lower down we met again and again with the most violent winds, necessitating long and weary delays in the desert. There was some trouble with Mongol brigands going on in this neighbourhood, and on one occasion shots were fired at us from the bank, though our boatmen and escort were uncertain whether they came from brigands or from soldiers signalling us to stop; the river being wide, however, and the current swift we did not trouble to enquire. In many places when tied up to the north bank we found the ground pitted with small holes, the work of the liquorice root diggers. This is an old industry which has revived considerably of late owing to a foreign firm commencing to buy the produce for export. The liquorice-producing areas in the world appear to be limited in extent, and this is one of them. Twenty-four hours above Paot'ou the Wula Shan mountains are reached, a bare rocky range running a little inland along the north side of the river, and a prominent landmark from afar. In this neighbourhood the Ordos bank, hitherto uninhabited desert, begins to be populated, and Mongols and Chinese are to be seen with many camels, sheep, and ponies grazing on poor-looking downs. As Paot'ou is approached farms and villages become numerous on the north bank, and the plain between river and mountains is a vast corn-field.

Paot'ou Chen (also known as Hsi Paot'ou) is a large walled town lying a little way back from the Yellow River in the corn-growing plain which slopes up towards the Tach'ing Shan, a continuation of the Wula Shan. It is remarkable in many respects; in the first place it is essentially a new and growing place, unlike the dilapidated and hoary old towns of Kansu, and is the centre of a fertile corn-growing area which a generation ago was unoccupied except by a few Mongols and their flocks. There is probably plenty more good land waiting to be opened up further west, north of the Yellow River, and the curious spectacle may here be witnessed of the Chinese colonising Canadian-like prairies within the borders of their own republic. Secondly, as well as being a cleaning and repacking centre for the Tientsin wool trade like Shihchu Shan, it is evidently a commercial centre of considerable and increasing importance for the import and export trade of the vast hinterland to the west. We found more evidence of trade activity in this isolated town than in any city in Kansu. Unfortunately, situated as it is on the very outskirts of Chinese civilization, Paot'ou appears to have suffered greatly from the prevailing

PLATE XLV

PONIES EMBARKED FOR THE JOURNEY ROUND THE ORDOS

ON THE YELLOW RIVER NEAR PAOT'OU

PLATE XLVI

MONGOLS MOVING CAMP

MONGOLS MOVING CAMP

lawlessness of the past few years, which fact, however, only makes its commercial prosperity all the more remarkable. It evidently owes its importance to its position as the most westerly outpost of Chinese trade in this direction, and like Kueihua Ch'eng, is one of the starting-points for caravans going west. The Mahomedans appear to form an important element in the trading community. There was no civil official at the time of our visit, but a large garrison of soldiers; the inhabitants seem a rough lot, as is to be expected in a frontier town.

At Paot'ou our river journey came to an end and we hired carts to convey our baggage to Kueihua Ch'eng, distant four marches, the usual stages being, Salach'i 90 li, T'aossu Ho 70 li, Pihsuehchi 90 li, and Kueihua Ch'eng 80 li. The road runs east across an undulating cultivated plain accompanied by the Tach'ing Shan range on the north. Except for some marshy patches of grass land which have to be crossed, the going is good, and I have never known Chinese carts to travel faster, our ponies frequently having to trot to keep up with them. The traffic was surprisingly busy on the road which evidently carried a bigger trade than any trail in Kansu. The inhabitants are apparently all Chinese, but at a farm where we stopped for a meal the owner and his wife though dressed in Chinese clothes could only speak Mongol; and another sign of the former Mongol population is a picturesque lamasery on the mountain side, which from its appearance might equally well have been situated on the Kokonor border. The Mongol lamas are very like their Tibetan colleagues, as is shown by the accompanying photographs (see frontispiece) of a so-called Devil Dance, which were taken at a big monastery in Eastern Inner Mongolia, and represent the "Dance of the Black Hat," the commonest religious dance in Tibet. It represents an incident in Tibetan history namely the killing of King Glangdarma, the notorious persecutor of Buddhism, by the lama Dpalgirdarje in A.D. 842; the lama danced before the King in the costume shown in the photographs, concealing in his broad sleeves a bow and arrow. The photographs facing pages 200 and 202, which were taken at the same Mongolian monastery, also represent purely Tibetan ceremonies, namely the *torma* offering for warding off devils, and the circumambulation of the monastery by the figure of the coming Buddha seated in a car drawn by an elephant, in this case a mock one. The extent of Asia covered by that curious form of Buddhism known as Tibetan Lamaism is very large, stretching as it does from the northern frontiers of India to the southern borders of Siberia, and from Ladak to the confines of Manchuria.

Kueihua Ch'eng is another busy commercial town serving a hinterland extending to Kashgar, Kobdo, Ili, and Uliassutai. Near by lies the old Manchu garrison fortress of Suiyuan, which gives its name to the new territory of Suiyuan; the latter includes parts of Inner Mongolia and Northern Shansi, and has its counterpart further east in the territory of Chahar, comprising portions of Eastern Inner Mongolia and the Kalgan and Jehol regions of Chihli. These territories are administered on military lines. Kueihua is a good starting-point for a big-game shooting trip into the mountains further north, where remarkably fine sheep, a sort of *Ovis argali*, and wapiti can be secured, as well as the roe-deer and goral common in North China. With the Kalgan railway extension pushing on towards Kueihua, this is some of the best and most accessible big game ground in China nowadays.

We changed our carts at Kueihua Ch'eng and hired new ones to take us through the mountains to railhead at Feng Chen, distant four long marches. The first stage is a march of 90 li to the mountain village of Shihjen Wan, the trail continuing east across the plain for six or seven hours and then running up a shallow valley for the rest of the way. Many of the higher mountain slopes were snow-clad, though the season of the year was only late September. On the following day another long march of 90 li up a valley and over a low pass brought us to the hamlet of Wuli Pa, lying on a sort of plateau of moorland country, the beginning of the grass lands of Eastern Inner Mongolia. It snowed heavily most of the day and we arrived cold, wet, and tired to find the roughest of accommodation in a large cart inn. The third stage is still longer, called 110 li, to the village of T'iench'eng Ts'un, but the trail lying partly across grass country one can travel fast. The road descends through flat open valleys to a lake, where good wild-fowl shooting

PLATE XLVII

PONY FAIR ON THE CHINESE-MONGOLIAN BORDER

PONY FAIR ON THE CHINESE-MONGOLIAN BORDER

PLATE XLVIII

ON THE ROAD BETWEEN PAOT'OU AND KUEIHUA CH'ENG

ON THE ROAD BETWEEN KUEIHUA CH'ENG AND FENG CHEN

can be had, and then ascends to another grassy plateau. Herds of Mongolian ponies (the "China pony" of the Treaty Ports) were to be seen, but the good pony country lies much further north-east, beyond Kalgan and Dolonor. The following day, September 26th, we accomplished our last march, 60 li to Feng Chen. It was freezing hard in the early morning, and we decided we had just completed our journey in time; for winter on these steppes of High Asia is very severe. The trail continues across the grass lands for two hours' march, and then runs down a broad cultivated valley plain for the rest of the way to Feng Chen, an un- walled township, and the railhead of the Peking-Kalgan-Kueihua extension line.

A construction train took us down to Tatung Fu, an important town of Northern Shansi, where we were lucky enough to strike the weekly express, which runs through to Peking in one day. This was the end of our long journeys, and the reader, having accompanied us as far afield as Chengtu in Szechuan and Hsining and Liangchou in Kansu, is probably as tired of reading about them as the writer is of recording their description.

CHAPTER XIV

SOME OBSERVATIONS REGARDING FOREIGN MISSIONS IN THE INTERIOR OF CHINA

Chinese interest in foreign things—Need of reform in type of Christianity taught to Chinese—Hostile attitude of Roman Catholics towards Protestants —Methods of Catholics—Celibacy—Chinese *versus* foreign dress—Unity of Catholic and disunity of Protestant Churches—Claims for compensation— Educational work—Advantages of a non-religious mission—Selection of missionaries—Missionary holidays—Spread of Anglo-Saxon ideals by missionaries in China.

CONSIDERABLE mention has been made in these pages of missionaries and their works, the excuse for which is the importance which the missionary question assumes nowadays in the interior of China. It is doubtless presumptuous for an outsider to venture to criticise the work of missionaries, with which he can have but a very superficial acquaintance, but as one who has seen a great deal of missionary enterprise in the more distant and backward provinces of the interior, and on the principle that a cat may look at a king, the writer ventures to devote a short chapter to the following random observations on the subject. Lest, however, the views expressed be considered anti-missionary, he would first explain that he is a profound admirer of the good work done by the Protestant missionaries in educating and healing the Chinese, and generally in leavening and improving things in China, the effects of which are apparent from Peking to Canton and from Chengtu to Shanghai, and is only in equally profound disagreement with some of their evangelising work and methods. The large sums provided annually by the home societies in Europe and America are indeed well spent from the former point of view, though it is perhaps doubtful whether they have really accomplished very much good from the latter.

The missionary problem has been entirely altered of recent years by the changes which have taken place in awakening China, especially since the Revolution of 1911.

The difficulty used to be, how to overcome the antipathy of the Chinese for everything foreign, and to induce the people to consent to listen to the foreign preacher; today the problem is, how best to utilise in the cause of Christianity the interest and admiration displayed by the Chinese for the foreigner and his works, including everything foreign from missions to machine guns. In the distant interior this enthusiasm for foreign things is sometimes mistaken for a rush to enter the Christian Church, because the missionary and his Western home are often the only foreign objects available locally. The disappearance of the antipathy to the foreigner does of course offer a great opportunity for missionary work, and the question arises whether this opportunity is being turned to the best advantage from the point of view of Christianity.

In the first place it would appear that there is urgent need for reform in the type of Christianity which is being nowadays propagated amongst the Chinese. It seems unnecessary and unfair that they should continue to be taught all the old literal beliefs and narrow bigoted doctrines now for the most part discarded in Europe, the truth of which is probably not accepted by one non-missionary out of a hundred in China. Anyone acquainted with the old-fashioned theology of the average missionary in the interior of China will scarcely need further evidence of the need of this reform, but the following extract from the last edition (at the time of writing) of the *China Mission Year Book* may be quoted, the reference being to the progress made by a certain Protestant Mission, "The reality of demon possession and healing by prayer are now fully recognized."

The Westernised form of Christianity is obviously unsuited to become a native religion in China, and though his foreign status is nowadays one of the chief assets of the missionary, it would seem that it should be his object to disassociate his religion as much as possible from everything foreign, and divest Christianity of all its foreign trappings, if he wishes to found a native Christian Church in China, which shall be independent of the moral and financial support of foreigners, propagate itself, and stand on its own legs (and only by this means can the most optimistic missionary hope that the Chinese will ever become genuine Christians); but the efforts of many Protestant missionaries appear to be rather directed towards the establishment of a foreign church in which the Chinese are taught to ape the foreign style of worship, with unsatisfactory if not ridiculous results.

The Catholics and Protestants are great stumbling-blocks to one another in China, and the latter would probably generally admit that the former are usually more hostile to them than the heathen Chinese and are their most formidable enemies. It is unfortunately a fact that in many places the foreign Catholics work directly and unceasingly against the foreign Protestants, with disastrous results for the Christian spirit of their respective flocks. Though the Roman Catholic priests have long since lost the official status they used to enjoy, the power of the Catholic Church continues to increase in the interior of China. In many Catholic missions today disputes between converts are still adjudicated upon by the foreign priests or bishops without the interference of Chinese officials, and punishments and fines are even imposed, the latter going to increase the wealth of the local Catholic establishment. The amount of land owned by the Catholic Church in out of the way parts of China nowadays is truly remarkable; the properties of the Protestant missions are for the most part covered with schools, hospitals, churches, and the comfortable bungalows of the missionaries; the Catholic priests on the other hand pay scant attention to their personal comfort; but their lands are usually let at a profitable rate to Chinese farmers, converts or others, and by this means many of the Catholic establishments are nowadays probably independent of financial support from Europe. In this respect therefore the Catholic Church may be said to be now indigenous in China, but the management is still entirely in the hands of the foreigners, and one can imagine what an orgy of plunder of Church property would follow the withdrawal of the foreign fathers and bishops. The power of the Catholics is generally speaking much greater than that of the Protestants, and in the case, say, of a lawsuit, a Protestant convert stands but little chance against a Catholic (this is of course in part due to the more correct attitude adopted by the Protestant missionaries in the matter

PLATE XLIX

THE "CHINA PONY" ON HIS NATIVE STEPPES

THE "CHINA PONY" ON HIS NATIVE STEPPES

PLATE L

SCENE AT A LAMA FESTIVAL, EASTERN INNER MONGOLIA

SCENE AT A LAMA FESTIVAL, EASTERN INNER MONGOLIA

of interference on the side of their converts in material matters). In spite of recent changes the Catholic Church in China remains to no small extent an *Imperium in Imperio*; and one cannot but admire and wonder at its power, based as it is nowadays rather on the remarkable unity and organization of the Church, and on the self-sacrificing zeal and ability of its priests, than on the support of foreign governments.

The methods of the Catholic missionaries in China are very different from those of the Protestants, and in a way they are markedly more successful; though some allege that their registers of converts contain whole families, all the members of which are far from being Christians; while their opponents consider that they but substitute one form of idolatry for another and replace the worship of Buddhist idols by that of images and pictures of Jesus Christ and the Virgin (and the writer has himself seen Chinese Catholics, who have apparently got a little mixed in their ideas, prostrating themselves and burning joss sticks before a picture of the Virgin in exactly the same way as their heathen brothers perform similar ceremonies before their idols). The Catholic plan is to work as far as possible through the rising generation, and to create new Catholic families rather than to convert old ones. To accomplish this end they collect children by various means in their so-called orphanages educate them as Catholics, marry them to one another, and if possible provide them with land to cultivate as a means of livelihood. The result has been that the Catholic Faith has taken root as a native religion more firmly than the Protestant, and Catholic communities have come into existence, the members of which adhere to one another and their faith in a manner only to be compared, as far as China is concerned, with the unity and religious zeal of the Mahomedans; such communities, united for purposes of mutual protection under the leadership of a foreign priest, are often a power to be reckoned with locally. On the other hand adult converts as often as not join the Catholic Church, or enroll themselves as "enquirers," in order to obtain the protection afforded by this powerful organization. This enrolling of enquirers is at times a gross abuse of the Church, both Catholic and Protestant. Cases are on record where people guilty or accused of crimes against the Catholics register themselves as enquirers with the Protestants, and *vice versâ*, with the sole idea of obtaining protection. In justice to the Protestant missionaries it should be stated that with them they seldom secure it.

The success of the Catholics is certainly due in part to the manner in which they enter into the lives of the Chinese people and preach their doctrines unobtrusively from amongst them; in contrast to the Protestant missionary, who usually lives a Western life in a Western home, cut off from contact with the orientals amongst whom he is working. In this connection it may be noted that the China Inland Mission, one of the largest and oldest and in the opinion of many still the finest and purest of all the Protestant missions established in China, originally adopted to a great extent the Catholic method of working from amongst the Chinese; but latterly they appear in many cases to have been affected by the example of the newer and more wealthy missions, and to have taken to the "foreign bunga-low" method (which does not, however, meet with the approval of all the members).

The celibacy of the Catholics is also greatly to their advantage and enables them to merge themselves with the Chinese in a way impossible for the Protestant missionary, encumbered with family ties and a European home. Especially in the old bad days of anti-foreign risings the single priest, quite prepared to suffer martyrdom, had a great advantage over the Protestant missionary, who, though himself probably equally ready to suffer for his faith, was hampered by his wife and children, and was usually com-pelled to beat a hasty retreat under conditions of terrible suffering for the latter. Further the celibate priest living on the merest pittance in Chinese style is a much more economical instrument for missionary propaganda than the Protestant living as a European, the cost of whose main-tenance with his family in foreign style accounts for a large proportion of the missionary funds collected at home.

The Catholics always work in Chinese clothes, as also used the Protestant missionaries, especially those of the China Inland Mission—until recently. After the Revolution of 1911 most of the Protestant Societies instructed or encouraged their missionaries to adopt foreign dress, on the supposition that now that the Chinese themselves were taking to everything foreign, including even foreign clothes, it was absurd and inadvisable that the foreigner should continue to disguise himself in Chinese dress. But there has been a considerable reaction against foreign food and foreign dress of recent years since the people got over their first revolutionary enthusiasm, and in the distant interior nowadays Chinese are practically never seen in foreign clothes. The wisdom of the missionary in giving up his Chinese gown for foreign dress and thus emphasizing his foreign status and that of his religion is therefore open to question, especially as the abolition of the queue has removed the chief objection to Chinese clothes, which are on the whole cheap and serviceable. It is safe to assume that a large proportion of the crowd listening to a foreign missionary preaching in foreign dress are far more interested in his clothes and his boots than in what he is trying to tell them.

Another advantage which the Catholics have over the Protestants lies in the unity of their Church compared to the many sects of the latter; not that this multitude of creeds really surprises the Chinese, who are accustomed to sects of all kinds in their own affairs; but it cannot fail to impair the respect of the heathen for the Protestant religion, especially where two neighbouring Protestant missions are not on good terms with one another, as is sometimes the case, more particularly with some of the newer and less regular missions. Wherever the Chinese enquirer may be throughout the length and breadth of China and beyond, he finds the Catholic priest preaching the same doctrines, whereas his Protestant teachers may be Anglican, Presbyterian, Methodist, Baptist, Lutheran, or Congregational, to quote the recognized denominations (sometimes roughly divided up by the Chinese into the Great Wash, the Little Wash, and the No Wash), each of which again may be subdivided into different missionary societies with varying ideas of their work; or he may strike one of the smaller and more irregular missions, such as the Seventh Day Adventists, the Tongues Movement Mission, the Faith Mission, the Church of God Mission, etc., some of which hold very strange beliefs, and may offer to instruct him in foreign languages by giving exhibitions of its foreign members rolling in fits upon the ground, or insist on his attempting to cure cataract by prayer instead of visiting the nearest foreign doctor. The missionaries themselves allege that there is unity in essentials and difference only in form; but it is not always easy for the Chinese to distinguish between the two. The China Inland Mission leads the way in unity as in so many other respects, in that it includes followers of most denominations; but its policy is to appoint missionaries of different persuasions to different parts of the country so as to avoid the clash of creeds.

Some Protestant Societies, however, notably again the China Inland Mission, have one great advantage over the Catholics, and that lies in their principle of never claiming compensation for buildings and property damaged or destroyed in times of disturbance, whether anti-foreign or otherwise. In view of the fact that nowadays such damage is usually the work of brigands or rebels over whom the local authorities have no control whatsoever, and that such compensation is in most cases ultimately paid by the innocent local people amongst whom and for whom the missionary is working, to claim it seems an obviously un-Christian act. There are some who maintain that not to put in such claims only encourages the people in the dangerous idea that they can destroy mission property with impunity; but in these enlightened days such an argument is no longer sound, and the mission which follows the Christian principle of relying on its own good influence for immunity from attack, and is prepared to suffer if necessary without retaliating with a claim, scores heavily in the eyes of the Chinese and is not likely to lose in the long run by such a policy. In times of civil disturbance, such as are nowadays everywhere so common, the Chinese flock to the missions, especially the Catholics, to secure protection for themselves and their goods and compensation for their losses. This increases the popularity of the Churches for the moment, but it can scarcely be considered a healthy sign in the growth of a genuine native Christian Church. It would rather seem desirable that the missionaries and their converts should nowadays be entirely cut adrift from the support

PLATE LI

THE "CIRCUMAMBULATION BY THE COMING BUDDHA"
AT A MONASTERY IN EASTERN INNER MONGOLIA

THE "CIRCUMAMBULATION BY THE COMING BUDDHA"
AT A MONASTERY IN EASTERN INNER MONGOLIA

PLATE LII

BEHIND THE SCENES AT A LAMA DEVIL DANCE, EASTERN INNER MONGOLIA

BEHIND THE SCENES AT A LAMA DEVIL DANCE, EASTERN INNER MONGOLIA

of foreign governments, and the missionaries might well surrender, in practice, some of the ex-territorial privileges, such as the right to claim compensation, which were formerly, but are scarcely at present, necessary to their residence in the interior; the result would probably be fewer converts, but more genuine ones.

The financial connection between the home society and the native church is nowadays an important and delicate question. Most missionaries agree that the real object of their work is the establishment of an independent native church in which the foreigner will play no part, and many admit that after all these years of work the time has now come, if it ever will come, when the results obtained in that direction must be put to the test by the withdrawal of foreign management. The connected step of withdrawing foreign funds would probably be disastrous for the moment; and as a withdrawal of the former and not of the latter would probably, from a Christian point of view, be even more disastrous, a compromise has been arrived at in many missions whereby the converts are given a say in the disposal of Church funds collected locally, but not in the disposal of those which come from abroad. As the former are naturally very small compared to the latter, the concession is not a large one, and the Chinese are beginning in some cases to contrast the houses and salaries of the native ministers and evangelists with those of the foreign missionaries, whose support, family allowances, travelling and building expenses account for so much of the money collected from abroad. Of course it is only natural and right that the foreign money should go to support the foreign missionary, but difficult questions in connection with the native church are nevertheless raised thereby. Connected with the problem of the foreign missionary's position *vis-à-vis* the native church is the question of the future disposal of those extensive foreign compounds occupied by the missionaries and their families, which in some provincial capitals of the interior amount to regular foreign settlements, and which are totally unsuited to the needs of the native church. These large and expensive establishments belong, not to individuals, but to the church; but to which church, the wealthy foreign society, or the impecunious native one?

The medical work of the missionaries is productive of such an incalculable amount of good amongst the hundreds of millions of Chinese, who are otherwise at the mercy of accidents and disease, that it naturally stands far above all criticism. But their educational work is sometimes criticised from the point of view of its relative efficiency and religious bias, and raises difficult problems for the future. These latter are connected with the fact that education in China is a government proposition and that the government schools are progressing and increasing in efficiency every year—indeed they are not infrequently more efficient than the local missionary school, for the missionary who comes to China does not always possess either the necessary training or talents for a teacher. The time will perhaps come in the not far distant future when there will be no place for the two systems of education, missionary and government, side by side, and a fusion or trouble must ensue. The missionaries have to a certain extent burnt their boats by not resting content with primary education and by establishing even so-called universities, of course at great expense in the matter of land and foreign buildings; while the Chinese Government has recently begun to develop its policy in the matter by offering to recognize certain primary mission schools on conditions such as, no religious teaching or ceremonies to take place, no support from the mission, the buildings to be entirely separated from the mission, the name of the mission not to be associated with the school, no distinction to be made as regards the admittance of Christian and non-Christian children, etc. It is therefore evident that a satisfactory fusion of missionary and government educational work will prove a problem requiring careful and tactful handling.

Generally speaking the secular work of the missionaries, medical, educational, and charitable, is not unnaturally more appreciated by the Chinese than their evangelistic efforts, and the tendency sometimes discernible of making the former conditional on obtaining results for the latter is perhaps resented. Chinese who have returned after prolonged residence in Western countries have been known to express the opinion that the best minds in the West seem to show little belief in the miracles, but evince great interest in social reform, and to intimate that a medical or charitable mission from which religion were excluded (on the lines of a London hospital), or at any rate kept in the background, would be much appreciated.

Proper selection does not always seem to be exercised by the home boards of the societies in sending missionaries to China, and the idea would seem to be that anyone who subscribes to the necessary dogma is good enough to go and attempt to convert the Chinese. But in dealing with a people of such acute intelligence and ancient civilization the exact reverse is rather the case, and quality would appear to be much more important and desirable than quantity in missionary work. Many missionaries give one the idea of having taken up the work principally as a means of livelihood, and plod along in their daily round like clerks in a city office; and there are stations where such men have been working for decades with practically nothing to show in the way of a native church at the end; others are obviously not fitted by intellect or education for the work; others again, attracted by the romance of travel in unknown lands (and the writer has every sympathy with them), spend their time rushing round the country, preferably on the borders of Tibet, on the pretext of distributing texts and "scripture portions" in Chinese or some tribal dialect, the effect of which in converting the heathen is practically nil. Others again are scholarly men with liberal ideas and full of sympathy with the Chinese, and it is these who are doing the good work. But on the whole there is a remarkable variety in the standard of education and intellect amongst the Protestant missionaries in China; and the Catholic priests would appear to be well ahead of them in this respect.

Another point which may be criticised in connection with Protestant missions in China is the tendency they have to develop as societies. A Chinese convert is almost always referred to by the missionaries as a Church Member, and admission to their particular church usually takes place after the carrying out of some solemn rite, which the heathen probably compare in their minds to initiation into the Ko Lao Hui or other secret society. The society, or *Hui*, has always played an important, and not always a respectable, part in China, the land of secret affiliations of all kinds, and the fact that it seems impossible for a Chinese to become a Christian without joining some particular foreign *Hui*, and becoming Baptist, Methodist, Presbyterian, or whatever it may be, strengthens the common idea that he only joins such a society for material reasons. The average Chinese Christian would probably be surprised to find how many foreigners consider themselves Christians without belonging to any particular society or *Hui*.

It seems highly desirable in the interests of the missionary cause in these days of constant rebellions and civil strife in China that the foreign missionary in the distant interior should resist the temptation of acquiring local popularity and influence by interfering in internal politics from the safe asylum of his ex-territorial privileges. This is usually, but certainly not always, recognized in missionary circles in the interior.

Finally the extended summer holidays of the Protestant missionaries, when they abandon their work in the hot cities to retire for months on end to their hill resorts, are often criticised as making a thoroughly bad impression amongst thinking Chinese. The Catholic priests and most of the members of the China Inland Mission never dream of abandoning their work in this way, and naturally gain greatly thereby. Of course it is necessary for the foreign mothers and children to leave the hot and unhealthy plains during the summer, but, apart from the necessity or advisability of the latter being in the interior at all, it is scarcely a sound policy, from the missionary point of view, for the men to do likewise. Few other foreigners in China, whether merchants or officials, though often far less comfortably housed in the interior than the missionaries, think it necessary to give up their work in the hot weather in the way the latter are in the habit of doing.

But quite apart from the splendid work done by the missionaries for the Chinese, and apart from the criticisms which their methods sometimes invite, the fact must not be overlooked that it is the Protestant missionaries who have spread the English language throughout China and turned the eyes of the rising generation of Chinese in search of Western knowledge towards Great Britain and the United States, thus creating bonds of sympathy and friendship between the Chinese and the Anglo-Saxon races to the great and lasting advantage of both.

PLATE LIII

RELIGIOUS DANCE AT A LAMA MONASTERY, EASTERN INNER MONGOLIA

RELIGIOUS DANCE AT A LAMA MONASTERY, EASTERN INNER MONGOLIA

PLATE LIV

MONGOL WOMEN IN GALA DRESS

MONGOL WOMEN IN GALA DRESS

CHAPTER XV

RAILWAY PROJECTS IN SHENSI AND KANSU

The Lung Hai Railway—The T'ung Ch'eng Railway—The Kueihua-Ninghsia Railway—The Han Valley Railway—Other possible railway routes.

NOT a single rail has yet been laid in the whole of the vast region of N.W. China covered by the provinces of Shensi and Kansu, though the need of railways is keenly felt both for commercial and political reasons. In the absence of waterways, such as exist throughout Central and Southern China, means of communication are limited to carts and pack animals, methods of transport which are both slow and expensive, while the vast numbers of ponies and mules employed consume a large proportion of the grain grown in these provinces. This absence of proper means of communication cannot but prevent the commercial development of the whole region, and encourages brigandage and political instability. There is no more vitally urgent reform waiting to be carried out in China than the construction of railways to outlying parts such as Szechuan, Shensi and Kansu. It seems safe to assume that nowhere in the world are there such vast, well-populated, and comparatively wealthy areas still without railways of any kind. Four trunk-lines have been projected through Shensi and Kansu, and there are openings for others. The four projects will first be discussed, in the order in which the concessions or contracts were obtained, for needless to say they are all foreign enterprises.

(1) The Lung Hai Railway from Kansu to the coast, and its extension west to the confines of Turkestan.

In 1912 a loan agreement was arranged between the Central Government and a Belgian Syndicate (Compagnie Generale de Chemins-de-fer et Tramways) for the construction of a trunk-line from Haichou on the coast of North Kiangsu to Lanchou Fu in Kansu, a distance of more than 1000 miles, with the option of an extension to Suchou in the extreme west of the latter province. The line was to be an

extension east and west of the existing Kaifeng Fu Honan
Fu Railway (called the Pien Lo). Lung is the classical
name for Kansu province.

In 1917 the construction of this railway westwards from
Honan Fu had reached, and stopped short at, the village
of Kuanyint'ang, half a day's march beyond the district
city of Miench'ih Hsien in Western Honan, and about three
marches short of the Shensi frontier at T'ungkuan. From
here the route projected is somewhat as follows. Through or
across a range of mountains to Shenchou on the Yellow
River and thence along the big road to T'ungkuan. This
stretch presents no great engineering difficulties after the
passage of the Kuanyint'ang range, presumably by a tunnel,
beyond some deep cuttings in the loess, especially as
T'ungkuan is approached. From the Honan-Shensi border
the line will cross Shensi from east to west following the
fertile valley plain of the Wei River. This section is flat and
open, and much of the way the only work required will be
an embankment and a number of small bridges across the
streams which flow down from the Ch'inling Shan into the
Wei River, the railway keeping to the south of the latter.
Traffic will be heavy and remunerative, and the towns
touched at will include the great metropolis of the North
West, the city of Hsian Fu. From the Shensi-Kansu border
near Fenghsiang Fu the line will probably keep as much as
possible to the Wei valley up to Kungch'ang and Weiyuan,
whence it will pass through the watershed between the Wei
and T'ao rivers to Titao. From Titao it can either follow
the T'ao River down to the Yellow River, or, more probably,
it will cut through the mountains direct to Lanchou Fu.
This stretch contains a great many serious engineering
obstacles, and is said to entail more than forty kilometres
of tunnels; nevertheless it is apparently the easiest way of
ascending the three to four thousand feet from the plains
of Shensi to the plateau of Kansu, and is certainly less
formidable than the existing high road *via* P'ingliang, which
crosses the Liupan Shan at a height of some 9000 feet, and
passes for the rest of the way to Lanchou through most
difficult loess country. The chief difficulties met with on
the proposed railway route are the Wei River gorges between
Paochi in Shensi and Ch'inchou in Kansu, and the passage

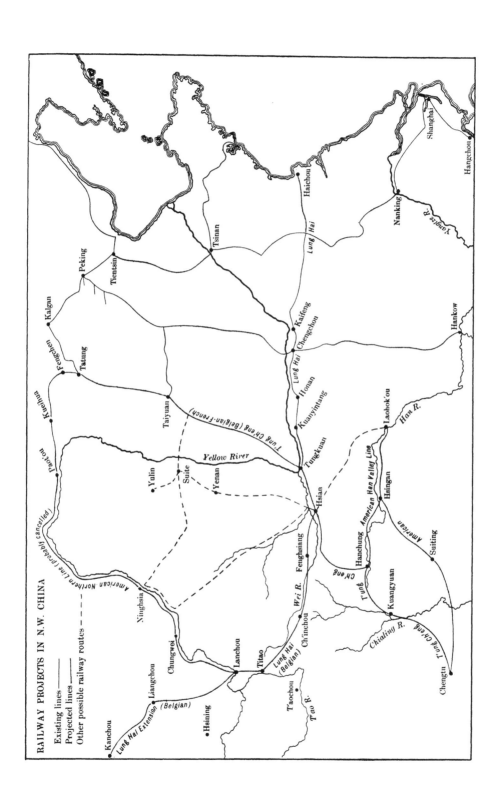

RAILWAY PROJECTS IN N.W. CHINA

Existing lines ————
Projected lines ————
Other possible railway routes – – – –

of the two watersheds, between Weiyuan and Titao, and between Titao and Lanchou.

As regards the extension west towards Turkestan, the chief engineering obstacle would seem to be the passage of the Wushao Ling, 10,000 feet; the P'ingfan valley provides an easy approach from the east, but the descent to the west is steep; there may, however, be a way round further north and east, as this range, the backbone of the Nan Shan, falls away in that direction. Further west the line can follow the main road, keeping if necessary a little further north on the edge of the desert, all the way to the frontiers of Turkestan without encountering any serious obstacle.

Generally speaking the Lung Hai Railway is a most attractive proposition through Shensi, but its construction through Kansu is likely to be very costly, and the traffic returns poor. However, sooner or later railway communication is bound to be established between China and Central Asia, connecting up with the Russian line from the Caspian Sea, and such a railway is more than likely to be an extension of the Lung Hai. For, whatsoever this great trunk line may be called, and by whomsoever it may be built, it is pretty well bound to follow the old fortified highway through Western Kansu along the narrow fertile belt between the deserts of Mongolia and Tibet, by which all trade and traffic between China and Western countries was once conducted. With the construction of this important trans-Asiatic trunk line, Kansu province will once more become, what it was in the past, the gateway from China to the West.

(2) The T'ung Ch'eng Railway, from Tatung in Northern Shansi to Chengtu in Szechuan.

In 1913 a loan agreement was arranged between the Chinese Government and a Franco-Belgian Syndicate for the construction of a trunk railway from Tatung in Northern Shansi, down the centre of that province via T'aiyuan to P'uchou on the Yellow River, thence via T'ungkuan and Central Shensi to Hsian, and thence via Hanchung to Chengtu in Szechuan. The period of construction was estimated at five years, but work has not yet been begun. This project is remarkable for its magnitude, but is in other respects not a particularly attractive proposition in view of the great engineering difficulties involved in passing from the Wei valley of Shensi into Szechuan and the doubtful amount of through traffic the line will carry. The contract is of a far-reaching nature, as it includes any extensions or branches for the construction of which the Chinese Government may require foreign capital.

Through Shansi the line will probably follow the important trade route across the Yen Men pass to T'aiyuan Fu and thence run down the valley of the Fen Ho to the plains of the Yellow River. There will apparently be no great engineering difficulties from T'aiyuan south, and this section should be remunerative.

At P'uchou the Yellow River will have to be bridged to reach T'ungkuan. From T'ungkuan through Central Shensi to Hsian and beyond the route is the same as that of the Lung Hai line, and the administration of the latter being the earlier concession will presumably grant running rights to the T'ung Ch'eng over this section.

The great obstacle is now reached, that is to say the passage of the Ch'inling Shan, the watershed between the Yangtzu and the Yellow River. This great barrier range is nowhere easy to cross in Shensi, and the least formidable passage, that from Hsian south-east *via* Lantien to Shang Chou in the valley of the Tan River, leads altogether in the wrong direction for the T'ung Ch'eng project. For the latter only two possible routes would appear to be available, firstly from Chouchih up the gorges of the Hei Ho, by tunnel through the watershed to Fop'ing, and thence down the gorges of the Ch'engku River to Hanchung, and secondly following the main road south from Paochi across the mountains to Feng Hsien. The first is probably too difficult to be practicable, and the second is the route likely to be followed. From Paochi the main road runs due south up a gorge which leads to a comparatively low gap in the main range of the Ch'inling Shan. But the rise is nevertheless something like 3000 feet or more in 50 li, and a long tunnel will presumably be necessary. The descent from the pass leads, however, not into the Han valley but to Feng Hsien on the head-waters of the Chialing Chiang, and the passage thence following the existing trail across the Han-Chialing divide to Liupa and Hanchung will be extremely difficult

PLATE LV

NATIVE PONY RACING IN INNER MONGOLIA : THE PADDOCK

NATIVE PONY RACING IN INNER MONGOLIA : THE PARADE

PLATE LVI

NATIVE PONY RACING IN INNER MONGOLIA : THE START

NATIVE PONY RACING IN INNER MONGOLIA : THE WINNER

and costly and require much tunnelling. The Chialing River, on the other hand, flows straight down into Szechuan, and a line down its limestone gorges to Kuangyuan, if practicable, is not unlikely to prove the easiest railway route into Szechuan from the north, or perhaps from any side. In that case Hanchung, which is mentioned in the loan agreement as a point to be touched at, could be connected up fairly easily by a line across the Han-Chialing portage in the neighbour-hood, that is to say from Yangp'ing Kuan to Mien Hsien. As regards a line south from Hanchung into Szechuan, the mountains on the Shensi Szechuan border in this neighbour-hood though rugged and intricate are not to be compared with the Ch'inling Shan as a barrier to communication, and are pierced by a line of gaps followed by the high road with passes less than 2000 feet above the valleys on either side. As regards the line from Kuangyuan through Szechuan to Chengtu, it is only safe to assume that it will not follow the existing high road, admirable as the latter is as an example of ancient engineering work in the mountains. Probably a route will be found down the Chialing Chiang to Paoning or beyond, and thence west to Chengtu.

(3) The Kueihua-Ninghsia-Lanchou Railway to Northern Kansu.

In the autumn of 1916 an American railway group secured the concession or contract for the construction of a certain mileage of railways in China, amongst which was the above line. The Peking-Kalgan-Kueihuach'eng railway, now constructed as far as Feng Chen, a day's march north of Tatung in Northern Shansi, and four marches short of Kueihua, was built by Chinese engineers with Chinese funds provided by the surplus earnings of the fine Peking-Mukden line. It was originally intended to extend this railway from Kueihua Ch'eng across the Gobi to Urga and thence to a junction with the Trans-Siberian line, a scheme which would have entailed years of unprofitable work in the deserts of Mongolia while many densely populated regions of China Proper were crying for railway communication; the present American project consists in a more useful extension of the same line in another direction, namely to the fertile plains of Ninghsia in Northern Kansu.

From the present railhead at Feng Chen to Kueihua

Ch'eng the line, if it follows the main road, will pass through mountainous but not difficult country. From Kueihua to Paot'ou it will run across flat corn-growing prairies, where the only work required will be an embankment. Once Kueihua and Paot'ou are reached there should be a fairly remunerative goods traffic, since this road carries a large trade to and from the vast north-west hinterland of Mongolia and Turkestan, whence camel caravans debouch into China Proper at these two points. From Paot'ou to Ninghsia will be flat going all the way except for the passage of the low ranges on the Kansu-Mongolia border near Shihchu Shan (Shihtsuitzu). This section will follow along the northern bank of the Yellow River, through a region which though partly desert contains an increasing population of Chinese settlers, and which is probably capable of great agricultural development with the assistance of irrigation works. Once Ninghsia is reached the trade of North-Western Kansu will be tapped, and, if it can compete successfully with the cheap transport by Yellow River boat and camel caravan across the desert, the railway will carry large quantities of wool collected from the grass-lands of Mongolia and the Kokonor down to Tientsin. From Ninghsia to Chungwei the line will run up the fertile and thickly populated plains along the Yellow River, with flat going all the way save for the passage of a low range near Kuangwu. The local traffic on this section should be heavy and remunerative, and the connecting of these isolated but comparatively wealthy plains by rail with the coast will be an event of great political and commercial importance to North China. From Chungwei to Lanchou the line would run through desert mountain country and will be neither easy nor profitable to construct until the capital is reached. An easier route, but also across desert, leads from Chungwei to Liangchou along the ruins of the Great Wall. On the whole this railway project is a not unattractive proposition, though there are many other regions in China where railway construction is far more imperative, and would be far more remunerative.

It is understood, however, that the above project has been abandoned as far as the American group is concerned, owing to the discovery that another Power possessed previously existing rights regarding the provision of funds for railway construction in that northern region should the Chinese require the assistance of foreign capital for the purpose.

(4) The Han Valley Railway.

As mentioned above an American railway group secured in 1916 the contract for the construction of a certain mileage of railways in China, but when it came to deciding on the actual lines to be so constructed, it was found to be no easy matter to avoid the previously existing railway rights of other Powers. Eventually, however, it was announced in the press in the spring of 1917 that a line from Laoho K'ou in Hupei up the Han valley into Southern Shensi, and across the divide south into Szechuan, had been fixed upon as one of the railways to be constructed by the American group. This line, opening up as it will the rich but backward upper Han valley, and thence penetrating into Szechuan, the goal of so many unrealised railway projects, from the north, is one of the most interesting and attractive of the many projected lines in China. Its passage up the Han valley should be highly remunerative, while the goods and passenger traffic likely to be secured by a line tapping the rich province of Szechuan has always been held by the planners of Chinese railways to be worth the greatest efforts.

From Laoho K'ou to Hsingan there appears to be the choice of two routes, neither very difficult, namely following the Han River to within a few marches of the latter city, or else outflanking the mountains on the Hupei-Shensi border by following a natural gap further west *via* Chuchi and Pingli. From Hsingan westwards the valley plain of the Yo River leading to Hanyin provides a natural railway route which outflanks the awkward mountain gorges of the Han River in this neighbourhood. From Hanyin a short tunnel will be required to regain the Han at Shihch'uan, whence there would seem to be no alternative, at any rate for the first part of the way, to a route along the difficult Han River gorges in order to gain the eastern end of the Hanchung plain, one of the most fertile and richest regions in China, near Yang Hsien. The latter portion of these gorges might perhaps be avoided by following a route *via* Hsihsiang, a rich and important city worth touching, and thence up the valley of the Muma Ho, debouching into the Hanchung plain near Ch'engku; only such a route would mean two more bridges over the Han.

A route south-west into Szechuan from Hanchung following the main road being barred to the Americans by the already existing Franco-Belgian rights in connection with the T'ung Ch'eng railway (though it is likely to be a long time before these rights can be made use of owing to the intervening barrier of the Ch'inling Shan), another road into Szechuan has to be sought for this project. According to Chinese reports there exists such a route, but only one, namely from Tzuyang on the Han River southwards up a valley, across the divide on the Shensi-Szechuan border, and down another valley to the neighbourhood of Suiting in Eastern Szechuan, whence Chengtu, Chungking, or other great centres in that province can be reached without great difficulty. It is alleged that apart from this route, and the main road further west, the ranges on the Shensi-Szechuan border, with peaks up to 8000 and 10,000 feet, are so precipitous as to render railway communication between the two provinces impossible.

In view of the immense difficulties confronting the engineers on the Szechuan section of the Hukuang railway system, which proposes to penetrate into Szechuan from Hupei, and of the barrier of the Ch'inling Shan which bars the way of the T'ung Ch'eng railway project in its course south from Hsian, it seems not unlikely that this American project, though the last of the three to appear on the scene, may be the first railway to reach Szechuan, and tap the riches of that wealthy but isolated province.

As regards other possible railways in Shensi and Kansu not yet. definitely projected, the most attractive is a line from the neighbourhood of Chingtzu Kuan in south-western Honan up the Tan River valley and across the Ch'inling Shan to Hsian. This is an ancient trade route, and provides the easiest passage across the Ch'inling Shan. Its construction will doubtless materialise in time, perhaps as a branch from the Peking-Hankow line, but inasmuch as a branch from that railway is already *en route* for Hsian *via* T'ungkuan (as a section of the Lung Hai) there is no immediate necessity for it. Another line will doubtless one day run north from

PLATE LVII

CHINESE TROOPS ON ACTIVE SERVICE IN INNER MONGOLIA

CHINESE TROOPS ON ACTIVE SERVICE IN INNER MONGOLIA

PLATE LVIII

ON A MAIN ROAD IN THE GRASS COUNTRY OF
THE CHINESE-MONGOLIAN BORDER

ON A MAIN ROAD IN THE GRASS COUNTRY OF
THE CHINESE-MONGOLIAN BORDER

Hsian up through Central Shensi to Yenan, Suitê, and Yülin, but though easy enough to construct this would not be an attractive project owing to the poverty of the country traversed. The Americans would perhaps have built it had their attempted exploitation of the North Shensi oil-field been successful. A more useful project would be a line connecting Northern Shansi *via* Suitê with Ninghsia in Northern Kansu, following the existing trail along the southern edge of the Ordos desert; though unremunerative until Ninghsia is reached, such a railway would be easy to build, and failing a similar line north of the Yellow River would be most useful in connecting Northern Kansu with the coast. Another route to Kansu, which presents no great engineering difficulties, but also passes through very poor country, lies from Hsian north-west across the loess plateau country and then up the valleys of the Ching and Huan rivers, across the loess divide in North-Eastern Kansu, and down another valley to Chungwei or Ninghsia. Finally when, in the far distant future, railway construction shall have reached a comparatively advanced stage in North-Western China, the railways of Kansu will doubtless be connected up with those of Szechuan by means of the valleys of the head-water streams of the Chialing River; the Yangtzu-Yellow River divide is far less formidable in Kansu than in Shensi, owing in part to the greater elevation of the country on either side. It is hardly worth while mentioning Tibet in connection with railway construction, but it may be noted that the easiest route for a line into that country from any direction probably lies from T'aochou or Hsining in Kansu, across the grass-lands of the Kokonor.

INDEX